Middleton's Tragedies

Middleton's Tragedies

A CRITICAL STUDY

by Samuel Schoenbaum

GORDIAN PRESS
NEW YORK
1970

ORIGINALLY PUBLISHED 1955
REPRINTED 1970

Library of Congress Catalog Card Number 71-128191
SBN 87752-132-8

To Richard Hindry Barker

Preface

IN the following pages it has been my object to inquire into the development of Middleton's tragedy: to arrive at a better understanding of the canon; to analyze the dramatist's handling of sources; to explore the influences that operated upon him, the traditions and conventions that shaped his work. But, more important, it has been my aim to provide a critical commentary on the plays themselves, with a view toward showing Middleton's special contribution to the tragedy of his age and to the literature of tragedy as well. I have tried also to call attention to the moral order which seems so clearly to underlie the action of the plays. Particular attention has been given to the characterization and to the dramatist's ironic method, which is an expression of his morality and perhaps the most striking single feature of his work.

This study is divided into two parts. In the first section I have presented a critical discussion of the five tragedies which seem to me to make up Middleton's contribution in this genre: *The Revenger's Tragedy, The Second Maiden's Tragedy, Hengist King of Kent, Women Beware Women,* and *The Changeling.* I may possibly be taken to task for writing at length on two anonymous plays which have in the past been attributed to Middleton but by no means universally accepted as his work—plays which have been assigned to other dramatists as well. Although it might be unreasonable to expect that ascriptions based almost exclusively on internal evidence will ever be regarded as certain, I do feel that stylistic tests are useful when applied with discretion and safeguarded by adequate checks. I have avoided the clumsy qualification, "if indeed this play be Middleton's," whenever *The Revenger's Tragedy* or *The Second Maiden's Tragedy* has been mentioned in Part One. It will, I trust, suffice for me to acknowledge here that the two plays have not been proved beyond question to be Middleton's work. However, the cumulative impression derived from a wide variety of evidence—tests of diction and metrics, parallels of phrase and thought, comparisons of dramatic technique, characterization, and point of view—favors Middleton strongly enough for *The Revenger's Tragedy* and *The Second Maiden's Tragedy* to be accorded at least provisional places in the canon and discussed alongside his undisputed works. The criteria and the results of the various tests are presented in Chapters V and VI. In Chapter VII, I have considered Middleton's collaboration with Rowley, and I have discussed briefly several plays in which Middleton's hand has been sought, in my opinion unjustifiably.

For quotations from Middleton's works I have used the best modern texts: Nicoll's *Tourneur* (for *The Revenger's Tragedy*); Greg's *Second Maiden's Tragedy;* Bald's *Hengist, A Game at Chess,* and *Honourable Entertainments;* and Bullen's *Middleton* for the rest of the works. The last is inadequate by present-day standards but the definitive edition remains to be issued; meanwhile, Bullen's text is the best and most easily accessible. The original quartos have been consulted when close textual study has warranted such a check. In quoting, in general I have followed the spelling and punctuation of my sources, except that superior letters have been lowered and archaic abbreviations spelled out. I have also silently corrected any obvious misprints. Titles are given in modern spelling and capitalization.

It is a pleasure to record my numerous obligations. The editors of *Philological Quarterly* and *Modern Language*

Quarterly have kindly allowed me to draw upon material in articles previously published. I have been given permission to quote passages from *Selected Essays 1917–1932* by T. S. Eliot, Copyright 1932, by Harcourt, Brace and Company, Incorporated, and from Samuel Putnam's translation of *Don Quixote*, published by The Viking Press, Incorporated, in 1942.

For their careful reading of my manuscript, their advice and corrections, I am grateful to Professors Alfred B. Harbage of Harvard University, Oscar J. Campbell and Maurice J. Valency of Columbia University, and Matthias A. Shaaber of the University of Pennsylvania. I wish to thank Professor Alfred Adler of Brooklyn College for help in translating from the Italian sources. My debt to Richard Hindry Barker, first my professor and now my friend, is greatest and also most personal. To him this book is dedicated.

SAMUEL SCHOENBAUM

Contents

PART ONE

The Plays

I. *The Revenger's Tragedy*

THOMAS MIDDLETON began writing for the stage at the turn
of the seventeenth century. In 1602 his name is associated
with two tragedies which have not survived. According to
Henslowe's *Diary*, he wrote *Randal Earl of Chester*, or *The
Chester Tragedy*, for the Admiral's Men and collaborated
with Munday, Drayton, Webster, and Dekker on *Caesar's
Fall* (apparently also called *Two Shapes*), for the same company.[1] But Middleton's creative energies were at this time
devoted primarily to a series of comedies, designed to appeal to the fashionable audiences that attended the perform-
ances of Paul's Boys and the Children of the Queen's Revels.

In plays which are uneven in quality, occasionally tedious
but often brilliant, he analyzes contemporary manners, especially as observed in the seamier side of London life. The
mood may vary from the harsh realism of *Your Five Gallants* to the uproarious and fantastic farce of *A Mad World,
My Masters;* from the bitter anger of *The Phoenix* [2] to the
dispassionate cynicism of *A Trick to Catch the Old One*.
But the subject matter remains fairly constant from play to
play. Middleton interests himself not so much in folly as in
vice, not so much in fopperies and affectations as in impos-
tures and cony-catching. He depicts a world of amoral
rogues driven by lust, greed, or desire for social advancement: scapegraces pursuing eagerly a career of sensual in-
dulgence or engaged in a relentless struggle for acquisition

or prestige. Wealth, land, and women—the symbols of value—slip quickly from gull to knave, to be wrested away by knaves of superior cunning.

The underworld and Bohemian circles of London and the world of the shopkeeper—the dregs and the middle class—comprise the milieu of these plays. Middleton's underworld is made up of scoundrels who live by their wits and prey upon one another. His middle class consists of incorrigible upstarts and social climbers: toothdrawers' sons infatuated with finery, wives who yearn for recognition at court, merchants who dream of cheating young heirs. The gentry dissipates itself in extravagance; all sense of "degree" has been lost. The view of Jacobean society is not a pleasant one, but the atmosphere is brightened by the dramatist's command of ingeniously ironic effects, by the geniality of some of his sinners, and (in the best plays) by his ability to create as central figure a Witgood or Follywit: the rogue who is clever rather than vicious, who is perhaps even appealing.

Sometime during this period of the City comedies, probably between 1604 and 1607,[3] Middleton's imagination turned away temporarily from the familiar shops and taverns of London to dwell upon the decadent splendor of a nameless Italian court. The conventions of comedy give way to the conventions of revenge tragedy; the extreme violence of the tragedy of blood replaces the essentially trivial reversals of farce. Art based firmly on a realistic appraisal of the social scene is succeeded by the grotesque expression of a view of reality that seems nightmarish and perverse. *The Revenger's Tragedy* is, indeed, a remarkable and complex work—in so many ways unlike the City comedies and yet at the same time akin to them; in some respects very different from any other play produced by the Jacobean age, yet also the culmination of attitudes and conventions long established.

I

Because of its complexity *The Revenger's Tragedy* has stimulated much controversy, and discussion has often obscured rather than illuminated the issues involved. Critics of Elizabethan drama have classified *The Revenger's Tragedy* as genuine tragedy "second only to the masterpieces of Shakespeare and Webster," [4] as the supreme example of "thoroughgoing, unadulterated" melodrama,[5] as "a kind of melodramatic farce." [6] The author has been called humorless; [7] he has been praised for his sense of the comic.[8] One reader criticizes his draftsmanship as "spasmodic and uncertain," the plot having "the air of being fabricated after a recipe." [9] Yet another can say: "It is . . . superlatively well plotted. It vies in this respect with the best of Jonson, with 'The Maid's Tragedy,' and with 'The Traitor.' " [10] The play has been disparaged for relying too heavily upon the conventions of revenge tragedy; [11] it has been commended for departing from the same conventions.[12] Boyer feels that "the separate scenes hold the attention, but are not carefully connected." [13] However, Wells asserts that "the play . . . has never been surpassed for logical consistency." [14] To Oliphant *The Revenger's Tragedy* is the work of "a stern and uncompromising moralist." [15] "Full of thrills and unspeakable juxtapositions," writes Thorndike, "it is governed by a sheer delight in horror and unrelieved by any moral standard." [16] To Vernon Lee the characters are "mere vague spectres"; [17] to Nicoll they are, for the most part, true and living; [18] to Eliot they are "distortions, grotesques, almost childish caricatures of humanity." [19]

When there is so much disagreement concerning the nature of a literary work, it is perhaps not surprising to find differences—extreme differences—about its quality. William Archer, who dislikes Elizabethan drama generally, is entirely revolted: "I will only ask whether such monstrous melodrama as *The Revenger's Tragedy*, with its hideous sexuality and its raging lust for blood, can be said to belong to civilised literature at all? I say it is a product either of sheer barbarism, or of some pitiable psychopathic perversion." [20] Prior's evaluation is more moderate. "After making all allowance for over-simplification," he writes, "it is nonetheless the case that the play gives occasion for the fine and brilliant things in it, though it cannot be said that it is a fine and brilliant play." [21] But to Oliphant *The Revenger's Tragedy* is "one of the literary and dramatic masterpieces of the period. . . . It is . . . one of the most perfect works of art— an art too that is noble in its austerity." [22]

Several of these conflicting statements may, no doubt, be the result of misinterpretation or insensitivity. But the difficulties are perhaps more the result of the complexity of *The Revenger's Tragedy* itself—a play that is at once farcical and tragic, conventional and unique, barbaric and austere, sternly moral and strangely perverse. Although discussed frequently for more than a century, it remains something of a mystery: its meaning in doubt, its place in the Jacobean drama still not fully explored, its position in the literature of tragedy as yet undetermined.

II

The scene of *The Revenger's Tragedy* is that Italy which Elizabethans regarded with mingled horror and fascination. "O Italie," exclaims Nashe, "the Academie of man-slaughter, the sporting place of murther, the Apothecary-shop of poyson for all Nations: how many kind of weapons hast thou inuented for malice?" [23] There Robert Greene "sawe and practizde such villainie as is abhominable to declare." [24] From Italy, inveighs Marston, the traveler brings cosmetics, paints, and poisoning, "Aretine's pictures, some strange luxury,/ And new-found use of Venice venery." [25]

But if young masters returned with vicious habits, they also brought back gossip: tales of intrigue and duplicity, violence and sensuality; accounts of the atrocities of despots, of incest and the slaughter of kinsmen. Perhaps some had learned of Ezzelino da Romano, who mutilated the entire population of Friola, or of the gracious Gianpaolo Baglioni, who murdered his father and had incestuous relations with his sister, or of Sigismondo Malatesta, Lord of Rimini, who encouraged the arts and slew his three wives. Others may have been told how the *condottiere* Werner von Ürslingen proclaimed himself "the enemy of God, of pity, and of mercy." Still others may have heard the legend of how fifty courtesans and valets gamboled naked after chestnuts on the Vatican floor, then mated before Pope Alexander VI and his offspring, Cesare and Lucrezia Borgia: the same Alexander VI whose corpse was found a blackened and swollen mass, the result, it was rumored, of some dreadful poison intended for two cardinals but through some error taken by the Pope himself.[26]

Through Geoffrey Fenton's translation of Guicciardini's history of the Italian wars, Englishmen could familiarize themselves with the depravity and remorseless ingenuity of Cesare Borgia, who with overtures of peace enticed Vitellozzo Vitelli and De' Ferme to a banquet, where they unsuspectingly met death; who, more terrible yet, had reportedly enjoyed his own sister Lucrezia. Oral and written reports described the impudence of Vittoria Accorombona, who took Bracciano as her mate within a fortnight of her husband's murder—a murder to which she had been accessory. English and French renderings of sensational Italian *novelle* contributed to the general impression of the iniquity of Renaissance Italy. "It is nowe a priuie note amongst the better sort of men," declares Nashe, "when they would set a singular marke or brand on a notorious villaine, to say, he hath beene in *Italy*." [27] *Inglese Italianato è un diavolo incarnato* runs the Italian proverb which gained currency in England and appeared in the writings of Ascham, Greene, Howell, Parker, and Sidney.

What appalled the Elizabethans particularly, however, was not so much the monstrousness of the crimes themselves, as that curious combination of refinement and bloodlust on the part of the villain: a combination which made for ingenuity rather than passion, for unbridled egotism and a sense of frigid detachment, for a defiance of gods and men. Italy produced the Machiavellian who held religion but a childish toy. "The Italyans," writes Moryson, ". . . are close, secrett, crafty, and the greatest dissemblers in the world." [28] And Nashe enumerates such "Italionate conueyances" as

to kill a man, and then mourne for him, *quasi vero* it was not by my consent, to be a slaue to him that hath iniur'd me, and kisse his feete for opportunitie of reuenge, to be seuere in punishing offenders, that none might haue the benefite of such meanes but my selfe, to vse men for my purpose and then cast them off, to seeke his destruction that knowes my secrets; and such as I haue imployed in any murther or stratagem, to set them priuilie together by the eares, to stab each other mutually, for feare of bewraying me; or, if that faile, to hire them to humor one another in such courses as may bring them both to the gallowes.[29]

Murder may be a convenient political expedient, but it is also a stimulant for the imagination of an artist, and so the Italian acquired a reputation for his skill in poisoning: his ability to devise envenomed letters, to anoint sedan chairs with deadly poisons, to mix with sweetmeats mysterious white powders which were very pleasant to the taste and quite gradual in their effect. Webster's Lodovico yearns for no ordinary revenge upon Brachiano:

> T'have poison'd his praier booke, or a paire of beades,
> The pummell of his saddle, his looking-glasse,
> Or th'handle of his racket—ô that, that!
> That while he had bin bandying at Tennis,
> He might have sworne himselfe to hell, and strooke
> His soule into the hazzard! O my Lord!
> I would have our plot bee ingenious,
> And have it hereafter recorded for example
> Rather than borrow example.[30]

Such a disinterested taste for wickedness, along with the sensational consequences of that taste, left a deep impression upon the Elizabethan mind, and especially upon the sensibilities of the dramatists—providing the diverse talents of such playwrights as Marston and Ford, Webster and Shirley, with magnificently lurid material for studies in evil. Renaissance Italy became early the most popular setting for Jacobean tragedies of blood. It is extraordinary when the manners of a foreign nation are able to influence so strongly a literature essentially native in tradition.

III

The Revenger's Tragedy appears to have a basis in actual events, may indeed be derived in part from a notorious episode in Florentine history.[31] Middleton had probably heard or read of the career of Alessandro de' Medici, the cruel and licentious Duke who for more than five years, from 1532 until 1537, controlled the destiny of Florence. His nights were given to profligacy. Attended by his chamberlain L'Unghero and his minion Giomo da Carpi, he would appear vizarded at banquets, dances, and revels—orgies where the youth of Florence abandoned themselves to debauchery, suppers costing five hundred to a thousand florins, masques where the most alluring young women were assembled to entice him. Still dissatisfied, the Duke lusted after the beautiful Luisa Strozzi, but his efforts to seduce her were scornfully rejected. A few nights after one such episode Luisa was convulsed with abdominal pains while dining with her sister Maria. She died two hours later—perhaps, as Varchi asserts, sacrificed by her relations to preserve the honor of the family; [32] perhaps, as Segni believes, poisoned by a hired instrument of Alessandro. [33]

The Duke's favorite and constant companion during the last months of his rule was his cousin, Lorenzo de' Medici, called Lorenzino because of his slightness. Lorenzino had insinuated himself into Alessandro's confidence by affecting effeminacy, by providing new mistresses and proposing newer pleasures. When Alessandro yearned for the attractive and virtuous widow of Alemanno Salviati, a young woman who had previously scorned him, Lorenzino went so far as to promise the Duke that he would persuade her to submit to his lust—even though she was Lorenzino's own sister, Laudomia. On the evening of January 5, 1537, he informed Alessandro that Laudomia had agreed finally to meet him late that night, at Lorenzino's secret chambers adjoining the Medici palace. Stirred by the prospect of pleasure, Alessandro donned his green satin robe lined with sable and his perfumed leather gloves, and accompanied Lorenzino to his quarters. There the Duke unbuckled his sword and reclined on the bed. Lorenzino took his leave, and returned a few minutes later. But, instead of Laudomia, he brought with him the ruffian Scoronconcolo, a devoted follower whom Lorenzino had rescued from the gallows. In a brutal struggle Alessandro was stabbed through with a short sword, slashed across the face and temple, pierced through the throat by

Scoronconcolo's knife, which the assassin turned round and round while the Duke in his agony bit down on Lorenzino's thumb. Finally Alessandro expired and Lorenzino fled on horseback to Bologna. The Duke's body was not discovered until the next evening.[34]

In these events may be seen the possible basis for several elements in *The Revenger's Tragedy*. The poisoning of Luisa Strozzi brings to mind the poisoning of Gloriana for refusing to become the Duke's mistress. Lorenzino's efforts on behalf of Alessandro are paralleled by Vindice's attempts to debauch his own sister, Castiza, while acting as pander for Lussurioso. Finally, the circumstances of Alessandro's death bear some resemblance to the murder of the Duke in the secluded lodge to which he had repaired, at Vindice's behest, in expectation of finding there a young woman ready to satisfy his lust. Accounts of Alessandro's rule may also have provided the author with background material for his conception of a Renaissance Italian court, but for this he could just as well have turned to the works of contemporary dramatists, and especially to the plays of John Marston.

I V

The vogue of Italianate tragedies of violence owes much to Marston, whom Swinburne aptly describes as "the most Italian of our dramatists." [35] In a series of eccentric plays— harsh, satiric, frequently bloody and as often incoherent— Marston selected Italy as the setting for intrigues concerning deposed dukes and heartless despots, lustful duchesses and child-slaying avengers. Of these dramas *Antonio's Revenge* and *The Malcontent* are perhaps the most significant. In *Antonio's Revenge* Marston first combined an Italian milieu with the theme of vendetta; in *The Malcontent* he empha-

debt to Marston

sized the nastiness of sex, indeed, of life itself. In both plays the background is the court, and Marston created a picture of Italian court life to which the author of *The Revenger's Tragedy* was much indebted. It is a world of parasites and knaves, of cynical jesters and sinister Machiavellians, all engaged in endless machinations and a ruthless struggle for power. But it is also a world of lechers and wittols, luxury and revels: "sweet sheetes, waxe lights, Antique bed-posts, Cambrick smocks, villanous Curtaines, Arras pictures, oylde hinges, and all the tong-tide lascivious witnesses of great creatures wantonnesse." [36] Its viciousness, according to Malevole, exceeds that of a bordello, where sin soon displays her ugly form and surfeit dissipates sensual longings—while "in an *Italian* lascivious Pallace, a Lady gardianlesse,

> Left to the push of all allurement,
> The strongest incitements to immodestie,
> To have her bound, incensed with wanton sweetes,
> Her veines fild hie with heating delicates,

Soft rest, sweete Musick, amorous Masquerers,/ lascivious banquets, sinne it selfe gilt ore,/strong phantasie tricking up strange delights,/presenting it dressed pleasingly to sence,/ . . . thus being prepar'd, clap to her easie eare,/ youth in good clothes, well shapt, rich,/ faire-spoken, promising-noble, ardent bloudfull,/ wittie, flattering: *Ulisses* absent,/ O *Ithaca*, can chastest *Penelope*, hold out?

III, ii, p. 179

It is a world, too, of cruelty and sudden death. "Enter *Piero*, unbrac't," reads the stage direction for the opening scene of *Antonio's Revenge*, "his armes bare, smeer'd in blood, a poniard in one hand bloodie, and a torch in the other, *Strotzo* following him with a corde." [37] Glorious bridal mornings become Stygian nights; poison is slipped into carousing bowls; tongues are plucked out; children are butchered and their severed limbs placed before their fathers' eyes. "Murder and torture," exults Antonio over his helpless opponent: "no prayers, no entreats." [38]

V

Such a milieu forms the background for *The Revenger's Tragedy*, but in Middleton's play the atmosphere is even more heightened. The motifs popularized by such works as *Antonio's Revenge* and *The Malcontent* are, indeed, carried beyond the limits of Marston's bizarre art to make up a fantastic picture of Mediterranean opulence and decay. *The Revenger's Tragedy* is the most extreme of the Elizabethan portrayals of Italy. It is the result not so much of historical study and contemporary observation as of a vivid and intense imagination operating upon fact and gossip to create a world that is scarcely realistic at all, but rather fantastic and grotesque. The play tells us little about Renaissance Italy, more about the concept of Italy that some Elizabethans shared, and a good deal about the state of mind of the dramatist himself.

The setting is one of dazzling artificial brightness, as night is made noon by the glare of tapers—and also of unnatural darkness, as the light of day is obscured to shroud deeds of evil. Perfumed courtiers parade richly in three-piled velvet and cloth-of-gold; royal mistresses luxuriate in silks and precious jewels and cloth-of-silver trains. Life is a round of sensual delights. "O thinke vpon the pleasure of the Pallace," Vindice urges his sister,

> Secured ease and state; the stirring meates,
> Ready to moue out of the dishes, that e'en now quicken
> when their eaten,
> Banquets abroad by Torch-light, Musicks, sports,
> Bare-headed vassailes, that had nere the fortune

> To keepe on their owne Hats, but let hornes were em.
> Nine Coaches waiting.   II, i, 222–28

But no pleasure is sweet unless it has a taste of sin; and so by day the Duke rides privately forth to secret assignations in hidden lodges "guilty/ Of his fore-fathers lusts, and great-folkes riots." There music, perfumes, and feasts excite the senses to wantonness. The night is given to revels and lust:

> Now tis full sea a bed ouer the world;
> Theres iugling of all sides; some that were Maides
> E'en at Sun set are now perhaps ith Toale-booke;
> This woman in immodest thin apparell
> Lets in her friend by water, here a Dame
> Cunning, nayles lether-hindges to a dore,
> To auoide proclamation.
> Now Cuckolds are a quoyning, apace, apace, apace,
>   apace.
> And carefull sisters spinne that thread ith night,
> That does maintaine them and their bawdes ith daie!
>   II, ii, 152–61

Vizarded masquers dance, healths go round, ladies' cheeks flush with wine. There is whispering and laughter; then lecherous courtiers and their willing partners silently withdraw, while male bawds keep watch at the stairhead. Should persuasion fail, innocence is violated or beauty snuffed out with poison, for impudence is goddess of the palace. Midnight is the Judas of the hours, when chastity is betrayed to sin. A man might be rich if he had "all the fees behind the *Arras;* and all the farthingales that fal plumpe about twelue a clock at night vpon the Rushes" (II, ii, 90–92).

In the "accursed Pallace" there is no remorse for wickedness, no fear of vengeance, no thought of a life after death. The aims of existence have been narrowed to the fulfillment of degraded ambitions and the pursuit of new sensual experiences. Moral restraints have been either perverted or destroyed; romantic love has ceased to be: "All thriues but chastity, she lyes a cold." Apparently Castiza's only suitor is Lussurioso, Italy's "lecherous hope." "Wert not for gold and women;" reflects Vindice bitterly,

> there would be no damnation,
> Hell would looke like a Lords Great Kitchin without
> fire in't.
>
> II, i, 278–79

The scriptures are cited to justify incest; men are hanged for telling the truth; the most upright man sins seven times a day. Flattery and bribes make a mockery of justice. "Fayths are bought and sold,/ Oths in these daies are but the skin of gold" (III, i, 6–7). The functioning of the judicial machinery has been reduced to hollow routine, as judges solemnly weigh evidence while the Duke summarily determines the fate of the prisoner. The phraseology at times reflects, as Lockert observes,[39] the inversion of moral values:

> A man that were for euill onely good;
>
> I, i, 88
>
> My haires are white, and yet my sinnes are Greene.
>
> II, ii, 360
>
> Best side to vs, is the worst side to heauen.
>
> III, v, 222

And always, in the midst of revels, appears the motif of the skull, mute reminder of evils done and retribution that is to strike. Portents of destruction loom over the riots of the court: blazing stars light up the heavens, thunder crashes. The orgies of the palace provide an ideal setting for the working out of murderous intrigues, for "in this time of Reuells tricks may be set a foote." Lussurioso, newly installed as Duke, basks in the flattery of his obsequious followers. Seated proudly at his banqueting table he calls out for diversions—"We're ready now for sports, let 'em set on"— not realizing that he calls for his own death. For Vindice has promised earlier,

And when they thinke their pleasure sweete and good,
In midst of all their ioyes, they shall sigh bloud.

v, ii, 23–24

The lecherous old Duke, prepared to meet pleasure in a perfumed mist, kisses the poisoned lips of a skull and brings to
himself lingering torment and the terrible revelation of his
wife's infamy. In this one dreadful moment lies the essence
of *The Revenger's Tragedy*—the union of cruelty and sexuality, the blending of the motif of lust and the motif of
death.

VI

If the setting is Italy of the Renaissance, the conventions are
those of revenge tragedy, conventions which Thomas Kyd
introduced upon the Elizabethan stage and which were
modified by the playwrights who came after him. In *The
Spanish Tragedy* (*ca.* 1584–*ca.* 1589) [40] Kyd offered, for the
first time in English popular drama, revenge as the basic
theme of a complex intrigue. The Senecan ghost, the motif of
madness, and hesitation on the part of the avenger are his innovations. He exploited the melodramatic effectiveness of
bloodshed (there are ten deaths) and made skillful use of
irony, especially in the scene where Pedringano goes to his
death confident that he will be saved by the man who, in
reality, wishes most to have him destroyed. The Kydian
formula was repeated in *Titus Andronicus*. In *Hamlet*
Shakespeare centered the entire action around the personality of the revenger. Chettle made his central character, Hoff-
man, the villain, and substituted a skeleton for the ghost. In
Antonio's Revenge Marston elaborated the intrigue to include a whole series of revenges and counter-revenges, and
made disguise an essential part of the avenger's plans.

By the time of *The Revenger's Tragedy* the conventions of the form, essentially a narrow one, had already hardened into tradition, the possibilities for innovation virtually depleted. Yet what Middleton contributed to the pattern is significant. He emphasized savagery, making the play "a distinct forerunner of the new school of true horror tragedies." [41] He introduced, as Bowers points out, a new type of protagonist: the self-deluded avenger who is not aware that his own character is tainted, who does not foresee that he is destined to perish. [42] Most important, Middleton adapted to the revenge tragedy formula the ironic method that he had perfected in the City comedies.

Irony had from the first been implicit in the situations of the vendetta plays, and ironic twists accompanied naturally the unraveling of the plot; but the role of irony was incidental, a by-product of melodrama. In *The Revenger's Tragedy* irony becomes the aim rather than the means of achieving a particular effect. Almost every scene contains a variation of the biter bit theme. "The narrative illustrates with ingenious variety," Bradbrook notes, "in how many ways a villain may be hoist with his own petard." [43]

The result is a tour de force, a work of schematized brilliance, in which the conventions of revenge tragedy are manipulated to form a pattern of the utmost complexity. Vindice, for example, uses disguise not once, but on three separate occasions, appearing as pander, malcontent, and masquer. Prior compares the dramatist's method "to a chess problem posed by an expert who assumes that his audience knows the conventions which govern the restricted movements of individual pieces and the possibilities of the game, and then demonstrates the solution in such a way as to encompass the maximum number of variant situations latent in the problem." [44] Yet the intrigue never collapses into obscurity, the action never falters in its headlong pace. If certain artistic values are of necessity sacrificed, the play remains nevertheless unique among Jacobean dramas. Neither romantic nor realistic, it is formalized and artificial, an experiment in technique, an exercise in the stylization of conventions.

VII

Bradbrook counts twenty-two instances of ironic reversals in *The Revenger's Tragedy*,[45] but the use of irony is not limited to situations. It also underlies the wordplay, the juxtaposition of phrases,[46] the reflective asides. Even the title harbors an ironic double meaning: "*The Revenger's Tragedy* is," as Parrott and Ball point out, "not only the tragedy accomplished by the revenger, but the tragedy which overtakes the revenger in the corruption of his own nature." [47]

Ironic reversals are indeed frequent. Lussurioso, for example, finds himself attracted to the virtuous Castiza and seeks a pander to assist in the intended seduction. Since he has a flair for irony, Lussurioso turns to Hippolito, his mortal enemy and Castiza's brother, asks him to suggest a suitable male bawd. Hippolito recommends his brother Vindice, who appears before Lussurioso disguised as a certain Piato. The Duke's son then naïvely betrays himself by commissioning a brother to ruin his own sister, and basks in his sense of irony in the presence of the very man who plans his ironical undoing:

LUSSURIOSO: That was her brother
That did prefer thee to vs.
VINDICE: My Lord I thinke so,
I knew I had seene him some where— . . .
LUSSURIOSO: We may laugh at that simple age within him.
VINDICE: Ha, ha, ha.

LUSSURIOSO: Himselfe being made the subtill instrument,
To winde vp a good fellow.
VINDICE: That's I my Lord.
LUSSURIOSO: That's thou.
To entice and worke his sister.
VINDICE: A pure nouice!
LUSSURIOSO: T'was finely manag'd.

I, iii, 148–51, 155–63

Later "Piato" tells Lussurioso that the Duchess expects to lie with her bastard stepson that night. Enraged by this affront to his father's honor, Lussurioso breaks into the Duchess' chamber. There he finds not Spurio, but the Duke himself, who fears an attempt upon his life. Thus Lussurioso's solicitude for his father's reputation is rewarded by imprisonment.

Ambitioso and Supervacuo (sons to the Duchess by a previous marriage) want Lussurioso executed and their brother Junior, who has been jailed temporarily for rape, freed. They manage to obtain the ducal signet, present it to the prison officers, bid them urge the executioner to hurry —but they forget to indicate whom they wish killed. Thus, Junior, whose release they so much desire, goes off to his death, the news being brought even as the two brothers quarrel over who deserves credit for the ingenious maneuver:

AMBITIOSO: Was not this execution rarely plotted?
We are the Dukes sonnes now.
SUPERVACUO: I you may thanke my policie for that.
AMBITIOSO: Your policie, for what?
SUPERVACUO: Why wast not my inuention brother . . . ?
AMBITIOSO: Heart, twas a thing I thought on too.
SUPERVACUO: You thought ont too, sfoote slander not your thoughts
With glorious vntruth, I know twas from you.
AMBITIOSO: Sir I say, twas in my head.

SUPERVACUO: I, like your braines then,
Nere to come out as long as you liu'd.
AMBITIOSO: You'd haue the honor on't forsooth, that your wit
Lead him to the scaffold.
SUPERVACUO: Since it is my due.
Ile publisht, but Ile ha't in spite of you.

III, vi, 1–5, 10–19

Lussurioso realizes eventually that "Piato" is unreliable. Although he should have better sense, he consults Hippolito once more, and this time learns of a discontented brother, Vindice. Lussurioso sends for him; Vindice returns undisguised, posing as a malcontent. Lussurioso informs the two brothers of his pander's treachery, confides in them how the "ingreatfull villayne" proposed the debauching of Castiza, then sought "of his owne free will" the corruption of both mother and daughter. "Oh villaine," cries Hippolito; Vindice remarks, simply, "He shall surely die that did it." Lussurioso defends his unassailable virtue, charges Vindice with the murder of Piato (IV, ii). "Do you marke it," Vindice says later, with obvious relish, "And I must stand ready here to make away my selfe yonder—I must sit to bee kild, and stand to kill my selfe, I could varry it not so little as thrice ouer agen, tas some eight returnes like Michelmas Tearme" (v, i, 5–8).[48]

When Lussurioso finally becomes duke, Vindice and Hippolito see their opportunity to destroy him. They will appear as masquers at the revels that have been proclaimed in celebration of his accession. They will dance their measures and, at the right moment, draw their swords, slay the profligate Duke, purge the court of corruption. But Ambitioso and Supervacuo have devised a similar plan: they too will don vizards and masquing suits, take part in the revels, steal out their swords at the proper instant—and then seize the coronet. But they arrive too late. The rhythm of the second dance is broken by the groans of the dying; Vindice and Hippolito have already accomplished the slaughter. The newly arrived conspirators proclaim themselves dukes, turn their swords against one another, complete the purgation of the court. Thus, those who have come to murder are themselves murdered. It is almost, but not quite, the final irony.

Antonio is now duke. Few others have survived the slaughter, but among these are Vindice and Hippolito. Standing alongside the corpses of their enemies, they enjoy now their moment of triumph. They have avenged a father disgraced, a mistress poisoned, a sister tempted. They have destroyed evil, but in the process they have themselves become evil, stained with a bloodlust exceeding the bloodlust of their opponents: they are destined soon to fall victim to their own cleverness. Pleased with their own wit, appreciative of the "quaintness" of their own devices, they hover near Antonio, their secret bursting within them. Antonio cannot help marveling at how the old Duke came to be murdered:

ANTONIO: It was the strangeliest carried, I not hard of the like.
HIPPOLITO: Twas all donne for the best my Lord.
VINDICE: All for your graces good; we may be bould to speake it now,
Twas some-what witty carried tho we say it.
Twas we two murdred him.
ANTONIO: You two?
VINDICE: None else ifaith my Lord nay twas well managde.
ANTONIO: Lay hands vpon those villaines.
VINDICE: How? on vs?
ANTONIO: Beare 'em to speedy execution.
VINDICE: Heart wast not for your good my Lord?
ANTONIO: My good! away with 'em; such an ould man as he,
You that would murder him would murder me.
                                              v, iii, 136–48

It is the last, the cosmic, irony.

But the irony of *The Revenger's Tragedy* is, as has been

noted, not a matter of situation alone; it permeates the dialogue as well. Irony underscores Vindice's words to the Duke in the trysting lodge:

DUKE: What Lady ist?
VINDICE: Faith my Lord a Country Lady, a little bashfull at first as most of them are, but after the first kisse my Lord the worst is past with them; your grace knowes now what you haue to do; sha's some-what a graue looke with her—but—

III, v, 139–43

It lurks in seemingly casual conversation:

LUSSURIOSO: Thy name, I haue forgot it?
VINDICE: *Vindice* my Lord.
LUSSURIOSO: Tis a good name that.
VINDICE: I, a Reuenger.
LUSSURIOSO: It dos betoken courage, thou shouldst be valiant, And kill thine enemies.
VINDICE: Thats my hope my Lord.   IV, ii, 189–95

It springs from the mistaken words of the bemused characters. "Stay, yonder's the slaue," cries Lussurioso when he comes upon a form that appears to be the drunken "Piato," but which is, in reality, the corpse of his murdered father:

VINDICE: Masse there's the slaue indeed my Lord; Tis a good child, he calls his Father slaue.
LUSSURIOSO: I, thats the villaine, the dambd villaine.

V, i, 37–40

In Vindice's meditations on the skull of Gloriana—his contrast of present luxuries and sensual pleasures with the imminence of death, of life's fleeting physical beauty with the irreparable decay that is to come—we have, as Lockert remarks, "the quintessence of satiric irony." [49] But it would be tedious to include further illustrations of Middleton's irony in this play: *The Revenger's Tragedy* is perhaps the most notable example in Jacobean drama of deliberate and sustained reliance upon the ironic method.

VIII

Although the author calls his play a tragedy, the dramatic types that participate in the ironic reversals are, it would seem, associated more properly with farce. They are not so much living characters as embodiments of abstract qualities, symbols of lust and ambition, chastity and hypocrisy. Even Vindice, the protagonist, is unreal: a fiercely energetic incarnation of the spirit of revenge. The figures who make up the play lack variety and complexity; they have neither nobility nor humanity. Plotting and counterplotting, betraying each other and themselves, they are puppets hurled from one situation to another, automata whose misfortunes stir sardonic mirth rather than terror or compassion. Painted with the broad strokes of caricature, they are fantastic creations: monstrous, it is true, but also amusing.

There is an insistent note of ludicrous exaggeration. The pander "Piato" has "beene witnesse/ To the surrenders of a thousand virgins" (i, iii, 54–55). The Duke, "a parcht and iuicelesse luxur," will need not days or weeks, but months to confess his sins. Lussurioso's "heate is such," remarks Vindice,

> Were there as many Concubines as Ladies
> He would not be contaynd, he must flie out:
> I wonder how ill featurde, vilde proportiond
> That one should be: if she were made for woman,
> Whom at the Insurrection of his lust
> He would refuse for once, heart, I thinke none.
>
> I, i, 90–96

"He [the Duke] yeelds small comfort yet," grumbles Spurio during the trial of Junior,

> hope he shall die,
> And if a bastards wish might stand in force,
> Would all the court were turnde into a coarse.
>
> I, ii, 38–40

In death, as in life, these figures are without dignity, evoke no sympathy. Unable to understand why "a man should lie in a whole month for a woman," Junior goes off to his execution complaining,

> My fault was sweet sport, which the world approoues,
> I dye for that which euery woman loues.
>
> III, iv, 86–87

—and dies "full of rage and spleene." Vindice's final words reflect not pain, but self-satisfaction, perhaps even elation:

> Yfaith, we're well, our Mother turnd, our Sister true,
> We die after a nest of Dukes, adue.
>
> v, iii, 168–69

Such obstinate good cheer, under such uncomfortable circumstances, does not accord well with a tragic view of life but is entirely compatible with the methods of farce. The laughter of *The Revenger's Tragedy* may be, as Wells suggests, "infernal," [50] but it is laughter nonetheless.

I X

If the characters and situations are often broadly comic, the language is not of the kind usually associated with farce. The verse is, indeed, Jacobean blank verse of the great period before the decadence: poetry of an order encountered most frequently in the supreme tragedies of the age. Such is the impression that remains with the reader—in spite of the careless alternating between verse and prose; in spite of the naïvely aphoristic couplets that jingle discordantly in the most splendid passages; in spite of lines that are too long or too short, of syntax that is occasionally awkward, of metre that is at times impossible.[51]

Perhaps Collins was the first to liken the style to flame, when he remarked on the "words which burn like fire," on

"the fierce and fiery splendour" of the poet's genius.[52] Swinburne, too, was entranced by "the fiery jet of his molten
verse, the rush of its radiant and rhythmic lava," [53] and since
his time, commentators have almost always made the flame
analogy. It remains entirely apt. As in the opening scene the
torches illuminate the sin-ravaged faces of the royal household, so too the language, flamelike, flashes through the
blackness of human corruption, lighting up folly, searing
and lacerating evil. The dialogue smolders and crackles
in fierce exchanges:

VINDICE: Shall we kill him now hees drunke?
LUSSURIOSO: I best of all.
VINDICE: Why then hee will nere liue to be sober?
LUSSURIOSO: No matter, let him reele to hell.
VINDICE: But being so full of liquor, I feare hee will put out
all the fire.
LUSSURIOSO: Thou art a mad beast.
VINDICE: And leaue none to warme your Lordships Gols
withall;
For he that dyes drunke, falls into hell fire like a
Bucket a water, qush, qush.   v, i, 49–57

It burns in lines of intense metaphorical concentration:

Throwne inck vpon the for-head of our state
i, ii, 7

And fed the rauenous vulture of his lust,
i, iv, 50

CASTIZA: I haue endur'd you with an eare of fire,
Your Tongues have struck hotte yrons on my face;
Mother, come from that poysonous woman there.
MOTHER: Where?
CASTIZA: Do you not see her? shee's too inward then:
ii, i, 258–62

My wrath like flaming waxe hath spent it selfe,
ii, ii, 315

> Nay and you draw teares once, go you to bed,
> Wet will make yron blush and change to red:
> Brother it raines, twill spoile your dagger, house it.
>
> IV, iv, 51–53

> A drab of State, a cloath a siluer slut,
> To haue her traine borne vp, and her soule traile
>   i'th durt.   IV, iv, 80–81

It blazes in passages of scorching eloquence:

> Let blushes dwell i'th Country. Impudence!
> Thou Goddesse of the pallace, Mistris of Mistresses
> To whom the costly-perfumd people pray,
> Strike thou my fore-head into dauntlesse Marble;
> Mine eyes to steady Saphires: turne my visage,
> And if I must needes glow, let me blush inward
> That this immodest season may not spy
> That scholler in my cheekes, foole-bashfullnes,
> That Maide in the old time, whose flush of *Grace*
> Would neuer suffer her to get good cloaths;
> Our maides are wiser; and are lesse ashamd,
> Saue *Grace* the bawde I seldome heare *Grace* nam'd!
>
> I, iii, 7–18

"It never cools," Barker writes, "never burns itself out. It is as though the author had written the whole play at a single sitting as the expression of a single mood." [54]

The effectiveness of the verse may be owing to a bold ellipsis—"for this time wipe your Lady from your eyes," (I, iv, 78)—or to the ingenious figures that suggest the metaphysical poets:

> For had hee cut thee a right Diamond,
> Thou hadst beene next set in the Duke-doomes Ring,
> When his worne selfe like Ages easie slaue,
> Had dropt out of the Collet into th' Graue.
>
> I, ii, 169–72

> Her honor first drunke poyson, and her life,
> Being fellowes in one house did pledge her honour.
>
> I, iv, 15–16

Its strength may derive from the grotesque images:

> If he but winck, not brooking the foule obiect,
> Let our two other hands teare vp his lids,
> And make his eyes like Comets shine through bloud;
>
> III, V, 213–15

> Are you so barbarous to set Iron nipples
> Vpon the brest that gaue you suck?
>
> IV, iv, 9–10

But the verse is always daring, always startles the imagination with its power and originality.

Reference is made again and again to poison and disease, fire and light and darkness, metals and precious stones. This last group of images at times imparts to the verse a kind of hardness: "the unpleasant tang of cold metal on the tongue." [55] But the essence of great dramatic verse can scarcely be isolated and analyzed. One need say only that the poet has succeeded in devising the perfect instrument for expressing the bitterness, the passion, the splendor of his nightmare vision. By so doing he has been able to leave behind one of the most remarkable achievements of the Jacobean stage.

X

This curious fusing of blank verse of tragic grandeur, farcical situations, and melodramatic violence sets the play apart from the rest of Jacobean drama, gives it indeed a status that is unique. *The Revenger's Tragedy* may perhaps be best described as macabre art and, one might add, the sort of macabre art usually associated with the Middle Ages. For, although the background of the play is Renaissance Italy, the point of view suggests more often the medieval heritage. A heritage that was always close to the Elizabethans, it was to exert a profound influence upon the literature of the Jacobean age—a time when many thinking men were given to skepticism, looking back with melancholy to the past rather than hopefully awaiting the future.

Lussurioso, Supervacuo, and the other figures with the oddly descriptive names certainly do not belong to history. The immediate source of several names is Florio's Italian dictionary,[56] but the types themselves have a longer pedigree. They may possibly derive from the classical tradition of satiric comedy; more likely, however, they go back to the medieval tradition of allegory, and especially to the morality plays, with their Wanton, Lust, and Iniquity. The remarkably effective opening tableau of the ducal family and train is little more than a procession of the Seven Deadly Sins in Jacobean trappings. The author's preoccupation with sex in general and woman's frailty in particular stems not, as Marston's does, from the tirades of Juvenal and the Roman satirists, but rather from the Biblical inheritance and the medieval condemnation of the sensual life. There are only two classical references in the play—a mention of the Phoenix [57] and a vague allusion to the sirens—but Middleton repeatedly associates lust with Judas and Lucifer, the breaking of God's commandments, and loss of salvation. Vindice's famous address to his mistress' skull is little more than a characteristic sermon of the Middle Ages transformed by the magic of Jacobean blank verse:

> here's an eye,
> Able to tempt a greatman—to serue God,
> A prety hanging lip, that has forgot now to dissemble;
> Me thinkes this mouth should make a swearer tremble,
> A drunckard claspe his teeth, and not vndo e'm,
> To suffer wet damnation to run through e'm.
> Heres a cheeke keepes her colour; let the winde go
> whistle,
> Spout Raine, we feare thee not, be hot or cold

Alls one with vs; and is not he absurd,
Whose fortunes are vpon their faces set,
That feare no other God but winde and wet?
                                III, v, 58–68

These lines recall themes dwelt upon by the medieval preacher, who would "point his audience to the skulls and bones of the departed, bidding them reflect how through the mouth once so delectable to kiss, so delicate in its eating and its drinking, through eyes but a short while before so fair to see, worms now crawl in and out. The body or the head, once so richly attired, so proudly displayed, now boasts no covering but the soil, no bed of softness, no proud retinue save worms." [58]

The dramatist's imagination, it has been said more than once, flourishes in the charnel house. To Spencer *The Revenger's Tragedy* is "the skull's apotheosis." [59] "Its motive," Eliot writes, "is truly the death-motive, for it is the loathing and horror of life itself." [60] Perhaps, however, criticism has gone too far. The insistence upon dissolution is not entirely somber but appears, as has been remarked, in conjunction with broadly comic situations. Even the death scenes themselves are lightened by a note of ghastly merriment. Supervacuo threatens a prison officer with the bleeding head of his youngest, and most cherished, brother. "Villaine," he cries, "Ile braine thee with it" (III, vi, 106). Harsh puns and bitter repartee accompany the whole episode of the Duke's murder. His final words are played upon by Vindice with malicious humor:

> DUKE: I cannot brooke—
> VINDICE: The Brooke is turnd to bloud.
>   III, v, 234–35

This grimly mocking treatment of death contributes to the macabre mood. One may, indeed, say even that *The Revenger's Tragedy* suggests in several ways the *danse ma-*

cabre, a theme that captured the imagination of the later
Middle Ages.

At first the Dance of Death was impersonal,[61] but it began to reflect personal horror and fascination when the
medieval outlook of stoicism mingled with Christian hope
gave way to the Renaissance justification of life in terms of
this world, when death became more final and immeasurably
more terrifying. Kurtz describes a late version of the Dance
in the church of the commune of Bar. "The dancers," he
writes,

are . . . worldly people clothed in elegant costume, the men in
close fitting trousers and jacket and hood in fashion at the end
of the XVth century.

The men and women, holding each other by the hand, dance
a sort of farandole to the sound of the tabor-pipe that the musi-
cian plays while beating a drum at the same time. Death, an
emaciated figure armed with bow and arrow, strikes down the
dancers one after the other. One woman has been shot through
the breast; her dancing partner is stretched out dead on the
ground. Little demons gambol on the heads of the dancers,
awaiting the opportunity to take possession of the soul which
escapes from the mouth of the dying. . . . On the right the
angel of judgment, Saint Michel, weighs the souls of the dead,
the book of life in the other balance. A demon puts his fork on
the scales in order to overbalance the soul. . . . God appears
above hell in his halo and indicates with his hand the balance of
justice.

To the left of this scene are three persons. One, clothed in a
long robe with a stick in his hand, is evidently the "Docteur"
who speaks the lines written under the picture. He addresses his
neighbor, a lay person in elegant costume, who points to the
Dance and is inclined to participate. The "Docteur" seems to
wish to prevent him from entering the "terribla dansa."

"The meaning of this allegorical tableau," Kurtz goes on to
remark, "is clear. Worldly life is a dance, a farandole, which
turns the thoughts of man from death, and conceals the sad
reality and the terrible consequences of sin, judgment, and

the eternal punishments. In the midst of the joy and freedom of the dancers, Death strikes at random noblemen and ladies, and the demons await the passage of the soul of the sinner." [62]

The Revenger's Tragedy has essentially the same message and conveys it in essentially the same terms. Almost all the important elements are here: the macabre atmosphere of mingled mirth and horror; worldly life represented as a revel turning man's thoughts away from the inevitability of death and the consequences of sin; the luxurious exteriors of the courtly revelers; Death, symbolized by the skull of Gloriana, lurking in the background or joining the dance in the masque of revengers. There is but one significant deviation: the deaths in *The Revenger's Tragedy* are not random, but derive inevitably from the irony which constitutes the framework of Middleton's moral order.

The characters who make up the play consider themselves very clever and worldly. They scheme and engage in intrigues; they pride themselves on their superior wit. But, as we have seen, they err quite grossly, quite stupidly—even when Vindice is not at hand to spoil their plans. For their little world is part of a larger universe which they are incapable of understanding. They do not realize that even as they strain eagerly after pleasure they invite disaster, must succumb ultimately to the inexorable moral order. Vindice himself, the cleverest of them all, the instrument of divine vengeance, has been corrupted and must eventually fall. The wheel has to come full circle; an omnipotent God and His angels weigh the souls of the sinners in the scales of judgment and mete out appropriate punishments. Vindice may be regarded as a kind of "docteur," pointing out the moral to the audience, warning all potential sinners.

The movement of a dance is suggested by the technique of the play. The pace never slackens; one startling situation follows another with ever increasing rapidity. The formalized, almost abstract, treatment of conventions contributes to the regularity and artificiality of the dance pattern. The ironic reversals are like variations on a theme; the repeated allusions to luxury and revels, sensuality and death, resemble musical motifs, recurring and blending. But it is in its final scene that *The Revenger's Tragedy* comes closest to being a dramatized Dance of Death. While a comet gleams balefully in the heavens and thunder reverberates, the masked avengers go through their last gyrations, courtly riot gives way to bloodshed, the laughter of the revelers to the moans of the dying.

It is altogether unlikely that Middleton ever visited the commune of Bar and saw there the unknown artist's tableau of the Dance of Death. Rather, because he was deeply attracted to the macabre and molded, perhaps more than he was aware, by the medieval heritage, he turned to a theme at once familiar and unusual—a theme rich in dramatic potentialities, ideally suited to the expression of his own sardonic attitude toward life. He uses the conventions of Elizabethan revenge tragedy as his framework, and Renaissance Italy as his setting. But he appears determined to divest his work of any topical relevance.[63] The background is neither the Venice of *Antonio's Revenge*, the Parma of *'Tis Pity She's a Whore*, nor the Rome and Padua of *The White Devil*. It is merely "Italy," and this we know only from a few casual references. For Middleton is telling a timeless parable of man's wickedness and God's punishment for sin.

X I

The Revenger's Tragedy is a difficult work upon which to pass judgment. One may relate the author's mood to the mood of his age. One may trace the forces that shaped his art: the traditions that he inherited from the past, the attitudes that he shared with his countrymen, the methods that he learned from his fellow playwrights. Yet, when all has been said, the play defies classification. Neither melodrama nor tragedy, neither farce nor satire, it has attributes of all these genres. It is the result not so much of an outer frame of reference as of some inner vision. *The Revenger's Tragedy* anticipates surrealist art, is perhaps essentially less akin to other Jacobean plays than to the grotesque fantasies which haunted the imagination of Hieronymus Bosch when he conceived his *Temptation of Saint Anthony*. The play has the accomplished draftsmanship of a Dali, but unlike Dali's work, it has passion and a message.

The Revenger's Tragedy has all the virtues of fantastic art and its weaknesses as well. It is unusual and effective; it is technically dazzling—perhaps too dazzling. We are aware always of the author's striving after originality, his desire to give a new and more sensational twist to any standard situation. And so we become interested less in what the characters are doing than in what startling interplay the dramatist will provide next for his automata, what new reversal will take place in the ensuing scene. Although the ironic method was essential to Middleton in setting forth his concept of the divine retribution for sin, he perhaps became infatuated with his own technique. The irony usurps the reader's attention; it becomes unintentionally the end, rather than an artistic embellishment, and detracts ultimately from the play's more serious purpose. Such preoccupation with technique is evidence, perhaps, of immaturity, of a precocious delight in displaying virtuosity.

The play suffers also from a narrowness of appeal, owing to the limitations of the author's view of life. It is as if his entire emotional energy were channeled into his loathing for humanity. There is no love, no pity: only anger and disgust and satanic laughter. Now a hatred of life may be, as Eliot believes, a significant phase of life itself,[64] and therefore valid material for creative expression. But there is no reasonable explanation for the hatred in this work: it is a scream that pierces the night, and communicates little more than shrill horror. It appears to be based neither on observation nor experience, but rather on some hidden, inexplicable torment. Other writers have experienced a loathing for mankind, though rarely with such intensity; few have communicated it so well. But the poet has not made it relevant to the relationships into which men enter, to the problems which men face. "[It] is such a vision as might come," remarks Eliot,

to a highly sensitive adolescent with a gift for words. . . . The cynicism, the loathing and disgust of humanity, expressed consummately in *The Revenger's Tragedy*, are immature in the respect that they exceed the object. Their objective equivalents are characters practising the grossest vices; characters which seem merely to be spectres projected from the poet's inner world of nightmare, some horror beyond words. So the play is a document on humanity chiefly because it is a document on one human being.[65]

The Revenger's Tragedy is a finer work than a *Titus Andronicus*, because it has poetry and a point of view. But the play is inferior to a *Hamlet*, because its point of view is a fragmentary and inadequate one, because it lacks the most compelling type of dramatic interest: a concern for people. *The Revenger's Tragedy* is in its own way very great, but it is not an example of the greatest type of art.

As Middleton goes on to develop his conception of tragedy, he does not revise materially his estimation of humanity nor does he acquire compassion. The figures in his later plays are often weak and contemptible, driven by the baser impulses, devoid of any moral sense. But the author's mood ceases to be one of agonized revulsion. He seems no longer to say, "How revolting life has become, how loathsome are the passions to which men yield," but rather, "This is the way life is, these are the passions that destroy men." The macabre atmosphere gives way to a realistic atmosphere characterized by an attention to homely detail. If the verse loses concentration and intensity, it gains in subtlety and fluency. Middleton is able now to translate his ironic view of life into terms of character. He probes with infinite delicacy the emotional recesses of men and women, specializing in the psychology of sexual relationships and abnormal states of mind. Although he remains fascinated by the manifold ways in which the sinner may set in motion the forces that destroy him, he never again attempts anything quite like *The Revenger's Tragedy*.

II. *The Second Maiden's Tragedy*

THE MOST IMPRESSIVE single feature of Middleton's later work is his growing concern with the inner lives of his characters: their motives and preoccupations, their struggles with conscience, and—more important—with the primitive impulses that tend to overwhelm them. These plays reflect, as Bradbrook observes, "Middleton's interest in the way the mind works." [1] He excels in analyzing irrational conduct, especially as it appears in relationships that have their basis in sex. He portrays men and women whose reasoning faculties and ethical scruples are unable to withstand the lures of pleasure and the pressures of physical attraction. They yield —only to find themselves caught in emotional entanglements which bring anguish as well as gratification, which indeed eventually destroy them. Middleton charts the careers of these personages with remorseless objectivity, setting forth the successive stages of their inexorable decline, recording the ultimate deterioration of their moral fibre.

Such a view of man diminishes rather than enlarges him. Middleton does not proclaim the final victory of the human spirit over the forces of evil; instead he portrays the enervating effects of evil upon those who succumb to it. If his characters are transformed in the course of the action, they are transformed for the worse. They become meaner and harder, more apt to exchange recriminations than to express lofty sentiments. "No one in these plays cries 'I am Duchess of Malfi still,'" writes Ellis-Fermor. "No one speaks over the dead and dying those tributes which Shakespeare, Webster,

Ford put in the mouths of the bystanders, often even of the very foes who have destroyed them. Their lives are indeed 'a black charnel' but they do not redeem themselves in death; their deaths are of a piece with their lives and become them no better." [2] In this conception of tragedy heroics can have little place, and the periodic outbursts of melodramatic bloodshed appear superfluous, perhaps even inappropriate, alongside the more compelling drama of inner turmoil. The picture of humanity that Middleton presents is certainly not a reassuring one, but it is usually consistent and it is always unsentimental. Perhaps because it is the result of observation and understanding rather than of a theory of psychology, it rings true. As Bradbrook remarks: "Compared with the characters of earlier plays, Middleton's are fuller, more natural and human." [3] The only concessions are to sensationalism. Were it not for these Middleton might have been credited with formulating a drama that was truly psychological.

As a play, *The Second Maiden's Tragedy* no doubt has weaknesses. It lacks unity of action, the two stories being joined together in a clumsy and arbitrary fashion.[4] Furthermore, the main plot is less interesting than the underplot—certainly a defect. But in the remarkable lesser action of *The Second Maiden's Tragedy* Middleton reveals for the first time an interest in mental processes and emotional disturbances. The pattern of the situations in which the characters become involved is, moreover, precisely the same pattern which Middleton uses, to more impressive effect, in *The Changeling* and *Women Beware Women*. A key work in the development of Middleton's art, the play merits close examination.

I

In the year 1611 or not long before, Middleton read in *Don Quixote* a *novella* which embodied that ironic view of life to which he was so profoundly attracted. But, unlike Middleton's City comedies, the "Story of the One Who Was Too Curious for His Own Good" imparts its ironies in terms of character and human relationships. One cannot determine with any assurance the extent to which the dramatist's source influenced permanently his approach to character and situation. There can, however, be little question that he was impressed deeply with his material, for on several occasions he follows the original almost word for word. Although Cervantes' *novella* is familiar enough, a fairly detailed summary will be of use in tracing Middleton's treatment of his source.

The story tells of two Florentine gentlemen, Anselmo and Lotario, who are devoted friends. Anselmo falls in love with the beautiful and wellborn Camila; using Lotario as emissary, he wins her hand in marriage. For a while they live together happily, but Anselmo at length becomes disturbed. He confides in his friend, tells him that he is tormented with the desire to prove whether or not his wife is truly as virtuous as she appears, implores him to make trial of Camila by wooing her. Lotario objects. "Tell me, Anselmo," he asks,

supposing that Heaven or good fortune had made you the master and lawful owner of a very fine diamond to whose quality and purity all the lapidaries who had seen it had testified, stating in unison their common opinion that in quality, purity, and fineness it was the best that nature could produce in the way of such a stone; and supposing, further, that you yourself believed all this to be true, without knowing anything that would cause you to believe otherwise, would it be right for you to wish to take that diamond and place it between a hammer and an anvil and there by force of blows and strength of arm endeavor to see whether

or not it was as hard and fine as they had said it was? And supposing that you went through with this and the stone withstood
so foolish a test, would you thereby be adding anything to its
worth and the esteem in which it was held? Whereas, if it should
break, a thing that could happen, would not all be lost? It would
indeed; for certainly its owner would be looked upon by every-
one as a man of little sense.[5]

But Anselmo remains unmoved, and his friend finally agrees
to do his bidding.

At first Lotario evades his obligation, telling Anselmo that
his wife has resisted all advances, when indeed none has been
made. But Anselmo eavesdrops and sees that the pair ignore
one another. When he later taunts his friend as unfaithful to
his word, the embarrassed Lotario swears that he will keep
his promise. The husband goes off for a week, and Lotario
now notices Camila for the first time and finds himself en-
chanted by her beauties of mind and body. Although he
struggles against the emotions that she arouses within him,
he cannot help falling in love. Lotario woos her in earnest,
praising her beauty, importuning her compassion. At first
Camila is distressed, but she gradually yields and eventually
surrenders herself entirely to her lover's will. When Anselmo
returns, he does not perceive what is missing there—"the
thing that he had treated so lightly yet had treasured most."

Although the affair is, on the whole, conducted with discretion, it does not escape the notice of Leonela, Camila's
maidservant; she becomes, indeed, her mistress' confidante.
Aware of the power that her knowledge permits her to exercise, Leonela brazenly admits her own gallant to the house
and entertains him in her room. One morning, as he steals
away at daybreak muffled in his cloak, Lotario catches a
glimpse of him and rashly concludes that Camila has been
false. In a jealous fury he rushes to Anselmo—tells him that
he has erred about Camila, that she has yielded to his entreaties, that she is ready now to lie with him. He urges the

credulous husband to feign a journey and then, from the privacy of his closet, observe his wife being solicited by his friend.

Lotario soon has reason to regret his impetuosity. For Camila is concerned about her servant's shamelessness; it might conceivably do injury to her reputation. And so, when she meets Lotario, she informs him immediately of the gallant who frequents the house, spends the night in Leonela's embraces, and then sneaks off at dawn. Lotario now confesses his fault and begs forgiveness, but he finds himself at a complete loss in dealing with the situation that he has created. Camila is able, however, to formulate an ingenious stratagem, designed to turn the expected revelation of her infamy into a dramatic confirmation of her virtue. The next day, as planned, Anselmo takes up his hiding place behind the draperies, before Camila and Leonela enter. There he hears his wife inveigh against her suitor's wicked passion, threatening indeed to slay Lotario with a dagger. Anselmo sees her lament, swoon, and recover. When Lotario arrives, Anselmo listens attentively to his wife's impassioned defense of her honor; he watches as she turns upon Lotario with an unsheathed dagger and, finding herself unable to pierce him, thrusts the instrument into her own side and collapses in a faint. As she lies outstretched upon the floor, bathed in her own blood, Anselmo can truly rejoice in the good fortune of having for his wife a second Portia. One need scarcely mention that the wound is superficial.

For some time afterwards the guilty pair are able to enjoy one another without fear. But one night the husband hears footsteps in Leonela's room. He investigates, finds the door locked, manages to force his way in—just as the maid's lover slips off by leaping from the window. Anselmo is so enraged that he threatens Leonela with death, but she puts him off by promising to inform him the next morning of something astonishing. When Anselmo returns to his wife's chamber and tells her all that has passed, Camila is terrified; she fears, as well she may, that her secret will be revealed by Leonela. At dawn Anselmo is surprised to discover that the maid-servant has managed to escape by tying some sheets together and fixing them to the window. He is even more puzzled when he finds that Camila, too, has run away, taking her jewelry along with her. But when he is told that Lotario has gone off that very night with all the money he possessed, Anselmo feels that he is losing his mind.

Eventually the foolish husband learns the truth, and dies "a victim of the grief which his ill-advised curiosity had brought upon him." The repentant Lotario is later killed in battle. Camila, having fled to a convent, is unmoved by her husband's passing, but the news of her lover's death so sad-dens her that she takes the veil and, within a short time, dies "of sorrow and melancholy."

II

It is easy to see why the tale of the overcurious husband would appeal to Middleton. The story is rich in the irony which had already become Middleton's specialty in the City comedies—the irony which invests the careers of those who stumble blindly upon the road to inevitable disaster because they cannot foresee the consequences of their own actions, because they continually place themselves in predicaments from which they cannot escape. It is an ironic pattern of which Cervantes is keenly aware, for he underscores it more than once in the course of the story:

and so [Anselmo] went on adding link after link to the chain by which he was binding himself and assuring his own dis-honor; for the more Lotario dishonored him, the more he held that he was being honored.

He [Lotario] implored . . . her advice as to what he should do to get out of the intricate labyrinth in which, through his impetuosity, he had become involved.

He [Anselmo] himself led home by the hand the one who had wrought the destruction of his good name, in the belief that he was bringing with him one who had exalted it.[6]

For the most part Middleton follows the sequence of events in his source faithfully. At one point he goes so far as to reproduce, virtually intact, the ironic image of the diamond, taking pains only to condense it:

> must a man needes in having a ritch Diamond
> put it betweene a hammer and an Anvile
> and not beleeving the true worth and valiew
> breake it in pieces to finde owt the goodnes
> and in the findinge loose it.
>
> ll. 315–19

There are some minor omissions and alterations, such as the curious changes of name. Only Leonela remains; Anselmo becomes "Anselmus" and Lotario is transformed into "Votarius." Camila is referred to simply as the "Wife." The maidservant's lover, nameless in Cervantes, is called Bellarius. Middleton strengthens his role in the intrigue, making him the bitter enemy of Votarius. Of greater interest is the one major deviation from the source: Middleton's conclusion is entirely his own.

In the play the climactic scene is the sham encounter between wife and lover, while the husband eavesdrops. But Middleton gives the episode a wildly melodramatic twist. As in the source, the Wife is to remonstrate against her paramour's impudence and defend her own reputation. But in the play she plans to turn the dagger upon her lover rather than herself. Votarius is not to be harmed, however, for Leonela has been asked to provide him with "some pryvie armour." The maid at once reveals the entire scheme to Bellarius, who urges her to forget the armor and ready a poisoned dagger for the Wife. The plot is successful; indeed, it is too successful. Votarius is slain, and the husband, convinced of his wife's virtue, kills the maid who had slandered her.[7] Anselmus and Bellarius then turn upon one another; during the struggle *"the Lady purposely runs betwene, and is kild by them both."* The two men wound each other mortally. At first Middleton apparently intended to have Anselmus die happy in his newfound faith, and to let Bellarius linger on a few moments to tell the whole story. But, in an insertion, Anselmus revives briefly to hear the account, then expires proclaiming: *"The serpents wisdome is in weemens lust."*

Middleton's conclusion can hardly be regarded as an advance upon Cervantes. Indeed, it mars the play seriously because it is violent—almost preposterously violent—in an entirely unnecessary way. For the tragedy lies essentially not in the conventional retributive justice terminating in death, but rather in the debasement of the leading figures themselves, in the perversion of their own characters. "Man has some ennemy still that keepes him back/ in all his fortunes, and his mynde is his," Votarius reflects on Anselmus' position, ironically unaware that he too has such an enemy within:

> and thats a mightie adversarie, I had rather
> haue twenty kinges my enemies then that [port] part,
> for let me be at warr with earth and hell
> so that be frendes with me.

ll. 435-40

Once submitting to the pressures of their impulses, these figures become possessed. "Somewhat Comaundes me," the Wife cries out in anguish, "and takes all the power,/ of my self from me" (ll. 567–68). Sin has become its own Nemesis and the sinner his own destroyer. The ironic pattern is almost identical with that of the City comedies. But it does differ in one very important respect: it evolves not so much from the external clashes between the principals as from their inner struggles and—more important—their abnormal emotional conditions. And it is in this respect that Middleton is able to take a hint from his source and improve upon it, making it indeed into something profoundly worthwhile.

III

The Camila of Cervantes' story is the conventional intriguing adulteress of the romantic *novella;* she is scarcely characterized at all. Lotario is more fully developed. "A thousand times," Cervantes writes,

he felt an impulse to leave the city and go where his friend would never see him again and he would never see Camila, but the pleasure he found in gazing upon her prevented this and kept him there. Struggling with himself, he made an effort to reject and not to feel the happiness which the sight of her gave him.

When alone, he would indulge in self-reproaches for his folly, calling himself a bad friend and a bad Christian. He would argue the matter in his mind, making comparisons between himself and Anselmo, and he always reached the same conclusion: to the effect that Anselmo's madness and rashness outweighed his own treachery, and if he could find an excuse before God as in the eyes of men for what he now thought of doing, then he need fear no punishment for his offense.[8]

Lotario takes no pleasure in Camila's triumphant deception of her husband, "for he kept remembering what a deceived man his friend was and how unjustly he had wronged him." [9] But it is the husband, Anselmo, who is the most interesting figure in the source. He is regarded frankly as the victim of an obsession, as one suffering from a mental sickness. "For some time now," he confides to his friend, "I have been wearied and oppressed by a desire so strange, so out of the ordinary, that I marvel at myself." [10] Anselmo finds himself incapable of following reasonable advice; he realizes that he is being driven by an irrational force. "You must take into consideration," he tells Lotario, "that I am suffering from that infirmity which some women have who are seized with the desire to eat earth, plaster, charcoal, and still worse things that are disgusting enough to look at and even more so to eat." [11]

In *The Second Maiden's Tragedy* and the later plays, Middleton takes up personages such as these—a Lotario, perplexed and morally weak; an Anselmo, tormented by inexplicable passions. Treating them with greater subtlety than he found in his sources, he creates a truly impressive gallery of studies in abnormal psychology. And, even as early as *The Second Maiden's Tragedy*, he explores an area his source left untouched: the personality of the female sinner. As Ellis-Fermor remarks, "it will be seen that Middleton's capacity for tragedy is inseparable from his other supreme gift, his discernment of the minds of women; in this no dramatist of the period except Shakespeare is his equal at once for variety and for penetration." [12]

Middleton's Anselmus is pretty much the Anselmo of Cervantes. He believes sincerely that his wife is chaste, yet he is curious—one might say pathologically curious—to learn more about her. She has not, after all, had the opportunity to stray, and Anselmus is eager to know how she would behave if faced suddenly with temptation. "What labour ist," he asks,

> for woman to keep constant
> thats neuer tride or tempted? whers her fight!
> the warr's within her brest, her honest anger
> against the impudence of flesh and hell,
> so let me knowe the ladie of my Rest
> or I shall neuer sleep well.   ll. 291–96

He refuses to desist, even though his friend tells him what he might expect:

> good sir thinck ont,
> Nor does it tast of wit to trye their strengthes
> that are created sicklie, nor of manhood
> we ought not to put blockes in weemens waies
> for some to often fall vpon plaine ground.
>
> ll. 319–23

In *The Second Maiden's Tragedy*, however, Anselmus' obsession has one consequence that is lacking in the source: it affects his sex conduct. So preoccupied has he become that he neglects his wife, finds himself unable to maintain a normal marital relationship with her. Instead "he walkes at midnight in thick shadie woodes/ wher scarce the moone is starlight" (ll. 369–70). Anselmus "has lost his kindnes,

> forgot the waie of wedlock, and become
> a straunger to the ioyes and rites of love,
> hees not so good as a lord ought to be.
>
> ll. 377–80

Anselmus' wife is quite attractive ("a worke of beautie") and she is younger than her husband. "Looke you," Votarius asks her,

> like one whose lord should walke in groues
> about the peace of midnight! Alas madame
> tis to me wondrous how you should spare the daie
> from amorous clips, much less the generall season
> when all the worldes a gamster.   ll. 479–83

Like so many of Middleton's women, the Wife is at heart fiercely sensual, needing only to be aroused. Keenly aware that she is being mistreated by her husband, she stays up for him at night, stands, "cold and thinly cladd," watching from the window as he paces below in the moonlight. Yearning for the love and affection denied her, she responds eagerly to the most hesitant advances. Indeed, when she senses Votarius slipping away, she becomes the aggressor, will not let him go:

> WIFE: you will not offer violence to me sir
>   in my lords abscence; what does that touch you
>   if I want comforte?
> VOTARIUS: will you take your answer?
> WIFE: it is not honest in you to tempt woman,
>   when her distresses takes awaie her strengthe,
>   how is she able to withstand her enemye
> VOTARIUS: I would faine leaue your sight and I could possible
> WIFE: what ist to you (good sir) if I be pleazd
>   to weep my self awaie? and run thus violently
>   into the armes of death, and kisse distruction
>   does this concerne you now.   ll. 526-37

After she has become Votarius' mistress, the Wife displays no sense of guilt; she is, in fact, less concerned about her adultery than about having to share her secret with her maid. Like Beatrice she is solicitous about her honor after she has lost it. "Tis easie/ to draw a ladies honor in suspision," she chides her lover,

> but not so soone recouerd and confirmd
> to the first faith agen from whence you brought it,
> your wit was fetcht owt abowt other busines
> or such forgetfullnes had never ceazd you.
>   ll. 1466-71

And later, shocked by her servingwoman's impudence, she regards herself with the self-pity of outraged gentility:

> o the wronges
> that ladies do their honors when they make
> their slaues familier with their weaknesses.
>   ll. 1566-68

Like Beatrice she becomes the deed's creature; she is as much in her servant's clutches as Beatrice is in the power of De Flores. "She has betrayed her husband," Barker writes, "but at the same time she has betrayed herself." [13]

Votarius is typical of Middleton's later sinners: the irresolute man of good intentions who becomes emboldened and
deceitful once he has embarked upon his shameful course. He
objects to his friend's request, yet carries it out. Once engaged in his mission he hesitates, tries to prevent himself from
succumbing to the Wife's allurements, yet fails and gradually—one might say inevitably—drifts into sin. As he goes
on, his character is gradually debased by the relationship into
which he has entered. At first he is conscience-stricken by
his betrayal of trust, terrified by the prospect of facing the
very man who but a short time earlier was his most intimate
companion:

> his very name shootes like a feaver throughe me
> now hott now cold, which cheek shall I turne toward
> him
> for feare he should read guiltyness in my lookes?
> ll. 860–62

But Votarius' friendship soon turns to hatred. If at first he
could not look at Anselmus for shame, he now shuns him
out of disgust and resentment:

> I do not like his company now, tis irksome
> his eye offendes me, mee thinckes tis not kindlie
> wee two should liue together in one howse: . . . .
> then let the worst giue place, whom shee'as least need
> on
> he that can best be sparde, and that's her husband.
> ll. 913–15, 921–22

He is racked by jealousy, finds Anselmus' familiarity with
his own wife offensive: "I do not like his ouerbouldnes with
her/ hees to famylier with the face I loue" (ll. 923–24). He
berates his mistress, quite unjustly, for carrying on an affair
with a man that he happens to see wandering through the
house. Later, thoroughly demoralized, he resorts to lies
and deceptions in his dealings with Anselmus. "My very

thought's my poison," he tells himself at one point, and indeed it is.

All three figures in the domestic story are remarkable studies. If Middleton is indebted greatly to Cervantes for Anselmus, he makes more of Votarius than he found in his source, and the Wife is almost wholly his own creation. The dramatist's achievement becomes even more impressive when one considers that the entire action occupies only four scenes.

I V

The main action of *The Second Maiden's Tragedy* concerns the fortunes of Lord Govianus in his struggle with a lustful Tyrant who first deprives him of his throne and then challenges him for the love of his Lady. Deserted by his followers, Govianus fears that he will lose his mistress as well. "O shees a woman," he says, "and her eye will stande/ vpon advauncement" (ll. 68–69). But his Lady remains defiantly true, even though by yielding she may share a kingdom and have jewels worth ten cities. The lovers are ordered confined to "seuerall Roomes,"

> wher he may only haue a sight of her
> to his myndes torment, but his armes and lips
> lockt vp like fellons, from her.
> l. 248²⁻⁵

However, they gain the friendship of the guard and are permitted free access to one another.

The Tyrant meanwhile persists in his courtship. First Helvetius, the Lady's aged father, is sent off to plead with her. The old man scolds his daughter, urges her to accept the usurper, if not as her husband, at least as a lover after she marries. But when Govianus suddenly appears discharging a pistol, Helvetius is at once converted to a life of virtue; indeed, he welcomes the deposed King as his son-in-law. The Tyrant turns next to Sophonirus, a wittol and court parasite, bids him use both words and jewels to lure the lady. Sophonirus is, however, even less successful than his predecessor, for he manages only to lose his life at Govianus' hands.

His patience now at an end, the usurper resorts to violence. He looses a band of armed ruffians upon the house in which the lovers are confined, and it is soon apparent that the Lady must either die or be carried off, a sacrifice to the Tyrant's lust. "My lord," she tells her beloved after a brief prayer, "be now as sodaine as you please sir/ I am ready to your hand" (ll. 1306–7). But Govianus fails her by falling into a swoon: as the Tyrant's men beat upon the doors, the Lady finds that she must take her own life.

At first the news of the Lady's suicide discourages the usurper. It is after all a setback, and a less enterprising suitor might conceivably be inclined to give up at this point. But the Tyrant is, if anything, persistent, and he determines to possess the Lady in death, if not in life. And so he makes his way at midnight into the cathedral that houses her tomb. There he has a few soldiers rip open her monument and steal out the body. The Tyrant believes that he may be able to have life dissembled upon her face, for he has

> once read of a *Herod* whose affection
> pursued a virgins loue, as I did thine
> whoe for the hate she owd him kilde her self
> (as thow to rashlie didst,) without all pittie:
> yet he preserud her bodie dead in honie
> and kept her longe after her funerall.
>
> ll. 1855–60

He hires "a Picture drawer/ A ladies forenoone Tuter" to anoint her, then seizes the corpse in his arms and presses his

lips against hers in order to "labour life into her." By so doing he clasps death: the Lady's face has been smeared with
poison, and the artist who stands alongside the usurper. is
Govianus. The Tyrant, in his last agonies, must watch his
rival being restored to his kingdom by a court grown tired
of depravity.

The story related in the Govianus-Tyrant-Lady scenes of
The Second Maiden's Tragedy is certainly a lurid and fantastic one. The reader is scarcely able to envisage material
more removed from the simple, and for the most part, realistic portrayal of adultery in the domestic episodes. The two
actions are, indeed, linked through a device that is entirely
artless and unconvincing: Govianus is the brother of the
overcurious husband, and his Lady, we learn, is the Wife's
sister. Aside, however, from a comment by the Wife late in
the play—

> ile ymitat my noble sisters fate
> late mistres to the worthy *Gouianus*
> and cast awaie my life as he did hers,
>   ll. 2079–81

—nothing is made of her relationship with the Lady, and
there is some doubt that the dramatist had any very clear
notion of such a relationship. It is perhaps superfluous to remark that Anselmus never strikes us as being a king's brother
and that none of the figures in the underplot seems even re-
motely related to the life of the court.

The scene in which the Tyrant embraces the poisoned
corpse of the Lady brings to mind the murder of the Duke
in *The Revenger's Tragedy*, and a number of other parallels
between the two plays—some quite remarkable—have been
pointed out.[14] Yet *The Revenger's Tragedy* and the principal action of *The Second Maiden's Tragedy* leave quite
different impressions. They are not the products of the same
mood; they do not share the same point of view. When Sir

George Buc gave *The Second Maiden's Tragedy* its title, he was thinking, no doubt, of Beaumont and Fletcher's *The Maid's Tragedy*. This designation is regarded by Greg as "not very appropriate." [15] Ward goes further: "Except that the subject is again the guilty passion of a tyrant," he writes, "the play bears no resemblance to Beaumont and Fletcher's tragedy." [16] But, if *The Second Maiden's Tragedy* cannot be classified as a sequel to *The Maid's Tragedy*, its main plot does show the very considerable influence of Fletcherian melodrama. It is an important influence—and one which is evident in all of Middleton's later tragedies and tragicomedies.

v

The makers of Elizabethan popular tragedy had tried, for the most part, to be faithful to the essential facts of human life. Their material had often been history or pseudo-history, the plays having some basis in what was believed to be fact —whether derived from pamphlets or Plutarch, oral reports or the chronicles of the Tudor historians. These plays are, to be sure, frequently naïve and uneven in quality, but they have the virtues of honesty and variety. They deal with domestic relationships and public affairs; they offer studies in ambition and conscience, love and lust, hatred and revenge. If the playwrights tended always toward the romantic and the sensational, they showed, nevertheless, an interest in portraying a wide range of human emotions and motivations. In Shakespeare and Marlowe the popular stage found its noblest voices, but it produced also a number of lesser figures of genuine ability—such men as Dekker and Munday and Heywood—whose talents were often obscured by haste, carelessness, and collaboration.

But by the second decade of the seventeenth century the age had changed and, along with it, the audience. Beaumont and Fletcher contributed to the outstanding adult company —the King's Men—but, unlike Shakespeare and their other predecessors, they were gentlemen by birth, training, and inclination, and they wrote to please a public that was now largely aristocratic. The new audience had a distaste for history and was not particularly stirred by tragedy. It wished to be amused rather than moved; it preferred eroticism to thought; above all, it craved novelty. Beaumont and Fletcher had the supreme good fortune to hit upon a formula which satisfied the new taste—a formula that placed a high premium on ingenuity and inventiveness, and could, in the right hands, be repeated indefinitely with minor variations.

The drama created by Beaumont and Fletcher is noteworthy for its originality, excitement, and theatrical effectiveness. The language is fluent and often beautiful; the stagecraft is polished—"slick" might be a better word—and occasionally brilliant. All that is lacking is credibility and integrity. The authors call their works tragedies and tragicomedies, but they may, perhaps, be more accurately described as entertainments: conceived as a means of stimulating jaded appetites, having little claim to depth or permanence.

The setting is remote and exotic: Rhodes or Messina, Iberia or Austracia. "The reader is transported to a no man's land," says Ristine,

beyond the ken of human experience, where men take on superhuman characteristics, where strange events happen, and imaginary history is made and unmade in the twinkling of an eye. The checkered fortunes of monarchs, generals, and lords and ladies of high degree engross his chief attention; war, usurpation, rebellion—actual or imminent—furnish a subordinate interest; while a comic touch or sub-plot is the diverting accompaniment of the romantic action. Love of some sort is the motive force;

intrigue is rife; the darkest villainy is contrasted with the noblest and most exalted virtue. In the course of an action teeming with incident and excitement, and in which the characters are enmeshed in a web of disastrous complications, reverse and surprise succeed each other with a lightning rapidity, and the outcome trembles in the balance.[17]

In the tragedies—*Thierry and Theodoret*, for example, or *The Maid's Tragedy*—the principal figures are unable to extricate themselves, and so suffer pathetic deaths. In the tragicomedies—plays such as *Philaster* or *A King and No King* —they live, saved at the last moment by the sudden descent of the *deus ex machina*, in the form of a convenient rebellion or remarkable disclosure.

One might reasonably object that this new type of tragicomedy—largely the creation of Fletcher—is at best a dubious literary genre. It is certainly facile and artificial, and in one sense it is quite false. For the audience is deceived into assuming that characters have died—indeed the other figures in the play mourn for them—only to learn finally that they live, that all will be well. We are given the sensations of tragedy and also a happy ending; we have been asked to shed tears over nothing. But this is perhaps taking too serious a view of what is essentially a commercial product. The characters never impress us as being real individuals with real problems, and so it matters little whether they survive or perish. The denouement is expedient rather than inevitable: *The Maid's Tragedy* could as easily have been a tragicomedy, while *A King or No King* might just as well have had a tragic conclusion.

Against a background usually restricted to the palace and its environs, the sensational is always happening. A king is told that he may be cured of impotence by killing the first woman who leaves the temple of Diana before the next sunrise; he waits outside—only to discover that the lady is his queen. A noble young courtier learns on his wedding night that his bride has sworn never to enter his bed, that she is indeed the mistress of the king, who has arranged the marriage. A brave general is exiled, robbed, and humiliated by the duke whom he has faithfully served; yet the old man offers to slay his own son for leading a rebellion against the tyrant.

There are all sorts of wonders. In a single play, *Thierry and Theodoret,* we hear of academes "in which all principles of lust were practis'd," of potions which, when given to the groom on the wedding night,

> Shall for five days so rob his faculties,
> Of all ability to pay that duty,
> Which new made wives expect, that she shall swear
> She is not match'd to a man.[18]   II, i, p. 19

We also hear of handkerchiefs that, if "once us'd/ Say but to dry a tear, will keep the eye-lid/ From closing, until death perform that office" (IV, i, pp. 50–51).

The audience is teased with a variety of piquant situations, involving incest and seduction, impotence and rape. In *A King and No King* Panthea and Arbaces confess their love for one another, discuss how far a brother and sister may go in expressing affection, hesitantly hold hands and kiss. Valerio, in *A Wife for a Month,* is ordered by the usurping tyrant to marry his beloved Evanthe, but he is permitted neither to consummate the union nor to disclose the reason for his abstinence, on pain of Evanthe's immediate death. On the wedding night she approaches her husband, bids him come to bed quickly, sues for his embraces—only to be informed that he is impotent. The central situation in most of the Beaumont and Fletcher plays is, indeed, sexual, with unusual emphasis placed upon the contrast between monstrous lust and stainless chastity. A recurrent theme is the unbridled passion of a tyrant for the virtuous wife or betrothed of a subject; it appears in *Valentinian, The Humourous Lieutenant, A Wife for a Month,* and *The Queen of Corinth.*

The drama is one of intense blacks and dazzling whites. Instead of a series of incidents leading up to a single denouement, we have a succession of high points. The scene, rather than the play, is the unit, and each scene has its own climax, its own tempest of conflicting passions.[19] Emotions are always near the breaking point; the plays overflow with tirades and laments, high-flown oratory and impassioned exchanges.

Since characterization must of necessity be a secondary concern, the dramatists rely usually upon stock figures. These include half a dozen easily recognizable types—types which have been pointed out frequently.[20] The hero is loyal and chivalric, but he is also sentimental and incapable of action, waiting to be relieved by friends or circumstances. He loves a beautiful girl whose chief distinction is a purity which is regarded as either miraculous or pathetic; he receives counsel from a gruff old soldier who feels ill at ease in the palace, who prefers displaying his wounds to begging ladies' favors. The others are less amiable types: the lustful despot, the sensual woman, the poltroon. But the consistency even of these simple stock figures may be violated for the sake of an immediate theatrical effect: Evadne's sudden conversion is unconvincing, but it does produce an exciting scene.[21] "The basis of these plays is," as Bradbrook observes, "an outrageous stimulation. Provided the characters are feeling intensely all the time, it does not much matter how or why." [22]

VI

The innovations of Beaumont and Fletcher were followed widely. Middleton responded to the new vogue by composing, between the years 1611 and 1618, a series of plays which exploit the stock situations of Fletcherian melodrama. Among these works are Middleton's weakest productions.

In *A Fair Quarrel* and *The Witch*, he joins serious actions with preposterous happy solutions, relies carelessly upon the fashionable artificialities and improbabilities which Beaumont and Fletcher popularized. But the influence of the new mode can also be seen in the main action of *The Second Maiden's Tragedy*. It has the sensationalism and unconvincing motivation, the spectacular effects and extremes of good and evil that one expects from Fletcher. It capitalizes, as Fletcher capitalized, on an unusual sexual situation which involves a striking contrast between lust and chastity. The principal figures—Govianus, the Tyrant, and the Lady—are all Fletcherian types, and the sudden transformation of Helvetius suggests the implausible conversions one encounters in the Beaumont and Fletcher plays. The unraveling is a compromise between tragedy and tragicomedy: we are supposed to be moved by the pathos of the Lady's death and then cheered by the happy restoration of Govianus. Actually, however, these scenes are never affecting; they are too unreal, too imitative, too deficient in conviction. Although more grisly and perverse than their originals, they comprise an entertainment similar to the entertainments of Beaumont and Fletcher.

The predominance of the Fletcherian school in Jacobean times created a most unfavorable situation for an artist with Middleton's gifts. He was by temperament a realist—but the new drama was wildly romantic. One of his greatest assets was his understanding of hidden motives, of the buried life— but the new theatrical fashion limited characterization to the superficial treatment of a few rudimentary types. He was interested in portraying a dark and frightening world in which a weak humanity struggles futilely against the terrible ironies that work against man's desires and aspirations—but the new mode stressed the artificial and the undisturbing, scarcely permitted the expression of a serious point of view.

One might possibly overestimate the influence upon Middleton of Beaumont and Fletcher and their followers. Barker feels that

he would occasionally have lapsed into sensationalism even if Beaumont and Fletcher had never written; for he was working within a dramatic tradition that was essentially alien to his genius. He was trying to transform the melodramatic tragedy of his age into something like psychological tragedy, and he was not sufficiently sure of himself to make the transformation complete. Hence the faults that mar even his best tragedies; hence the tendency of his critics to regard him as an author who was capable of writing great scenes but not great plays.[23]

The conventions of Elizabethan tragedy had not, however, entirely precluded an interest in characterization, had not entirely prevented the expression of a point of view; the age did produce a Shakespeare and a Chapman. It is Beaumont and Fletcher who reduced tragedy to the status of entertainment, who accentuated everything that was antithetical to Middleton's talents. And their success was so overwhelming that a professional dramatist like Middleton had of necessity to make concessions to their practices. No doubt he would have written sensational scenes had Beaumont and Fletcher never lived, but they would probably have been less frequent and less flagrant. It seems unlikely that he would have written anything quite so unconvincing or uninteresting as the Tyrant-Lady-Govianus story of *The Second Maiden's Tragedy*. In a different setting Middleton might well have been one of the supreme masters of tragedy. As it is, his work remains an extraordinary—if incomplete—triumph of genius over milieu.

VII

From 1611, the year of *The Second Maiden's Tragedy*, until *A Game at Chess* in 1624, Middleton relies upon verse as the principal medium of his plays: a verse quite unlike any that he had written previously. The difference between the earlier and later poetic styles may easily be seen by a comparison of two passages which appear in almost identical contexts and which serve much the same dramatic purpose. In the first illustration Vindice urges Gratiana to persuade her daughter to Lussurioso's lust; in the second Helvetius solicits his daughter to become the mistress of the Tyrant:

> Would I be poore deiected, scornd of greatnesse,
> Swept from the Pallace, and see other daughters
> Spring with the dewe ath Court, hauing mine owne
> So much desir'd and lou'd—by the Dukes sonne?
> No, I would raise my state vpon her brest
> And call her eyes my Tennants, I would count
> My yearely maintenance vpon her cheekes:
> Take Coach vpon her lip, and all her partes
> Should keepe men after men, and I would ride
> In pleasure vpon pleasure:
> You tooke great paines for her, once when it was,
> Let her requite it now, tho it be but some;
> You brought her forth, she may well bring you home.
>   II, i, 103–15

>   —base spirrited girle
> that canst not thinck aboue disgrace and beggarie,
> when Glorie is set for thee and thy seed
> advauncment for thy father, beside ioye
> able to make a latter springe in me
> in this my fowrscore sommer, and renew me
> with a reuersion yet of heat and youthe?
> but the deiection of thy mynde and spirrit
> makes me thy father guiltie of a fault
> that drawes thy birth in question, and een wronges

> thy mother in her ashes being at peace
> with heavne and man, had not her life and vertues
> bin seales vnto her faithe, I should thinck thee now
> the worke of some hirde servaunt: some howse Tailor
> and no one part of my endeuour in thee.
> had I neglected greatnes: or not rather
> pursued allmost to my eternall hazard,
> thou'd'st nere bin a lordes daughter.
>
> ll. 657–74

The first speech is stiff and rhetorical, lacking in smoothness and polish. But it blazes with passion and energy, rushing onward at a breathless pace, the images contracted in an attempt, as Eliot puts it, "to say everything in the least space, the shortest time." [24] It is a verse capable of producing striking, at times brilliant, effects; it succeeds—succeeds admirably—in expressing simple, fierce emotions. But it is less well suited to introspection or ordinary conversation; it does not lend itself easily to capturing nuances of character or recording the emotional impact of personalities upon one another. The second passage is less concentrated, less intense, perhaps also less memorable. Even though the speaker is expressing disappointment and anger, the tone is conversational, almost casual, in comparison with the first speech. But the verse is more finished; the lines are more fluid and flexible, the rhythms more subtle and varied. If it is less immediately impressive than the preceding passage, it seems more clearly adaptable to the expression of a wide range of thoughts and feelings. To secure its effects it relies on suggestion rather than on bold statement; it does not so much startle the imagination as stir associations. This technique is different at once from that of *The Revenger's Tragedy* and that of Middleton's contemporaries. "His language too gains its effects by different methods from those of the majority of the Elizabethans," writes Bradbrook; "he does not rely upon explicit statement or direct speech but upon implication; nor upon a gorgeous and elaborate vocabulary, but upon a pregnant simplicity which is perhaps more difficult to achieve, and is certainly found more seldom." [25]

"Pursued allmost to my eternall hazard" (l. 673)—such a line is entirely characteristic of Middleton's mature verse. The general meaning is immediately apparent, yet the full implications of the line remain somehow elusive. The words themselves can scarcely be regarded as unusual, but they are all abstract, all rich in overtones that evoke vague associations. Middleton is fond of such abstract words as *comfort*, *eternal, destruction, joy,* and *peace*—words that linger, re-echoing inexplicably in the memory.

Although images appear frequently in *The Second Maiden's Tragedy* and in Middleton's later plays, the range of figurative language is not exceptionally wide. Images derived from food and drink, gardens, diseases and death, temples, treasures, and the everyday activities of humble people—these recur again and again. Indeed, Middleton may repeat a figure from play to play, increasing its elaboration with each use:

> Andrugio? O, as welcome to my lips
> As morning dew to roses! my first love!
> > *More Dissemblers,* ii, iii, 37–38

> A kiss now, that will hang upon my lip
> As sweet as morning-dew upon a rose,
> And full as long;
> > *Women Beware Women,* iii, i, 104–6

> Uppon those lips the sweete fresh Buds of youth,
> The holie Dewe of prayer lyes like pearle
> Dropt from the opening Eye-lids of the Morne
> Uppon the bashfull Rose.
> > *Game at Chess,* i, i, 84–87 [26]

Middleton's images are never as obscure as Chapman's can be, nor are they as ingenious as the conceits of the metaphysicals; rarely does he display the esoteric lore of which

Webster is so fond. His imagery springs not so much from study as from reflection and, to a lesser extent, from observation. Yet the pictures that he creates are seldom precise, can seldom be visualized by the mind's eye. Consider this figure, from *The Second Maiden's Tragedy:*

>   and run thus violently
> into the armes of death, and kisse distruction.
>   ll. 535–36

A picture of some sort is no doubt suggested, but, as in the case of the rose images, it is too indefinite to be clearly envisaged; it appeals to our imagination rather than affording us the pleasure of recognition. Although one might easily point to a number of similar figures in Middleton's later works, a few further illustrations from *The Second Maiden's Tragedy* will suffice:

> in syluer nightes when all the earth was drest
> vp like a virgin in white Inocent beames,
>   ll. 371–72

>   I am like one
> removing from her howse, that lockes vp all
> and rather then she would displace her goodes
> makes shifte with any thinge for the tyme shee staies,
>   ll. 1321–24

>   —o thow faire Springe
> of honest and religious desyres,
> fowntaine of weeping honor, I will kisse thee
> after deathes marble lip,   ll. 1454–57

> were my sowle bid to ioyes eternall Banquet
> and were assurde to finde thee there a guest
> Ide sup with Torments, and refuse that feast;
>   ll. 2188 12-14

> wellcome to myne eyes
> as is the daye-springe from the morninges woombe
> vnto that wretche whose nightes are tedious.
>   ll. 2388–90

It can be seen that Middleton relies often upon personification and that his key words—*virgin, goodes, Springe, Banquet, Torments*—are rarely concrete.

There is another feature of Middleton's imagery that is equally important, but which is inevitably lost in quotation: the perfect appropriateness of the figure to the dramatic situation. "Ile neuer see her more," Votarius tells himself when he begins to find the Wife's charms greater than he can resist,

> I praisde the garden
> but litle thought a bed of snakes laye hidd in't.
>
> ll. 518–19

The reader recalls the words that Votarius has used just a few moments earlier, during his first reluctant overtures:

> the very Springes vpon you now
> the Roses on your cheekes are but new blowne,
> take you together y'are a pleasaunt garden
> wher all the sweetnes of mans comfort breathes.
>
> ll. 469–72

Propriety in the verse of Middleton's later plays is associated with his ability to convey through imagery the same ironic point of view that distinguishes his handling of character and situation. By means of metaphor and simile he makes observations or tells pointed little stories which have in common an ironic, at times sinister, twist. Derived principally from humble life, they are quite realistic and unpretentious. But they do much to establish an atmosphere, foreshadowing sudden reversals and ironic turns of fortune. They serve also as a commentary, emphasize indeed the larger ironies implicit in the interplay of wills and emotions.

In the lesser world of images bright days, filled with sunshine, teem with sudden storms. Through her neglect a foolish mother brings her son to the gallows and stands by weeping as he is punished. The rich man heaps his wealth by the sweat of another's labor; he of all men fears death especially, promises himself to repent when he is old—only to die suddenly in the prime of his life. The felon who has just shaken off his old irons cuts his neighbor's purse at the bench to deserve new ones. A widow dallies as she follows her husband's body to the cemetery, or contracts with a handsome young man at the graveside. The herb-woman sells away all her nosegays and sweet herbs, but returns home with a foul breath for her own pottage. A man goes off to rid another country of a plague, only to bring it home with him to his own dwelling.[27] Images of this kind—realistic, simple, often humble and always ironic—occur repeatedly in *The Second Maiden's Tragedy*. One may quote directly several of the more striking instances:

> —thers the kingdome
> within y'on vallye fixt, while I stand here
> kissing falce hopes vpon a frozen mowntaine,
> without the confines,   ll. 153–56

> like one that has a watche of curious makinge,
> thinckinge to be more cvnnynge then the workeman
> neuer giues ouer tampringe with the wheeles
> till either springe be weakned, ballance bowde
> or some wrong pin put in, and so spoiles all;
>   ll. 832–36

> his care shall watch to keep all straunge theeues owt
> whiles I famillierlie goe in and rob him
> like one that knowes the howse;   ll. 981–83

> for we often see
> condempnd men sick to death, yet tis their fortune
> to recouer to their execution
> and rise againe in health, to set in shame?
>   ll. 1299–1302

> tis for all the world
> like a great Cittie-Pye brought to a table
> wher ther be many handes that laie about

the liddes shutt close when all the meates pickt out,
yet standes to make a showe and cozen people.[28]
ll. 1872–76

Middleton's dramatic verse—different from that of the other great Jacobeans—achieves its own distinction; it is, indeed, perfectly fitted for Middleton's conception of tragedy, ideally suited to conveying his unique view of life. Middleton's poetic gifts have been recognized, but not by all his readers and not as fully as they deserve. Of the earlier critics, Hazlitt feels that Middleton has no style at all,[29] while Courthope is not inclined to seek "poetical sentiment or diction" in the plays of a dramatist who moves "in such a sphere of action and character." [30] But Schelling offers qualified praise,[31] and Herford is impressed with "language which disdains charm, but penetrates by remorseless veracity and touches of strange and sudden power." [32]

Today, as in the past, one finds curiously conflicting appraisals of Middleton's poetry. Eliot pays tribute, but with reservations: "Incidentally, in flashes and when the dramatic need comes, he is a great poet, a great master of versification." [33] Brooke feels that "Middleton had . . . no very individualized poetic style," [34] but to Oliphant "he is, in short, one of the most original of all the versifiers of the period." [35] Perhaps the differences are owing to the fact that Middleton's verse is so elusive, that one comes upon so few purple passages in his work. "In discussing Middleton's poetry," Bald points out,

one must emphasise the fact that it is essentially dramatic. Webster's poetry is frequently of the same order, as a single example will show. When the Duchess of Malfi bursts into reproaches against the malignant fate that has pursued her, Bosola's reply, "Look you, the stars shine still," is absolutely overwhelming in its effect, but the power of these words to reduce to insignificance any individual protest can scarcely be appreciated apart from their setting. Similarly, some of Middleton's most

powerful lines are almost meaningless away from their context.
. . . For this reason it is impossible fully to illustrate by mere
quotation Middleton's poetic range, but there are still numerous
lines and sentences which are outstanding for their imaginative
power and concentrated strength.[36]

Bald is writing primarily on *Hengist, King of Kent,* but his
remarks may be applied with equal relevance to any of Middleton's later plays.

VIII

The Second Maiden's Tragedy has not aroused much enthusiasm. There is no reason to believe that it was an outstanding
success on the Jacobean stage: no quarto was offered to an
expectant public during Middleton's lifetime. Indeed, the
play had to wait more than two centuries for publication,
and is yet to appear in a form which satisfies the needs of the
student and cultivated reader: a volume including a critical
introduction, an accurate text, and explanatory notes.[37]

One searches in vain for the analyses of scholars and the
judgments of critics. The play has been discussed—discussed,
indeed, fairly often—but not as literature. It has been treated
rather as a curiosity: an interesting specimen of Elizabethan
handwriting, a rare instance of a surviving early prompt-
book, a provocative subject for authorship inquiries. *The
Second Maiden's Tragedy* is ignored in all the shorter sur-
veys of Stuart drama, alluded to in a footnote of Ward's history, commented upon briefly and without fervor by Schelling. It is the inspiration for no appreciative essay, has never
been rhapsodized by a Swinburne or rediscovered by an
Eliot. The fullest critical evaluation appears in Barker's
Thomas Middleton and occupies four manuscript pages.

There are perhaps two fundamental reasons for this apparent oversight. Since *The Second Maiden's Tragedy* is an

anonymous play, the authorship of which has hitherto been regarded as highly controversial, it has not been included in collected editions and, aside from Barker's treatment, has not been discussed as part of the evolution of a writer's technique. Secondly, the play can scarcely be regarded as a great work. It imitates *The Revenger's Tragedy* without recapturing the intensity of *The Revenger's Tragedy;* it reproduces Fletcherian pseudo-heroics, but lacks the ingenuity and grace of which Fletcher is capable. To Schelling *"The Second Maiden's Tragedy,* if well written, is wanting in true dramatic force,—a want which neither heroics nor sensational situation can ever hope to supply." [38] Although the remark does an injustice to the subplot, it is certainly a fair pronouncement on the main story. Ward characterizes the play in a single word: "sensational," [39] and *The Second Maiden's Tragedy* is indeed sensational, even by Elizabethan standards. The main action is grotesquely melodramatic, while the underplot dissipates itself at the very close. "The tragedy," writes Barker,

like the tragedy in the *Fair Quarrel,* is complete long before the final scene. The characters have faced the consequences of their sin, have fully realized what they have done to themselves. There is no need for more. But just as in the *Fair Quarrel* Middleton insists on going on—insists on providing in this case, not indeed a happy ending, but a great deal of gratuitous slaughter. He has his characters plot and counter-plot, clash with swords in their hands and stab one another until no one is left alive to carry the dead bodies from the stage. He has apparently forgotten the real tragedy of the play in his desire for violence and death.[40]

Yet, in spite of these limitations, it is hardly possible to overestimate the importance of *The Second Maiden's Tragedy* in the development of Middleton's art. The play is written throughout in his mature verse, and the Anselmus-Wife-Votarius scenes reflect his mature characterization and his mature irony. In his greatest tragedies Middleton is to do the very same things but do them better. Only one important advance remains. Never again does the playwright make the mistake of clumsily uniting the intrigues of royalty with a story from domestic life. When Middleton turns once again to a court milieu, as in *Women Beware Women*, his dukes and duchesses are weak men and women and the atmosphere that he conveys is realistic and bourgeois. Although he deals with the most terrible of passions, he creates no Bussy D'Ambois, no Tamburlaine of lust. For an ironic and psychological view of life is scarcely compatible with the conventions of heroic drama. The transformation that Middleton accomplished in his later work is an impressive one. From the soaring bombast of Tamburlaine to the perfect stoicism of Claremont D'Ambois, from the epic wrath of Lear to the passionate defiance of Vittoria Corombona, Elizabethan tragedy had always been heroic. Middleton's last, great tragedies mark the decline of heroism on the Elizabethan stage and the uncertain emergence of realism and psychology in the poetic drama of England.

III. *Hengist, King of Kent, or the Mayor of Queenborough*

THE DECADE following the appearance of *The Second Maiden's Tragedy* was a busy period for Middleton, but one can scarcely say that his creative energies went into the composition of uniformly distinguished work. Middleton had developed his mature poetic style; he had arrived at his mature view of life. Yet his writing is frequently uneven, and a point of view emerges only fitfully. He worked unassisted; he also collaborated—with Rowley, with Massinger, possibly with Fletcher and Beaumont as well.[1] He wrote constantly: plays for the King's Men, the Prince's Men, and the Lady Elizabeth's Men; masques for the Inner Temple and the Merchant Taylor's Hall; civic pageants and entertainments for the City of London; even a prose pamphlet. Perhaps he wrote too much. It was at this time that Middleton produced such potboilers as *The Witch* (*ca.* 1615–16) and *No Wit, No Help Like a Woman's* (*ca.* 1613–15). But during these same years he composed two of his masterpieces: the uproarious *Chaste Maid in Cheapside* (1615–17) and, with the help of Rowley, the somber *Fair Quarrel* (1615–17).

During this decade of prolific activity Middleton concerns himself frequently with situations rich in tragic overtones and implications. Yet he wrote only one play which may be considered a tragedy, and some doubt has been expressed as to whether or not that work is indeed a tragedy. The play in question is *Hengist, King of Kent, or the Mayor of Queen-*

borough (*ca.* 1619–20).² It is described as a comedy on the title page of the original quarto. Bullen and Symons consider the play a tragicomedy, while modern commentators tend to classify it as either a tragedy (Bald and Boas) or chronicle history (Schelling and Barker).³ Although there is no apparent basis for regarding *Hengist* as a tragicomedy, one can readily understand the origin of the conflicting designations. *Hengist* is the result of a divided artistic purpose. It is something of an anomaly—a curious union of psychological tragedy, pseudo-history, and comic buffoonery. I should perhaps apologize for discussing such a work at length in a study concerned only with Middleton's tragedies. But since *Hengist* is as much a tragedy as a history play, it may, I feel, with some justification be treated here.

I

In *Hengist* Middleton turns to the legendary beginnings of English history, dramatizing the arrival of the first Saxons and their early struggles with the Celts for the possession of Britain. So far as we know, Bede, in his *Ecclesiastical History of the English Nation*, was the first to mention Vortiger, Hengist, and Horsa. Nennius elaborated their careers into myth in the *Historia Britonum*, and Geoffrey of Monmouth brought the legend to its final form in the *Historia Regum Britanniae*. The Elizabethans accepted the fabrication as authentic history, retold the story in their chronicles, included it in *Polyolbion* and the *Mirror for Magistrates*, *Albion's England* and *The Faerie Queene*. Middleton may have used as a source Henslowe's old play of *Vortiger*; we know that he took hints from Fabyan's *Chronicle* and Holinshed's *History of Scotland*. But he was indebted primarily to the *History of England*.⁴

In the *History of England* [5] Holinshed tells of the ambitious noble Vortiger [6] who, not content with his position of high authority among the Britons, sought the glory of a crown. As he had no legitimate title, his rise to power necessitated "indirect meanes and sinister proceedings." On the death of King Constantine, he prevailed upon the nobility to crown Constantius, the late King's eldest son. This Constantius, "dull of wit, and not verie toward," was ill-suited for public affairs, and Vortiger soon controlled the destinies of the realm.

But Vortiger was not content to be the force behind the throne: he wanted the pomp of majesty. Accordingly, he ordered the murder of Constantius and then, with a great show of public-spirited zeal, had the assassins hanged. Through such "diuelish meanes and vnconscionable practises" he stole the hearts of the people and was elected King of Britain. But he then had to pay the price of his transgression. He feared, resented, and persecuted the admirers of the murdered King. Many subjects, including the two younger brothers of Constantius, fled the kingdom to avoid the usurper's wrath, and Vortiger lived in constant dread of their return. His rule was indeed troubled. Scots and Picts invaded Britain, laid waste the countryside, pillaged and burned the towns. At last desperate, Vortiger summoned to his aid a host of Saxons from across the channel. They arrived in 449 and soon defeated the invaders from the north.

The leader of the Saxons, Hengist—"a man of great wit, rare policie, and high wisedome"—liked Britain so much that he determined to gain a kingdom for himself. The land generously given to him was fenced with garrisons. More Saxons were sent for, and among them arrived Hengist's daughter Roxena, "a maid of excellent beautie and comelinesse, able to delight the eies of them that should behold hir." And she came "speciallie to win the heart of Vortigerne with the dart of concupiscence, wherevnto he was of nature much inclined, and that did Hengist well perceiue."

The Saxon leader prepared a great feast for the entertainment of the King. At the height of the revels, the guests merry and flushed with drink, Roxena came before the King, offering him a golden cup filled with wine. Captivated by her charm and beauty, he soon "felt himselfe so farre in loue with hir person, that he burned in continuall desire to inioy the same." Forsaking his lawful wife, he married the pagan Roxena and gave to Hengist as a gift the fertile soil of Kent.

Vortiger's actions so displeased his subjects that they rebelled, deposing him in favor of his son Vortimer. The new sovereign began his reign with an impressive display of military skill. In four great battles he overcame the Saxons— slaughtering them, driving them into the sea, forcing them into the treacherous wastes of Colemoore. In "diuers other conflicts" as well, his success was so overwhelming that the Saxons were compelled to abandon their possessions and huddle together on the Isle of Tenet, there to be subject to the forays of Vortimer's ships. The King's exploits were viewed by his step-mother with alarm rather than pride; indeed, Roxena began to explore ways of shortening his career. Her efforts were rewarded. After a reign of six or seven years Vortimer died unobtrusively, of poison.

The people now restored Vortiger to the throne, and Hengist celebrated the occasion by returning with a great host of Saxons. But Vortiger was prepared to meet them: he had assembled an even mightier army of Britons. When Hengist learned of these preparations he altered his plans, resolving to depend upon cunning rather than strength. He requested a parley with Vortiger, to be held on May Day upon the plain of Salisbury. Before the meeting took place Hengist caused euerie one of his allowed number secretlie to put into his hose a long knife (where it was ordeined that no man should bring anie weapon with him at all) and that at the verie instant when this watchword should be vttered by him, "Nempt your sexes," then should euerie of them plucke out his knife, and slea the Britaine that chanced to be next to him, except the same should be Vortigerne, whom he willed to be apprehended, but not slaine.

At the day assigned, the king with his appointed number or traine of the Britains . . . came vnto the place . . . without armor or weapon, where he found Hengist readie with his Saxons, the which receiued the king with amiable countenance and in most louing sort: but after they were a little entred into communication, Hengist . . . gaue the watchword, immediatlie wherevpon the Saxons drew out their kniues, and suddenlie fell on the Britains, and slue them as sheepe being fallen within the danger of woolues. For the Britains had no weapons to defend themselues, except anie of them by his strength and manhood got the knife of his enimie.[7]

It is scarcely necessary to add that the day ended in total disaster for the Britons. Vortiger was taken prisoner and not freed until he had delivered to Hengist the greater part of the southern and eastern portions of his realm—the provinces of Kent, Essex, Norfolk, and Suffolk; the cities of London, York, Lincoln, and Winchester.

Stripped and humiliated, fearful of what lay ahead, Vortiger withdrew into Wales and built a strong castle on Breigh Mountain. But the end was near. Seeing their opportunity, Aurelius and Uther, the younger brothers of Constantius, returned to England, and the people flocked to them. Landing at Totnes, they marched through Wales to Vortiger's castle and burned it to the ground, destroying the King and all his followers. Aurelius was crowned in 481. He then proceeded toward York and met with Hengist and his forces at a place called Maesbell, past the Humber. The Saxons were vanquished—vanquished decisively—and, according to one account, Hengist fled to save himself. He was captured, led to Conningsborrow, and beheaded by decree of the bishop of Colchester.

The story of the rise and fall of Vortiger and the treachery of Hengist, taken from the bleak and shadowy origins of British history, has a rude, primitive power—perhaps even grandeur—that makes it worthy material for the tragic dramatist. It is a story of cunning and aspiring men, of lust and ambition, of the vicissitudes and peculiar ironies of fortune, of the turbulence and chaos that accompany civil disorder. Especially around the character of Vortiger, with his overweening political ambition, his dissatisfaction and Macbeth-like recoil into fear and brutality after his aims have been seemingly fulfilled—around such a character, evil but majestic, terrible but also pitiable in his final degradation, could a great tragedy have been written.

One might reasonably assume that material of this type would be especially well suited to Middleton's talents at this particular stage of his career. The dramatist had arrived at his mature conception of tragedy; he had mastered a subtle and flexible verse technique. He understood the base passions and uncontrollable impulses which overrule men's reason; he could create a dark and treacherous world. He could not fail to be aware of the ironies implicit in the career of a Vortiger or a Hengist. Yet Middleton is not entirely successful. With its acrid atmosphere and somber grandeur, *Hengist* is often frightening and always disturbing. It has arresting dramatic verse, several great scenes, and three very memorable characters. But it has also serious defects—defects owing partially to Middleton's own preoccupations and partially to the theatrical conditions of his time.

I I

Middleton opens his play with a presenter, Raynulph, Monk of Chester, who tells the spectators that they are about to witness a drama based upon actual historical events as described in the chronicles of early British history. Raynulph's rejection of the newer dramatic modes—"Fashions that are now Calld new/ Haue bene worne by more then you," (Chor. i, 11–12)—and his approval of older material and methods—"Ancient storyes haue bene best," (Chor. i, 10) —would seem to indicate that Middleton planned to offer his audience a chronicle play, a dramatic genre that had long since passed the peak of its popularity. The introduction of Raynulph and the mention of the "policronicon" are perhaps designed also to invest the play with an aura of historical authenticity.

The first scene of *Hengist*, couched in splendidly eloquent blank verse, shows a brilliant use of dramatic contrasts. Constantine is dead; Vortiger has had hopes of snatching the crown, but the people refuse to accept him while Constantine's three sons live. Now, as the tumult and shouting of an angry mob echo in the background, Vortiger enters and launches into a scornful tirade against that "wide throated Beast the Multitude." With great economy and powerful imagery, this soliloquy—the first speech in the play—unmasks Vortiger's pretensions and betrays the passionate intensity of his desires:

> How neere was I to a Scepter and a Crowne,
> Faire power was een vpon me, my desires
> Were tasting glory, till this forked rable
> With their infectious acclamations
> Poysoned my fortune.   I, i, 5–9

Vortiger's quite worldly sentiments are offset immediately
by the words of Contantius and his fellow monks, as they
enter in procession, singing a pious renunciation of earthly
glory:

> Boast not off high Birth or Blood,
>   To be greate is to be good;
>   Holy and religious thinges
>   Those are vestures ffitt for Kinges. . . .
>
>   It is not state; it is not Birth;
>   The way to heauen is grace on earth.
>   Sing to the Temple him so holy
>   Sinn may Blush to thinke on ffollye.
>
> I, i, 29–32, 37–40

While the mob cries out in noisy approval, Vortiger brutally
seizes Constantius and thrusts upon him the government of
the kingdom. Constantius' futile entreaties and anguished
protestations, his final unwilling acceptance, are framed in
lines of extraordinary distinction:

> Dare you receiue heauens light in at your eye Lidds
> And ofer violence to religion; take heede,
> The very Beame lett in to Comforth you
> May be the fire to burne you, on these knees
> Hardened with zealous praiers I entreate you,
> Bring not my Cares into the world agen,
> Think with how much vnwillingnes and anguish,
> A gloryfied soule departed from the Bodye,
> Wold to that loathsom gaole returne againe,
> With such great paine, a well subdude efection
> Re-enters worldly Buisnes.
>
> And ift be worthily held sacredlidge,
> To robb a Temple, tis no lesse offence
> To rauish meditations from a soule
> The Consecrated alter in a Man,
> And all their hopes will be beguild in me;

I know noe more the way to temporall rule
Then he thats borne and has his years Come to him
In a rough desart.   I, i, 69–79, 127–34

After bidding a touching farewell to his "Holy parteners,"
Contantius leaves as the trumpets sound a royal flourish. Vortiger remains alone on the stage. His reflections on his own
unbounded aspirations, contrasting vividly with the simple
humility of Constantius' leavetaking, bring the scene to an
impressive close. One can scarcely conceive of a more satisfactory opening. It is curious that its manifest poetic and
dramatic qualities have for so long passed unnoticed.

The vexations contrived by Vortiger to bedevil the King
are barely suggested by Holinshed, who indicates merely
that Vortiger, "abusing his [Constantius'] innocencie and
simple discretion to order things as was requisite, had all the
rule of the land, and did what pleased him." Middleton elab-
orates: he devises a whole series of brief but theatrically effective episodes illustrating Vortiger's futile attempts to
force the King to abdicate through sheer exasperation. The
simple ascetic garb worn by Constantius is taken from him,
and against his helpless will he is clothed in the luxuriant
robes of royalty. He is plagued by petitioners, besieged by
frivolous courtiers commanded by Vortiger to dance attend-
ance upon him. His fasting days, once observed scrupu-
lously, are denied him on the pretense that they are injurious
to his precious health. And although he has sworn abstinence,
inclining all his zeal toward heaven, Vortiger insists that he
marry in order to beget heirs. Perhaps the most striking of
these incidents occurs when Vortiger looses a pack of suitors
upon the hapless Constantius. Seeing the King approach, they
kneel with their petitions. He notices them and assumes that
they are praying. "How happy am I in the sight of you," he
declares, and proceeds to chide himself for lack of piety:

Here are religious soules that loose noe tyme;
With what Deuotion doe they kneele to heauen
And seeme to Check me that am soe remise.

I, ii, 82–85

He soon learns, however, that they are kneeling to him, and are concerned only with such worldly matters as the cost of pasturage, the enormities in wool, and the availability of brass buttons. He turns away in disgust. "Make your request to heauen," he admonishes them, "not to me."

In his portrayal of Constantius, Middleton reveals himself as the conscious artist—comparing sources, selecting interpretations, discarding material unsuited to his creative purpose. Holinshed had described the King as "too soft and childish in wit, to haue anie publike rule committed to his hands." For this reason he was made a monk during his father's lifetime.[8] But Middleton does not choose to depict Constantius as an ineffectual and pathetic innocent. Instead he apparently follows a hint from Fabyan's *Chronicle*, in which Constantius enters the monastery because of the "pure devocyon that he hadde to god and saynt Amphiabyl" [9]—an explanation which offered far more in the way of dramatic possibilities.

As a king, Middleton's Constantius is a tragic misfit. At times he recalls Shakespeare's mild and pious Henry VI, wandering off from the bloodshed and horror of Towton field to sit on a hilltop, lost in reverie, dreaming of a happy shepherd's life. But, even if Constantius emerges as a weak monarch, he manages to keep the respect of his audience. He retains his dignity—a dignity that Henry rarely impresses us as having. Passionately devout, fired by a true religious vision, Constantius is indeed a man of God. When Castiza is sent to tempt him, he makes so eloquent a plea for chastity that the girl resolves never to marry. "Y'haue mightily prevaild, greate vertuous Lord," she tells him,

Ime bound eternally to praise your goodness
I Carry thoughts away as pure from man
As euer made a virgins name immortall.
                              I, ii, 191–94

Under different conditions Constantius might well have
been a saint. As it is, he remains deeply sympathetic as he is
abused brutally by the unprincipled Vortiger.

Constantius is murdered by hired assassins early in the
second act, and Vortiger has at last realized his ambitions.
The lords of the realm accept him as their king, and he takes
the unwilling Castiza as his bride. But now his troubles begin,
for the murder of Constantius stirs the populace to rebellion.
Vortiger becomes frantic. "Prouide me safety," he cries:

Hark I heare ruin threaten me, with a voice
That imitates thunder.   II, ii, 19–21

But fortune is apparently still his friend. A fleet of adven-
turers is by chance cast up upon the shores of Britain, and the
voyagers, hardened and wily Saxons, offer their services to
Vortiger.

III

Hengist thus begins in much the same manner as the conventional English chronicle histories: "plays that," in Tillyard's
words, "had as a main concern the facts of history, that
sought to instruct the audience in the matter of the prose
chronicles." [10] Works of this type had become oddities, re-
quiring prefatory explanations before they could be offered
to a skeptical public. Yet, for more than two decades, this
curiously indigenous genre had aroused extraordinary enthusiasm. In 1592 Nashe, defending the drama of his age,
could say of its subject matter: "(for the most part) it is borrowed out of our English Chronicles, wherein our forefa-

thers valiant acts (that haue line long buried in rustie brasse and worme-eaten bookes) are reuiued, and they themselues raised from the Graue of Obliuion, and brought to pleade their aged Honours in open presence." [11]

The shortcomings of the chronicle plays are obvious enough. Their style is often pedestrian, their structure ramshackle; they are too diffuse, too crowded with character and incident. They embody a concept of history which we do not share and with which we cannot sympathize. Yet these humble plays had served their age well. For an England on the threshold of national greatness, they had given voice to the stirrings of national pride. They had made familiar the lives of the British monarchs; they had presented the pomp and pageantry of history—the alarums of battle, the exploits of heroes, the splendors of royalty. "Playes," writes Heywood,

haue made the ignorant more apprehensiue, taught the vnlearned the knowledge of many famous histories, instructed such as cannot reade in the discouery of all our *English* Chronicles: & what man haue you now of that weake capacity, that cannot discourse of any notable thing recorded euen from *William* the *Conquerour*, nay from the landing of *Brute*, vntill this day, beeing possest of their true vse. [12]

Perhaps even more important, the histories had provided moral instruction. The evils of civil war, the hard fate of the transgressing ruler, and the unpleasant consequences of excessive political ambition are recurrent themes. These plays are designed, Heywood declares, "to teach the subiects obedience to their King, to shew the people the vntimely ends of such as haue moued tumults, commotions, and insurrections, to present them with the flourishing estate of such as liue in obedience, exhorting them to allegeance, dehorting them from all trayterous and fellonious stratagems." [13]

Hengist also appears destined to follow the familiar pattern, for it sets out as a promising, if conventional, study of a man obsessed with lust for power, and offers every indication that it will consider the tragic results of criminal ambition upon both the protagonist and the commonwealth.

Middleton, as we know, read Holinshed, the chronicler whose political philosophy so thoroughly reflected Tudor thought, and who had such clear "understanding of cause and effect in human actions and of the vengeance exacted by God for sin, working out with arithmetical accuracy the relation of each sin to the divine vengeance." [14] And had not Holinshed shown deep concern with the evil effects of usurpation upon the state? For it is no small affair to depose God's anointed; Vortiger's wicked act disrupts the entire social order, bringing chaos and dissolution to the kingdom:

It chanced also the same time, that there was great plentie of corne, & store of fruit, the like wherof had not beene seene in manie yeeres before, and therevpon insued riot, strife, lecherie, and other vices verie heinous. . . . euerie man turned the point of his speare . . . against the true and innocent person. The commons also gaue themselues to voluptuous lust, drunkennesse, and idle loitering, whereof followed fighting, contention, enuie, and much debate. Of this plentie therefore insued great pride, and of this abundance no lesse hautinesse of mind, wherevpon followed great wickednesse, lacke of good gouernement and sober temperancie, and in the necke of these as a iust punishment, death and mortalitie, so that in some countries scarse the quicke sufficed to burie the dead.[15]

Holinshed states the moral quite clearly and with great insistence. But Middleton has little interest in politics; he avoids dealing with questions of public morality and chooses to ignore the implications of Holinshed's pious moralizing. For Middleton devotes himself almost exclusively to the private doings of men; if he is concerned with ethics, it is with the ethics of sexual relationships.[16] In *Hengist,* as in all his plays, Middleton's preoccupation must sooner or later reveal itself and take precedence over any other interest. Such specialization may be narrow and limiting, but Middleton's professional affiliations made it perhaps inevitable.

In his early career Middleton wrote, so far as we know, almost exclusively for the sophisticated private companies which catered to the tastes of the select audience. After 1608, when the Burbages acquired Blackfriars for the use of the King's Men, the distinction between the popular and private traditions gradually faded. By the time of Shakespeare's retirement, Elizabethan drama had become, for all practical purposes, the drama of the few. Middleton is, then, primarily the dramatist of a coterie—a coterie that cared little for history. Harbage's figures are illuminating:

In the public theatres, the plays, exclusive of three moral interludes, are in round numbers 49 per cent comedies, 30 per cent tragedies, and 21 per cent histories. . . . In the select theatres, the plays, exclusive of one moral interlude, are 85 per cent comedies and 15 per cent tragedies. In view of the prominence of history plays in our conception of the Elizabethan drama, it is notable that, so far as we know, none ever appeared in the coterie theatres.

"Except for Lyly's allegorical compliments to the great figures of Whitehall, and three or four scattered tributes to Elizabeth," Harbage goes on to say, "there is nothing in the sixty-seven plays of the select repertory to suggest pride in England or concern for national solidarity." [17]

I V

But, if the sophisticated audiences had little taste for history, they had a very distinct taste for sex. "Giue me a sceane of venery, that will make a mans spirits stand on theyr typtoes and die his bloode in a deepe scarlet, like your *Ouids Ars Amandi*," declares one of the genteel Blackfriars patrons in the induction to Day's *Isle of Gulls*, "there flowes the true Spring-head of Poetry, and the verie Christall fount of Parnassus." [18] For the period between 1599 to 1613 at least fifty-five coterie plays have survived. "In all but a few . . . ," writes Harbage, "the theme is sexual transgression, coupled in tragedy with treachery and murder, and in comedy with cupidity and fraud. It is a body of drama preoccupied with lust and murder or lust and money, and with the exhibition of the foolish and the foul." [19] To this body of drama Middleton contributed. He was a professional playwright aiming to please an audience whose tastes he understood and whose preoccupations he shared. In *Hengist* Middleton follows the dramatic structure of the chronicle history, but he loses sight of the purpose which, at least to some extent, justified that structure. As the play unfolds it becomes gradually apparent that *Hengist* belongs with the great majority of select repertory plays. It does indeed turn out to be a tragedy of lust and murder.

The earliest hint of the sex motif occurs briefly in the first act, when Vortiger thrusts Castiza upon the unwilling Constantius. With the arrival of the lascivious Roxena in the second act, the theme recurs with full orchestration and dominates the rest of the play. Although the rise of the wily and unscrupulous Hengist receives some attention, and although several scenes of comic horseplay are devoted to the amiable tanner Simon, the interest remains fixed, for the most part, on the strange interplay of passion and intrigue among Vortiger, Horsus, and Roxena.

Almost directly after Roxena's arrival, there takes place a curiously cynical and preposterous "test" for virginity. Horsus, Roxena's lover and Hengist's captain, comes with the first contingent of Saxons and helps put down the revolt against Vortiger. He is overjoyed when informed of his mistress' landing; but when he learns that Vortiger has been taken with her from first sight, he begins to quake. "I feele a paine like a Convulsion," he tells Hengist, "A Crampe at hart, I know not what name fitts it" (ii, iii, 216–17). When the pair enter arm in arm, the strain proves too great; Horsus collapses in an agony of distress. Roxena senses what is wrong. "Oh tis his Epilepsie, I know it well," she informs the onlookers.

> I holp him once in Germany, Comst agen?
> A virgins right hand stroakt vpon his heart
> Giues him ease streight But tmust be a pure virgin
> Or ells it brings no Comforth.   ii, iii, 249–53

Leaning at Horsus' side, she whispers to him, pleading for his cooperation:

> Oh sir shame me not
> Y'haue had whats pretious, try my faith yet once more,
> Vndoe me not at first in Chast opinion.
>
>   ii, iii, 272–74

Finally he agrees—just this once—to save his whore's credit. To the amazement and delight of the bystanders, he lifts himself up, declares himself so wonderfully restored that he longs for violent exercise. King Vortiger is most impressed.

A brutal and tortuous plot to eliminate Castiza dominates the two succeeding acts. When Horsus is assured by Roxena that she still loves only him, that she has designs upon Vortiger merely to keep her shame concealed, he agrees to help his mistress. Insinuating himself into the King's confidence, Horsus endears himself by suggesting a project for the removal of Castiza—a project that is soon carried out. They steal upon her as she stands alone on the palace grounds, reflecting—ironically—upon her husband's virtues:

> Though amongst liues elections that off virgin
> I speake noblest, yet't'has pleased Iust heaven
> To send me a Contented Blesedness
> In this of marriage which I euer doubted:

I see the Kings effection was a true one
It Lasts and holdes out long, thats noe meane vertue
In a Commanding Man, thoug in greate feare
At first I was inforcd to venture ont.
III, ii, 15–22

The King and his accomplice seize and blindfold her, then bear her away. Castiza is raped, unaware that it is her own husband who forces himself upon her.

Sometime afterward a gorgeous banquet is held at Hengist's castle. In the presence of Castiza's family, Vortiger proposes to some of the ladies at the table that they swear ignorance of any man's will but that of their own husbands. When they parry his request, he turns to Castiza, insists that she set an example. Then, seeing that she cannot take the oath, he denounces her savagely. The King next puts the test to the pagan Roxena who, having no scruples, steps brazenly forward and affirms her chastity. "Heer I take oath I am as free from man," she declares, "As truth from death, or sanctity from staine" (IV, ii, 259–60). The credulous Vortiger is now able to congratulate himself on winning a matchless virgin. "Oh thou treasure, that rauishes the possesor," he exclaims,

I know not where to speed so well agen
Ile keepe thee while I haue thee: heres a fountaine
To spring forth Princes and the seed of Kingdomes.
IV, ii, 261–64

The intrigue involving Vortiger, Horsus, Roxena, and Castiza seems to be entirely Middleton's invention. Horsus plays a minor role in the prose chronicles. Fabyan indicates only that he was either Hengist's brother or cousin, while Holinshed merely notes that Hengist had a brother, Horsus, who was slain in battle by Vortimer's brother, Catigerne. The elaborate scheme to discard Castiza has no historical basis; Holinshed remarks simply that Vortiger forsook his lawful wife to marry Roxena. Vortiger's sensual nature is, however, made clear by the chronicler, who finds time to point a moral:

the king was much giuen to sensuall lust, which is the thing that often blindeth wise mens vnderstanding, and maketh them to dote, and to lose their perfect wits: yea, and oftentimes bringeth them to destruction, though by such pleasant poison they feele no bitter taste, till they be brought to the extreame point of confusion in deed.[20]

But Middleton insists upon this aspect of Vortiger almost to the point of forgetting completely the other powerful drive established earlier in the play as a basic motivating force in Vortiger's make-up: intense, overreaching ambition. Middleton's preoccupation is so great that he is always intruding irrelevant allusions to chastity and infidelity, lust and ravishment. On one occasion he makes Horsus brood, with little dramatic pertinence, upon the possibility of unwitting incest:

> Mans scattered Lust brings forth most strange events,
> Ant twere but strictly thought on; how many brothers
> Wantonly gott, through ignorance of there Births
> May match with their owne sisters.[21]　　III, i, 90–93

　　In order to give full scope to the subtle and complex emotional involvements of Vortiger, Roxena, and Horsus, Middleton has to skim over such important historical episodes as the slaying of Constantius, the deposition and restoration of Vortiger, and the reign of Vortimer. These events are forced into the background—acted out in dumbshows, summarized in the choruses of Raynulph. The dramatist's preoccupation results in a total shift of emphasis as the play progresses: an historical drama becomes a melodrama of amorous intrigue, a study of ambition becomes a study of lust. Boas is certainly right, so far as he goes, in describing Middleton's plays as "dramas of sex complications." [22] It would be difficult to cite a more striking illustration than *Hengist* of how a single, consuming interest can divert an artist's energies from the course apparently intended. Here one may see embodied, perhaps more graphically than in any other single play of the period, the peculiar interest in problems of sexual transgression characteristic of so much of Jacobean drama.

Yet one does not come away from *Hengist*, or from any other of Middleton's serious plays, with the impression that he was doing merely what other, less gifted men were doing —exploiting, primarily for commercial gain, the rather specialized interests of a jaded and frivolous audience. No doubt he was deeply interested in sex; but, unlike so many of his contemporaries, he was concerned more with the consequences than the manifestations of sin. And, in spite of a preoccupation that must have been intensely personal, he manages usually to keep his artistic equilibrium. He is able to convey the impression of detachment—the "steady impersonal passionless observation of human nature," [23] as Eliot describes it. It is a detachment which has become a commonplace of Middleton criticism. He was probably neither more nor less concerned with sex than Marston; but, unlike Marston, who succeeds only in exhibiting his own divided feelings of attraction and revulsion, Middleton creates genuine characters that appear at times to possess what a psychologist might describe as unconscious minds.

It has been remarked more than once that Middleton's approach is realistic and ironic rather than romantic and sentimental; one might add as a corollary that it is clinical rather than sensuous. His treatment of sexuality is hardly suggestive in the way that Fletcher's so often is; Middleton's point of view is too stern, too tragic in its implications. He seems always to be aware of the sordidness of his material: he never clothes sin with splendor. "Compared with Webster," writes Barker, "he lacks grandeur; he never compromises with sin— he could never have portrayed the daring of a Flamineo or

the magnificent effrontery of a Vittoria Corombona." [24]
One can scarcely regard the Horsus–Roxena–Vortiger
scenes of *Hengist* as an exposition of wholesome domestic
relationships. But it would be just as unreasonable to suggest
that their purpose is erotic stimulation. They constitute a
serious study of the psychology of abnormal sexual passion
and a powerful *exemplum* of the terrible consequences of sin.

v

The most striking illustration of Middleton's interest in psychology is to be found in his characterization of Horsus. He
is the chief figure in the later scenes of the play, and his personality is delineated with extraordinary subtlety. He
emerges, indeed, as one of Middleton's most remarkable accomplishments. Horsus has an exceptional mind, perhaps
even a brilliant one. His wit is bitter and incisive. He is given
to reflection, makes penetrating observations on the forgetfulness of pride, the means men take to abuse themselves, and
the mischiefs that follow in the wake of lost honor. The
rape of Castiza prompts him to meditate on the strange ways
in which the imagination works:

> never was poore Ladye
> So mockt into false terror: with what anguish
> She lyes with her owne Lord, now she Could Curse
> All into barrenness and beguile herselfe by't;
> Conceyts a powerfull thing, and is indeed
> Placde as a pallat, to tast greife or loue
> And as that relishes, so we approue;
> Hence it Comes that our tast is soe beguilde
> Changeing pure blood, for som thats mixt, and soyld.
>
> III, ii, 117–25

Horsus is clearly superior to the men and women around
him; he is able to evaluate them—and himself—with remark-

able insight and detachment. He senses the dark passions which underlie Hengist's external calm and assurance. He understands, almost appreciates, Castiza's virtue. Vortiger is his puppet, a naïve sacrifice to his ingenuity—to be abused at his will, cuckolded at his pleasure. Yet, in spite of his abilities, Horsus is not his own master. He is driven by lust: a lust that is intellectualized and rendered strangely objective. Although his entire existence centers around Roxena, he has no illusions concerning her nature; he accepts her for what she is—a whore—and makes no effort to release himself from his enslavement. He does not sentimentalize or romanticize the fact that she follows him from Germany; he attributes it to "her Cuning,"

> The loue of her owne lust, which makes a woman
> Gallop downe hill as feareless as a drunkard.
>
> II, iii, 189–91

Indeed, at one point he contemplates making her whoredom public knowledge, so that he may be sure to have her for himself. Yet he does not object to Roxena's marriage to Vortiger, as long as he may enjoy her at will. "Tis a gallants Creditt," he declares, "to marry his whore bravely."

Had he wished, Horsus might have been another Hengist, ruling over London and York, Lincoln and Winchester: the rewards of his service. He realizes his own worth, knows what he may claim, yet allows what is due him to pass on to other, less deserving men. He deliberately chooses to follow Vortiger, basks with him in the glory of his triumph, shares with him the humiliation of his disgrace; but always he is near Roxena. He has no dreams of power; rather he envisages himself as a destructive force in the world—the cuckolder and despoiler, the calumniator of the chaste. Vicelike, he exults in his role:

> euery one has his toye
> While he liues here: some men delight in Building,

A tricke of Babell & will nere be left,
Some in Consuming what was raysd with toyleing
Hengist in getting honor, I in spoyleing.

IV, iii, 160–64

Yet he can also be tender, as when he relents for a moment
toward Castiza, or when he shows his compassion for Roxena in the final scene:

True, my hart findes it that sitts weepeing blood now
For poore Roxenas safetie.

V, ii, 28–29

As Barker points out, "Horsus is indeed a complex character
—a strange mixture of cruelty and affection, cynicism and
lust." [25] In some ways Horsus reminds one of Iago—an Iago
with greater humanity. He anticipates the later and even
more finely realized De Flores.

Vortiger is distinctly less complicated than Horsus, and
he is also less interesting. But he is nonetheless a compelling
figure: a curious amalgam of animal cunning and simple
credulity, fierce passion and childlike innocence. He longs
for a crown and tries to obtain one through an elaborate
Machiavellian scheme, but he is not quite clever enough to be
successful at intrigue and must at length resort to the cruder
and more direct method of murder. Once possessed of a
throne, he is surprised to discover that he has not found perfect peace, that there remain passions and appetites as yet un-
satisfied:

After I was a King
I thought I neuer shold haue felt paine more,
That there had beene a ceasing of all passions
And Common stings which subiects vse to feele,
That were Created with a patience fitt
For all extremityes; but such as wee
Know not the way to suffer, then to doot
How most prepostrous tis: whats all our greatenes
Iff we that prescribe bovndes to meaner men
Must not passe these ourselues.

III, i, 98–107

Bald speaks of "Vortiger's inherent kinship with the man in the street. He shares the common man's attitude of ignorance and wonder towards place and power, which he apostrophises as 'sweet power' and 'this dream of glory,' and he never outgrows it." [26] Although he is at first a great lord and later becomes a king, he retains the vicious snobbery that so often marks a plebeian mind. He is always conscious of the meanness and inferiority of those beneath him; the masses never cease to be "vlcers of realmes," a "wide throated Beast," the "Ranck rowt." Welcomed by the amiable Mayor of Queenborough at the gates of Thong Castle, Vortiger scorns his subject's greeting, spurns his gifts. "Forbeare your tedious and rediculous duties," he commands,

> I hate em as I doe the rotten rootes of you
> You inconstant rabble, I haue felt your fits,
> Sheath vp your Bountie with your Iron wits
> And get you gon.   IV, i, 15–19

Vortiger is half brute, almost entirely without moral sensitivity. Totally unconscious of his own unscrupulousness, he registers shocked amazement at Hengist's duplicity on Salisbury Plain. "Take me not Basely," Vortiger beseeches him,

> when all sence & strength
> Lyes bound vpp in amazement, at this trecherye,
> What Diuell hath Breathd this euerlasting part
> Of falshood into thee?   IV, iii, 57–60

Indeed, Vortiger is always being surprised, whether by the intensity of his own passions or the cleverness of Hengist, the treachery of Horsus or the lustfulness of Roxena. Bald's pronouncement—"Vortiger . . . is altogether of lesser calibre than Macbeth." [27]—is something of an understatement. It would be difficult to recall an Elizabethan villain-protagonist to whom Vortiger is superior in intellect or sophistication. Yet, if he scarcely qualifies as a tragic hero, he is nevertheless a powerful study of a primitive and passionate man.

Of the other figures (with the exception of Constantius, who has already been discussed) less can be said. At different times Castiza is made to take the role of temptress, reluctant bride, loving wife, and personification of chastity; it is little wonder that she never becomes a credible character. Roxena is more convincing. She is, like so many of Middleton's women, lecherous, crafty, and something of an egotist. She is, too, virtually amoral: she lies with ease, forswears herself without compunction. Her first love is Horsus, and she does remain, in her way, faithful to him. It is true that she marries another, but she takes Vortiger neither out of love nor lust. Rather, she marries to satisfy her craving for advancement and, more important in her view, to keep her shame concealed. The figure who gives the play its title is shadowy and less firmly grasped than either Vortiger or Horsus. The picture we have of Hengist is that of an affable and ambitious man, generous to his followers, loving to his daughter, but unprincipled and ruthless in his dealing with his superiors. We are, however, told also that there is more to his personality than appears on the surface: that he is proud and greedy, that he has a consuming thirst for power. But these aspects of his character are never really explored, rarely manifest themselves in action. Yet, in spite of these lapses, one can hardly quarrel with Bald's opinion of the play as a whole: "In the main . . . Middleton's characterisation is not merely convincing but penetrating. . . . Not only are the utterances of each character the natural outcome of the situations to which they belong, but they reveal so individual a bent of mind that they can belong to no one else." [28]

VI

At his best Middleton can create scenes that unite turbulent melodrama with passionate verse; scenes in which he strips his characters of every vestige of dignity, deprives them of every illusion, reveals as it were their very souls. Such a scene, perhaps the most grimly powerful in *Hengist*, occurs near the very end of the play.

Tricked out of his power by Hengist's treachery on Salisbury Plain, hounded by the victorious armies of Aurelius and Uther, Vortiger has been forced to retreat into Wales. There the usurper shuts himself up in his castle, accompanied only by the whore he has taken as his wife and the favorite who cuckolds him. No avenue of escape remains; their situation is desperate. Vortiger and Horsus appear on the battlements, look down at the enemies who surround the castle and make ready the wildfire that is to destroy them. Now, for the first time, Vortiger reflects on his evil past—questioning "things that horror long agon/ Resolud vs on," discovering that "Their is noe rest at all, But torment makeing." He turns like a cornered animal on the man who had offered him counsel and shared his secrets, denounces him as the sole cause of his own criminal acts, offers him up to appease the wrath of the forces below. "May thunder strike me from these walls my Lords," he shouts,

> & leaue me many leauges off from your eyes,
> If this be not the man whose stigian soule
> Breathd forth that Councell to me, & sole plotter
> Off all these false iniuryous disgraces
> That haue abusd the vertuous patience
> Of our religious queene.   v, ii, 76–82

But his hysterical efforts are futile. Indeed, they yield a bitter return, for they prompt Horsus to make a revelation more terrible than the torments of death itself:

HORSUS: What, has thy wild rage stampt a wound vpon me,
        Ile send one to thy soule shall never heal fort
VORTIGER: How to my soule
HORSUS: It shall be thy Mastertorment
        Both for the paine & the everlastingnes
VORTIGER: Ha ha
HORSUS: Dost laugh, take leaue ont, all eternitie
        Shall never see the doe so much agen
        Know thou art a Cuckold
VORTIGER: What
HORSUS: You Change to soone sir
        Roxena whom thast raisd to thyne owne ruine
        She was my whore in Germany
VORTIGER: Burst me open,
        You violence of whirlewindes
HORSUS: Heere me out ffirst
        For her embrace which yet my flesh sitts warme in
        I was thy friend & follower
VORTIGER: Deaffen me
        Thou most imperious noise that starts the world.

                                    v, ii, 111–30

While the fires race through the castle, Vortiger and Horsus turn upon one another with drawn blades, in a savage struggle to the death on the outer battlements. As they plunge their daggers into one another, hurling imprecations, Roxena enters terrified, pursued by flames that assume, in her imagination, the shape of Prince Vortimer, whose life she has taken by poison. She kneels to the dying men before her, begs them for help. "*Hersus* [29] looke vp," she pleads in final desperation, "if not to succor me/ To see me yet Consumd." But he can scarcely relieve her, and she cannot escape. Roxena dies, embraced by the flames that symbolize her lust. "Burne burne," Vortiger cries with his last breath,

                          now I Can tend thee,
Take time with her in torments, Call her Life
Affarr of to thee, dry vpp her strumpet blood
& hardly parch the skyn, let one heate strangle her
Another fetch her to her sence agen,
& the worst paine be only her reviueing
Follow her eternally: giue her not ore
But in a bitter shape: I shalbe Cold
Before thy rage reach me: oh mysticall harlott
Thou hast thy full due, whom Lust Crownd queene
                                              before
Flames Crowne her now, ffor a trivmphant whore.
& that end Crownes em all.

                              v, ii, 191–202

With its violence and terror, its unsparing picture of human degradation, this scene is certainly not a pleasant one. But its impact, to which a summary can hardly do justice, is undeniable.

                              V I I

Among the most notable of Middleton's achievements in *Hengist* is his masterful use of blank verse. This is the feature of the play which has, in the past, been most generally appreciated. The dialogue has an almost uniform stateliness, but striking poetic flashes, concentrated and rich in imagery, illumine the somber atmosphere. There are individual lines of remarkable power and incisiveness. Although their effectiveness is more apparent in context than in quotation, a few illustrations may be given:

                    she [fortune] has sent vs forth
        To thriue, by the redd sweate of our owne merritts:
                              II, ii, 40–41

        Why looke you sir I Can be as Calme as Silence
        All the whiles musick plays,   III, i, 132–33

To strip my wordes as naked as my purpose.

III, ii, 64

But there are longer passages as well, passages which show Middleton's ability to rise to an occasion that demands splendid poetry. Several of these have already been cited, but one may point also to such lines as Constantius' hymn to chastity:

Keepe still that holy and immaculate fire
You Chaste Lampe of eter..itye, tis a treasure
Too pretious for deaths moment to pertake,
This twinckling of short life; Disdaine as much
To lett mortality knowe you, as starrs
To kiss the pauements, y'haue a substance
As excellent as theirs, holding your pureness;
They looke vpon Coruption as you doe
But are starrs still; be you a virgin too

I, ii, 179–87

Horsus' reflections on the ambitions of Hengist:

the Earle of Kent
Is Calme & smooth, like a deepe dangerous water,
He has som secret way, I know his Blood
The graues not greedier, nor hells Lord more proud

IV, ii, 283–86

Vortiger's reaction upon seeing the Earl of Kent's castle:

Methinks it looks as if it mockt all ruin
Saue that greate Masterpeece of Consumation,
The end of time, which must Consume even ruin
And eate that into Cinders

IV, ii, 7–10

or Aurelius' order to raze Vortiger's sanctuary:

lett wild fire ruin it
That his destruction may appeare to him
Ith figure of heauens wrath at the Last day;
That murderer of our Brother.

V, ii, 2–5

The imagery is characteristically elusive—there are few pictures one can visualize—but it contributes to the prevailing mood. The snake and poison figures used so effectively in *Hengist* seem to hint at the hidden treacheries and ironies which "vnseene,"

> Lurke like the snake vnder the innocent shade
> Of a spread sommers leafe.
>
> IV, iii, 23–25

Occasionally there appears a homespun image that tells its own ironic little story:

> An Ill facde Iealousy, which resembles much
> The mistrustfullnes of an insatiate theife,
> That scarce beleiues he has all, though he has stripd
> The true man naked, and left nothing on him
> But the hard Cord that bindes him.
>
> III, i, 50–54

But such figures do not appear frequently in *Hengist*. The tone is graver, more eloquent than in Middleton's other plays. Indeed, the verse has a brooding passion and grandeur that make *Hengist* one of Middleton's finest poetic accomplishments.

VIII

Hengist is interesting also as an expression of Middleton's irony. There are the lesser ironies which are implicit in almost every situation, which give an ominous undercurrent of meaning to so much of the dialogue. Constantius mistaking the petitioners for religious votaries, Roxena "proving" her chastity, Castiza thinking of her husband's worth just as he is about to hurt her terribly—these moments have been noted earlier. Such lines as the following, spoken by Vortiger to Castiza in the midst of the banquet at which he plans to vilify her, take on a sinister ironic innuendo as we realize her perfect innocence and the essential truth of Vortiger's words:

> by all these blesings
> That blowes truth into fruitfulness, & those Curses
> That with their barrein Breaths Blast periurye
> Thou art as pure as sanctityes best shrine
> From all mans mixture, But whats Lawfull: mine.
>
> IV, ii, 143-47

There are larger ironies also. Vortiger gains a kingdom by treachery, only to lose it through his own naïveté. In Horsus he feels that he has found a true friend, but his hench-man follows him only to betray him:

> Ile follow you through the world, to Cuckold you
> Thats my way now.   IV, iii, 159-60

Vortiger takes as his wife a chaste and dutiful woman, but forsakes her to marry a pagan whore, thus invoking the wrath of his subjects—a wrath that can be allayed only by his death. The Earl of Kent, whose ambition could not be satisfied unless he possessed all, must in the end lose daughter, land, and life—everything. "A strange drowth," remarks his captor, Aurelius,

> & what a little ground shall death now teach you
> To be Content withall.   v, ii, 253-54

No agent of Nemesis is needed; the sinner betrays himself. "What Carefull wayes som take t'abuse themselues," observes Horsus at one point. "See," says the Gentleman in the last scene,

> sin needes
> Noe more distruction then it breedes
> In it owne Bosome.
>
> v, ii, 107-9

They ably sum up Middleton's ironic attitude toward life.

IX

Although its virtues are many, *Hengist* has not been well received by the critics. "The few who praise it," writes Bald, "do so half-heartedly, while the majority condemns." [30] Ward's brief comment is typical of the pronouncements of the earlier judges. "As a whole," he remarks, "the piece, though containing some fine passages, calls for no special notice." [31] In our own century *Hengist* has, until very recently, been ignored or slighted in discussions of Middleton. [32] But in 1938 R. C. Bald provided, for the first time, a complete and satisfactory text of the play. He bestowed high praise on *Hengist* and showed conclusively that, far from being a youthful experiment, it is "a product of the same mature power that created *Women Beware Women*, *The Changeling*, and *A Game at Chess*." [33] It is perhaps too early to predict the effect of Bald's edition on critical opinion. But, in his *Introduction to Stuart Drama*, Boas devotes more space to the play than it ever received before in a survey; and Barker, in his *Thomas Middleton*, treats it as one of the major works. "*Hengist* has faults which are only too obvious," Barker sums up:

Its quality is uneven; it has scenes of great brilliance like those devoted to Constantius in the first act, and scenes that are purely perfunctory like those devoted to Castiza in the fourth. It has, furthermore, comic scenes which—though amusing in themselves—are far too genial for so sombre a play. And yet at its best it has a dark grandeur that is not easy to parallel elsewhere in Middleton's serious work, not even in *Women Beware Women* and *The Changeling*. [34]

This is a balanced view; yet one might bear in mind that even the greatest of Elizabethan tragedies, such plays as *The White Devil*, *Macbeth*, and *The Changeling*, are uneven in quality and have scenes that are perfunctory.

It is, however, true that *Hengist* is not entirely successful, that it is not wholly satisfactory as either chronicle history or historical tragedy. As a chronicle play it embodies no point of view with regard to the philosophy of government and departs too frequently from the matter of history. As a tragedy it has all the faults that so often accompany the other genre. The action is too compressed; event follows event with bewildering rapidity as the dramatist encompasses a considerable span of time and much tumultuous action within the "too poore howres" of a play. *Hengist*, moreover, lacks a hero; instead of a single protagonist there are four major figures. The frequent shifts of interest and concentration—from Constantius to Vortiger, from Vortiger to Horsus to Hengist, and finally back to Vortiger—are confusing and misleading. The two titles by which the play has been known derive from the names of characters, but neither Hengist nor the Mayor can be looked upon as the principal figure in the play as a whole.

Simon is a sympathetic buffoon, and although the scenes in which he appears cannot be regarded as uproarious, they are genuinely comic and appealing. But there is far too much of him. As Bald remarks: "The underplot . . . fails to emphasise the tragic theme. It really constitutes an excess of comic relief, such as might have occurred if the Porter in *Macbeth* or the Gravedigger in *Hamlet* had been elaborated on a scale comparable to that accorded to Dogberry and Verges." [35]

It becomes apparent, as we examine *Hengist*, that Middleton is trying to do too many things at once. In an age that had so markedly altered its inclinations, the dramatist, attempting to reproduce an outmoded dramatic form, could not possibly capture the spirit of the original, could not indeed create a completely homogeneous work. The result was a peculiar mixture—a diffuse blending of tragedy and history, melodrama and farce, in which the individual parts are for the most part very fine, but the finished product is lacking in unity of purpose. The sudden deviation from state affairs to sex intrigue, owing partially to the tastes of the audience and partially to the dramatist's own preoccupation, is especially disconcerting. Perhaps it is this diversity and uncertainty of intent that have puzzled and divided those commentators who have attempted to fit the play into some category of dramatic expression.

However, the merits of *Hengist* far outweigh the defects, and its very faults have an interest of their own. They give us some clue to Middleton's elusive personality and help us to understand the perplexing milieu in which he worked. The play most certainly does not deserve the apathy or scorn with which it has been received by so many critics. No important Jacobean play has been as underrated as *Hengist*. It belongs with the half dozen or so outstanding works of a great dramatist.

IV. *Women Beware Women* AND

The Changeling

THE PECULIAR VIRTUES and defects of Middleton's art may be seen to excellent advantage in his last and, perhaps, his greatest tragedies. With *Women Beware Women* (*ca.* 1621) [1] and *The Changeling* (licensed May 7, 1622), the dramatist reached his full maturity. These plays are the fruits of a lifetime of practical experience in the theater and skeptical observation of the human scene.

In several respects the two tragedies are quite similar. Both reflect the playwright's continued preoccupation with the theme of lust; both are studies, to use Bradbrook's words, in "the progressive deterioration of character." [2] In neither play does Middleton create sympathetic figures; never does he regard his personages with anything but pitiless detachment and irony. Both works are impressive; indeed, in their own ways, even masterpieces. Yet for masterpieces they are curiously imperfect and uneven. Although they have scenes which possibly surpass even the greatest scenes in Webster, as plays they are not fully as satisfying as *The White Devil* or *The Duchess of Malfi*. Middleton apparently worked less deliberately than Webster; rarely does he impress us as being capable of prolonged and studious application. Unlike Webster, he kept no commonplace-look; he does not imitate Sidney and Montaigne, nor does he pride himself on his erudition. Even in his most significant work there appears much that is insipid or inconsequential. Alongside scenes of exquisite craftsmanship occur others of utter triviality. *Women Beware Women* and *The Changeling* are both marred by tedious, almost irrelevant subplots involving tiresome and offensive clowns.[3]

In his more sensational plays Middleton's usual method is to build inexorably toward a scene of crashing and spectacular melodrama: the masque in *The Revenger's Tragedy*, the excavation of the tomb in *The Second Maiden's Tragedy*, the burning of the castle in *Hengist*. But in *Women Beware Women* and *The Changeling* the most brilliant and overpowering episodes—the seduction of Bianca and De Flores' triumph over Beatrice—take place too early, and thereafter the action runs steadily downhill, except for an occasional moment of terror or beauty. Indeed, *Women Beware Women* falls entirely to pieces, while Middleton allows another, inferior playwright to complete the action developed so masterfully in the earlier scenes of *The Changeling*. It is as if the dramatist had lost interest in his own creations; as if his energies had suddenly, inexplicably, exhausted themselves. An entirely convincing explanation for this curious phenomenon is not easy to arrive at. Perhaps, and this would seem most likely, Middleton was finding it increasingly difficult—possibly even distasteful—to try to reconcile the sensational melodrama of his age with the psychological drama toward which he aspired.

Although the two plays have much in common, in several ways they are quite unlike one another. Of the great scenes of *The Changeling* there is a quality that approaches pure horror, while the most brilliant episodes in *Women Beware Women* reflect a mood not too far removed from the spirit of comedy. In the latter work our interest is divided equally among half a dozen characters. Bianca, the Duke, Leantio, and his mother all take important parts in the main action; Isabella figures most prominently in the tragic subplot;

Livia's role can scarcely be overestimated, for she is involved conspicuously in both stories. In the case of *The Changeling* there could have been no play without Beatrice or De Flores. The tragedy is their tragedy, and they dominate every scene in which they appear.

The verse of *Women Beware Women* is the most relaxed and luxuriant that Middleton ever permitted himself, and more than one critic has complained of the long-winded speeches. "The texture of the dialogue is richer," Barker writes, "there is more aphorism and more imagery. It is as though Middleton, in this one case, had tried to cultivate the more ornate, more florid style of Webster." [4] *The Changeling* is, on the other hand, notable for Middleton's most intense and severe dialogue. Perhaps Symons best describes its effect when he speaks of "fierce reticence," of words written at white heat, of "a restraint never paralleled elsewhere in his work; nowhere else are words used with such fruitful frugality, or so much said in so little." [5] Neither play could have been written by anyone but Middleton. Considered together, the two works testify to the range of his creative genius, to his unique powers and peculiar limitations.

I

The main plot of *Women Beware Women* is based upon a famous episode in Florentine history, a story so well known that the dramatist may have obtained his information from a number of accounts, oral or written. But the most striking incidents of the early scenes of the play are paralleled clearly in a single source to which Middleton probably referred—the *Ducento Novelli* of Celio Malespini, published in Venice in 1609. In *Novelle* 84 and 85 of Part II, Malespini relates the romantic story of Bianca Capello's elopement with Pietro

Buonaventuri, and her subsequent alliance with Francesco de' Medici, Grand Duke of Tuscany.[6]

Just opposite the banking firm of Salviati, so the narrative goes, stood the palace of the illustrious Venetian house of Capello, and there resided the gracious Bianca, young daughter of Bartolommeo Capello. Her beauty captivated one Pietro Buonaventuri, a Florentine youth of humble origin employed as a cashier in the bank. Bianca, in turn, admired the clerk's good looks and fine manners; she felt herself drawn toward him physically; she assumed he held a high position. Eventually, vows were exchanged, and the lovers felt free to enjoy each other clandestinely, Bianca confiding only in her old governess.

In the evening the girl would slip off—leaving her door slightly ajar—spend the night with her beloved, and re-enter unobserved just before daybreak. On one such occasion Bianca returned home and found that the door had been inadvertently slammed shut. Panic-stricken, she ran back to her lover, and shivering like a reed exposed to the winds, fell into his arms. At first Pietro could think only of signaling the governess, but the old matron did not respond to his frantic whistling. Now dawn was at hand; no time remained, for discovery meant death. Taking some money and a few belongings, the pair hurried into a barge and made their way to Florence. There Bianca and Pietro moved into the Buonaventuri house above St. Mark's Square, near the Church of the Annunciation.

Since the elder Buonaventuri was a poor citizen, and his wife too old to do hard work, the young couple's situation was miserable indeed. They could scarcely venture out—a price was on their heads—and the beautiful heiress was forced to perform the meanest household duties. These she did with patience and cheerfulness, for she loved her husband deeply.[7]

One day, as the Grand Duke Francesco rode forth in his carriage, passing beneath the Buonaventuris' window, he looked up and by chance his eyes met Bianca's. The Duke looked again; he leaned out from the carriage but he saw nothing, for the girl had modestly withdrawn. Francesco immediately made inquiries and learned of Bianca's misfortune. He felt compassion, and he also felt a desire to see her again. On morning drives to and from the Casino, he would look for her at the window; on the way to mass at the Church of St. Mark or the Church of the Annunciation, he would glance upward. But he would not rest until he had observed the girl more closely.

Francesco sought the help of a Spanish gentleman, Mandragone, who had been for many years his favorite companion. Mandragone, in turn, informed his wife, and together they resolved to lure Bianca to their palace by suggesting that the Duke might extend his protection to the distressed couple. The scheme worked admirably; none was more eager to cooperate than Pietro. Accompanied by his mother, Bianca was received graciously and shown many signs of favor, including a tour of the palace.

While Signa Buonaventuri rested below, Mandragona and her guest, laughing and arm in arm, explored the building. Although it was partly rebuilt and as yet not entirely furnished, Bianca could express only delight and admiration. At length, when they came to a pleasant little room overlooking the garden, a room with a fine bed, Mandragona excused herself for a few moments. No sooner was she gone than the Grand Duke suddenly appeared. Bianca shuddered and drew back. Now, for the first time, she realized why she had been summoned. Falling to her knees, she pleaded submissively, begging the Duke's pity, imploring him to consider that all she had left was her virtue. The Duke listened patiently, then raised the trembling girl. He had not come, he assured her, to stain her honor. Rather, he pitied her unfortunate state and wished only to help her, as she would soon discover. Then, bidding the pallid and confused girl be cheerful, Francesco departed. The Spanish lady now returned to comfort Bianca, asking her whether she had reprimanded the Duke properly, telling her laughingly of Francesco's merry pranks, of his compassion and power, of his ardent love for Bianca. The distressed young woman consoled herself with Mandragona's words and, not very long afterward, with the Duke's embraces as well.

The domestic arrangements among the three—mistress, paramour, and husband—were curious indeed. The Duke was not only chivalrous and discreet; he had also a strong sense of fairness and prided himself on his generosity. He certainly did not wish to do anything that might be suspected of impropriety. And so, when he saw that Bianca's love for her husband was deep-rooted and abiding, he made every effort to elevate the man's status and provide for his comfort. Pietro was put in charge of the Duke's wardrobe; he was showered with wealth and abundance, furnished with a handsome palace. He could enjoy his wife whenever he pleased—except, of course, when Francesco chose to lie with her. During those times Pietro would remain in his private lodgings on the ground floor, or come and go through his own entrance. For a while all three lived in perfect harmony. The Duke adored his beautiful mistress, Pietro gloried in his exalted station, and Bianca took pride in her husband's advancement.

Unfortunately, however, Pietro eventually became arrogant. He was young and handsome; he enjoyed the Duke's protection; he began to chafe under the indignity of cuckoldom. To divert himself he had numerous love affairs, and one of these, his amour with the widow Cassandra Buongiani, proved disastrous. The widow was a woman of high birth and proud family. Indeed, Pietro himself knew of two gentlemen in her circle who had lost their lives ignominiously by incurring the wrath of her relations. Yet he boasted openly that he had slept with Cassandra and laughed and grimaced in the face of Roberto de' Ricci, the widow's hot-blooded nephew.

When reports of Pietro's irregular conduct reached Francesco, he took the young man aside, told him of the complaints he had received, stressed the power and influence of Cassandra's family. Pietro might lie with the woman—one could scarcely object to that—but he need not boast of his conquest: to do so would be to invite death. But Pietro remained defiant, and his behavior toward Roberto became, if anything, more contemptuous. Finally the Duke was forced to tell Bianca that her husband would be banished unless he reformed. Bianca was heartbroken. She loved Pietro so much that the prospect of being separated from him for even a short time was unbearable. She pleaded with him, but her pleading served only to heighten Pietro's rage. "Let the Duke hang himself!" he screamed. Bianca was a whore; he would cut off the golden horns she had placed on his head; he would slit her throat. Pietro stormed out, leaving his wife in tears, lamenting the hour that she was born.

At the columns of the Holy Trinity he saw Roberto conversing with two Florentine gentlemen. Pietro drew one of his guns—he always carried a pair—and cursed the man who stood motionless before him. Since he was unarmed Roberto said nothing, but as soon as Pietro had left, he went with his companions to seek out the Duke at the Casino.

During Pietro's tirade Francesco had stood unobserved at the entrance; later he had seen his wife's tears and heard her laments. By the time Roberto found him at the Casino, the Duke had already concluded—however reluctantly—that Pietro must be removed. An appropriate course was soon decided upon. The next morning Francesco went on horseback to Pratolino, and Roberto was free to work out his revenge. He knew that Pietro would spend the night with Cassandra and leave shortly before daybreak. He knew also that the gallant would pass through a narrow alley on the way to his lodgings.

Roberto provided himself with a dozen henchmen armed with long knives. A boy was placed on the bridge of the Holy Trinity, to signal when Pietro approached. An hour before dawn the lover took leave of the widow and walked toward the bridge. He heard whistling—once, twice, a third time—but he paid no attention, for he was well armed. In his left hand he clutched a gun, barrel toward the ground; a sword was in his right hand. The bridge was now behind him and ahead loomed the narrow passageway that led to his lodgings. Two cloaked men appeared, but Pietro walked on. By then he had reached the midpoint of the alley. Four other men emerged from the shadows, and these were joined by six more: he was surrounded. "Kill him! Kill him!" a voice shouted—it was Roberto. Pietro defended himself bravely, shooting one of the attackers in the chest. But the alley was too narrow for Pietro to use his sword freely. He did manage to wound Roberto before a friend intervened, plunging his knife into Pietro's skull, splattering his brains upon the wall. The victim lay dead, and the band now carried Roberto to the Duke's sister, where surgeons dressed his wounds. His revenge was complete when, not long afterward, two of his masked followers put the widow Cassandra to death. Pietro's body was borne to the church of San Jacopo. Hysterical and despondent, Bianca was on the point of suicide when Francesco arrived to comfort her. He succeeded so well that, after her grief had subsided, she married him.

Malespini has little to say concerning the subsequent careers of the beautiful heiress and her illustrious paramour. For such information Middleton had to turn elsewhere. But it would seem apparent that the dramatist used Malespini for the first four acts of *Women Beware Women*. He did make changes. In the play the setting is Florence from the outset: the courtship of Bianca and her elopement have already taken place. Pietro's name is changed to Leantio, and his mother becomes a widow. Mandragone is replaced by Guardiano, and his wife and Cassandra are combined into a single character—the tremendous figure of Livia. Of greater significance, however, is the point of view which Middleton adopts toward his characters, a point of view considerably different from that of Malespini.

In its concern with passion and intrigue, revenge and sudden death, the story told by Malespini is typically Italian. Also characteristic is the author's attitude toward his personages. Bianca—"una gratiosa, e gentile figliula"—is an idealized portrait. It is true that she visits Pietro without her parents' consent and even lies with him, but she never doubts that he is an honorable suitor, and she does not give herself until vows have been exchanged. In Florence, Bianca endures with good cheer the humiliations to which she is subjected and tries—tries desperately—to preserve her honor. She does, indeed, become the Duke's mistress, but circumstances have perhaps made that inevitable, and, in any event, she remains devoted to her first love—eager for his advancement, anxious for his safety. The Grand Duke Francesco is the model of a Renaissance courtier: refined in his sensibilities, gracious in his manners, discreet in the conduct of his affairs. He is generous with his patronage and constant in his affections, but he is capable also of stern action when his own interests are threatened. By Christian standards his passion for Bianca may be a guilty one, but it is a perfectly appropriate and conventional expression of the code by which he lives, a late Renaissance variation of *amour courtois*. If anyone deserves reproach, it is Pietro. He has advantages—youth, a handsome appearance, winning manners— but his point of view is hopelessly bourgeois. Eventually he resents his wife's amour, even though her conduct of it is impeccable; he grows to despise his cuckoldom, even though it has profited him handsomely. His chief defect, in other words, is that he does not conduct himself like a gentleman. Rather than follow a restraining code of social behavior, he flaunts his emotions. Pietro boasts, threatens, slanders; he is subject to tantrums. He mistakenly associates honor with character and behavior, unaware that it is the gift of society, a reward for successful concealment.

There can be little doubt that Middleton understands Malespini's code, for at one point he has a minor character summarize it neatly. "Put case one must be vicious," Hippolito says,

> as I know myself
> Monstrously guilty, there's a blind time made for't,
> He might use only that,—'twere conscionable;
> Art, silence, closeness, subtlety, and darkness,
> Are fit for such a business; but there's no pity
> To be bestow'd on an apparent sinner,
> An impudent daylight lecher.   IV, ii, 5–11

But Middleton's attitude is different. Like Pietro he cannot take sin lightly, cannot believe that honor has little to do with character and conduct; his Bianca is able to lose her virtue only because she never really possessed it. The dramatist never confuses gallantry with sin. He fails to see the romance of Bianca's elopement from Venice, nor can he regard her affair with the Duke with sympathy. To him the

Reartio [margin annotation]

entire story has an unrelieved sordidness, and all the participants are base. The women become procuresses and "glistering whores," the men pimps and whoremasters.

It is not surprising, then, that Middleton could accept, for the final act of *Women Beware Women*, a version of the lurid and fantastic legend which Fynes Moryson records as sober fact in the manuscript chapters of his *Itinerary*. Before her husband's death, according to Moryson, Bianca bore Francesco a son, Antonio. Soon after the murder of Pietro the Duke took his concubine as his wife, and Bianca now sought to have her child legitimatized so that he would be eligible to succeed his father. She was opposed by the Cardinal Ferdinand, brother to the Grand Duke. On one occasion, "it happened that he [Ferdinand] came to Florence to passe some dayes merrily with the Duke,"

and they being to goe out hunting earely in a morning, the Duchesse sent the Cardinall a March payne for his breakfast, which he retorned with due Ceremony saying that he did eate nothing but that was dressed by his owne Cooke, but the Duke by ill happ meeting the messenger, did eate a peece thereof, and when the Duchesse sawe it broken, shee smiled and spake some wordes of Joy, but the messenger telling her the Cardinalls Answer, and that the Duke had eaten that peece, shee with an vnchanged Countenance tooke another peece, and hauing eaten it, locked herselfe in a clossett, and herevpon the Duke and shee dyed in one hower, and the Cardinall Ferdinand succeeded in the Dukedome.[8]

III

Meslier = source. [margin annotation]

For the subplot of *Women Beware Women* Middleton drew upon Meslier's *novella, Les amours tragiques, et estranges adventures d'Hypolite et Isabelle Neapolitains,* published in Paris in 1620. Meslier tells the pathetic story of Isabella, daughter of Fabritio, a gentleman of Naples. Her stepmother

Livia had been wed to a great lord, and her eldest son by this marriage, Pompeio, was heir to a considerable fortune. It was Fabritio's desire to advance his daughter by matching her with the youth, and of this Livia approved, for Isabella's beauty and intelligence were much esteemed. But the girl detested Pompeio; he was, indeed, a repulsive fool—so repulsive that his family kept him apart, isolated in a country house outside of Naples.

Isabella's most trusted friend was her uncle Hippolito, a handsome courtier of twenty or twenty-one. She doted upon him to the extent that he became virtually her sole companion; he, in turn, found himself drawn toward her irresistibly. It was in vain that they denied to each other that the emotion they felt was love; it was in vain that they struggled against a passion which could only be regarded as guilty. Finally, the unhappy Hippolito confessed to his sister, a nun who did not permit the demands of religion to interfere with her worldly interests. She soothed Hippolito, saying that he was not the first to undertake things forbidden, that the greater the difficulty the more exquisite the pleasure of fulfillment, and—most important—that he need not torment himself for she would manage the whole affair. Soon afterward, at her request, he appeared at the convent along with his niece. There the nun made a startling revelation: Isabella's mother had lain with the Marquess of Coria while Fabritio had been away; it was certain that Isabella and Hippolito had different blood. Shortly thereafter, the girl gave herself freely to her lover—perhaps not so much because of the nun's story as through the force of love and the blind tyranny of fate. It was in the convent, in the nun's cabinet, that the consummation took place. The marriage with Pompeio went forward as planned, but the lovers continued their amour under the very nose of the stupid husband, who found no man's company more pleasing than Hippolito's.

An old servant in the household was not so blind. She suspected that Hippolito and Isabella were lying together, and she shared her suspicions with Pompeio's guardian. He said nothing but saw to it that a trusted man was stationed in the house as a spy. Ultimately the pair's guilt became obvious. Still they made efforts—numerous efforts—to deceive their family and enjoy each other. Hippolito went so far as to have word given out that he had been killed and then visited Isabella nightly through a secret entrance. One night—a night they had fixed upon to elope to Cyprus or to Candy—they were surprised by the guardian. Hippolito managed to slip away, but for Isabella there was no way out. Her coffers and chests were ransacked, and a document she had prepared for her pursuers was found and read. In it she eloquently defended her love against the stain of incest, citing, as God was her witness, a number of proofs that her true father was the Marquess of Coria. But her cruel oppressor did not relent, and Isabella, deprived of her love, welcomed the poisoned pills held out to her and died with Hippolito's name on her lips. Beside himself with grief, her lover almost took his own life before his brother persuaded him instead to undertake revenge. The sudden death of the guardian defeated the better part of the plan, but he did slay Pompeio. Exiled and reduced to starvation, Hippolito eventually married a woman of some means and worse reputation. But he could not erase the memory of his Isabella, and his malicious wife, unable to endure this wretched, solitary existence with a man who feared and desired death at all times, took her husband's life by poisoning his soup.

In *Women Beware Women,* as in Meslier, Hippolito is attracted incestuously to the niece who has always cherished him. But when he reveals that he loves her "as a man loves his wife," she promptly rejects him. "I'll learn to live without ye," she cries, "for your dangers/ Are greater than your

comforts." As in the source, Hippolito confides in his sister
(here not a nun but the bawd Livia of the main action); and,
as in the source, Isabella is taken aside and told of her illicit
origins. But in the play Hippolito is not present—he knows
nothing of Livia's scheme—and so Isabella's sudden change
is a complete surprise. "Never came joys so unexpectedly,"
he reflects after she leaves, "To meet desires in a man." He
takes his niece as his mistress and, to cover their sin, she goes
on to marry the hideous fool that plays with a trapstick. Hippolito and Isabella remain lovers until Livia is driven to unmask them. "O, shame and horror!" she cries to herself when
her lover finally stands revealed,

> In that small distance from yon man to me
> Lies sin enough to make a whole world perish.
>
> IV, ii, 134–36

As for Livia:

> for her
> That durst so dally with a sin so dangerous,
> And lay a snare so spitefully for my youth,
> If the least means but favour my revenge,
> That I may practise the like cruel cunning
> Upon her life as she has on mine honour,
> I'll act it without pity.
>
> IV, ii, 145–51

It is noteworthy that Middleton's morality would not permit
—as Meslier's or Ford's would—investing perversity with
pathos. Thus a sympathetic tale of love thwarted by an in-
scrutable destiny becomes a sordid study of betrayal and
vengeance.

IV

Women Beware Women is perhaps the most unpleasant of
Middleton's serious plays. The *dramatis personae* include an

assortment of contemptible weaklings, figures with scarcely a redeeming feature. Their tragedy is not so much that they lose their souls, but that they barter their souls away too cheaply, as if they never realized they possessed them. They pursue lives neither of action nor of contemplation but, rather, of pure self-indulgence. They are all narcissistic, and in them lust and ambition, two of the dominant passions of Elizabethan romantic drama, have been debased into their meaner equivalents, libertinism and greed. They have no grand passions, only amours; they seek not kingdoms, but "advancement."

They never have to resort to violence for their amatory conquests; there is hardly enough virtue present to make force necessary. If they are young they depend upon the pressures of immediate physical attraction. If they are old they buy their love, and the price is not exorbitant. Livia provides herself with a desirable paramour half her age, and the cost is only rich clothes and a livery. The Duke wins and keeps Bianca, apparently because he is able to furnish her with luxuries that her husband cannot afford—cutwork for the bedchamber and silver-and-gilt casting bottles, green silk quilts, and silver basins and ewers. As compensation for the loss of his wife Leantio is made captain of a fort, an office even less remunerative than his meager factorship. If a seduction should require the help of bawd or pander, one can be had reasonably. Livia will betray innocence merely as an exercise for her ingenuity, and Guardiano will do likewise in the vague expectation of "riches or advancement." Leantio's mother, comments Bianca, is "an old wench [who] would trot into a bawd now/ For some dry-sucket, or a colt in march-pane." Her remark is perhaps unfair (the widow does not quite realize what is going on), but it contributes to the prevailing atmosphere of cynical materialism.

The most "romantic" episode described in the play is the elopement of Bianca and Leantio, but from the beginning the relationship between the two is depicted as wholly sensual. The girl has been brought up strictly, guarded with jealous eyes. But restraint breeds wandering thoughts—fantasies which prompt Bianca to run off with the first suitor who arouses her. "You have not bid me welcome since I came," she murmurs to Leantio after their arrival in Florence.

> LEANTIO: That I did questionless.
> BIANCA: No, sure—how was't?
> I've quite forgot it.
> LEANTIO: Thus.   [*Kisses her.*
> BIANCA: O, sir, 'tis true,
> Now I remember well; I've done thee wrong,
> Pray take 't again, sir.   [*Kisses him.*
>
> I, i, 142–48

It is already clear enough that the feeling between Bianca and Leantio could not be described accurately as love. That their marriage is based on physical appetite alone appears even more clearly in the next scene between the pair. Leantio finds, after several days, that he cannot tear himself away from his wife to go off on a business journey. "He struggles with himself," writes Barker, "much as the heroes of Shakespeare struggle, except that in their case the struggle emphasizes their nobility, in his only his weakness and lust." [9]

> 'Tis even a second hell to part from pleasure
> When man has got a smack on't: as many holydays
> Coming together makes your poor heads idle
> A great while after, and are said to stick
> Fast in their fingers' ends,—even so does game
> In a new-married couple; for the time
> It spoils all thrift, and indeed lies a-bed
> T' invent all the new ways for great expenses.
>
> I, iii, 5–12

At this very moment his mother and Bianca appear above at a window. "I've no power to go now, and I should be hang'd," he declares;

> Farewell all business; I desire no more
> Than I see yonder: let the goods at key
> Look to themselves; why should I toil my youth out?
> It is but begging two or three years sooner,
> And stay with her continually: is't a match?
>
> I, iii, 15–20

But he changes his mind once more, resolves to leave, chides Bianca when she begs him to stay another night:

> As fitting is a government in love
> As in a kingdom; where 'tis all mere lust,
> 'Tis like an insurrection in the people,
> That, rais'd in self-will, wars against all reason;
> But love that is respective for increase
> Is like a good king, that keeps all in peace.
>
> I, iii, 43–48

Still Bianca pleads: "But this one night, I prithee!"

v

The most remarkable scene of the play occurs in the second act. The seduction of Bianca is a tour de force, a triumph of sustained ingenuity not equaled elsewhere—not even in *A Game at Chess*—in the work of a playwright distinguished for his ingenuity. And yet, for all its cleverness, the scene never descends into artificiality or blatant theatricalism; never does it lose its atmosphere of homely informality. "This is one of those scenes," observes Lamb, "which has the air of being an immediate transcript from life." [10] The seeming casualness contributes to the bitterness of the final effect, for the reader is never permitted to forget that the amiable conversation serves only to cloak the most vicious and sordid

of intrigues. Malespini's narrative may have provided the
basis for the scene, but Middleton's handling of it reflects
his unique abilities. The most striking feature of the scene,
the chess game, is entirely his own.

When the Duke first spied Bianca at her window, his favorite, Guardiano, was at his side. Twice since then Francesco has spoken to his follower. The Duke is growing im-
patient, and Guardiano now turns anxiously to Livia for a
course of action. Livia takes pride in her cunning, and she
moves swiftly, with the skill of an accomplished bawd. She
has no difficulty in renewing her acquaintance with Leantio's
widowed mother, who readily accepts an invitation to the
kind gentlewoman's house and then permits her daughter-
in-law to be summoned also.

Bianca receives a cordial welcome. "I pray, sit down, forsooth," Livia entreats, "if you've the patience/ To look
upon two weak and tedious gamesters" (ii, ii, 273–74). But
Guardiano interposes to suggest that the visitor might derive
greater pleasure from a tour of the building. Although
Bianca hesitates politely—"I fear I came to be a trouble to
you," she declares—all present commend the proposal. The
young heiress still knows little of the ways of the world; she
does not for a moment question the motives of the courteous
strangers who seem so eager to make her feel at home. Not
once does she suspect that remarks dropped with seeming
unconcern are, in reality, designed to further an elaborate
and sinister plot. Bianca goes off with Guardiano to see the
rooms and pictures and—a special treat for the guest—the
remarkable monument. The two older women remain to
play a curious game of chess—a game which provides an
ironic commentary on the seduction about to take place
above:

> LIVIA: Alas, poor widow, I shall be too hard for thee!
> MOTHER: You're cunning at the game, I'll be sworn, madam.

LIVIA: It will be found so, ere I give you over.—[*Aside.*
        She that can place her man well—
MOTHER: As you do, madam.
    LIVIA: As I shall, wench, can never lose her game. . . .
        Here's a duke
        Will strike a sure stroke for the game anon;
        Your pawn cannot come back to relieve itself.
MOTHER: I know that, madam.   II, ii, 299–303, 305–8

While the game below goes forward, Bianca and Guardiano appear on the balcony. The decorations and ornaments have been impressive, but, Guardiano assures the young woman, an even fairer sight remains. He draws a curtain, reveals the Duke, then vanishes—leaving the astonished Bianca caught in Francesco's arms. Although she has been shown lascivious pictures "to prepare her stomach by degrees to Cupid's feast," Bianca is too surprised and frightened to be quite ready to submit to a lover. She struggles and protests; her breast trembles under the Duke's hand—but her pleadings serve only to intensify his lust. By turns he coaxes and threatens, whispering words of tenderness and love, declaring brutally that his absolute power enables him to command what now he humbly begs. Gradually Bianca's resistance crumbles, and the Duke's final appeal to her vanity and mercenary instincts is enough, apparently, to overcome her scruples:

> Do not I know you've cast away your life
> Upon necessities, means merely doubtful
> To keep you in indifferent health and fashion—
> A thing I heard too lately, and soon pitied—
> And can you be so much your beauty's enemy,
> To kiss away a month or two in wedlock,
> And weep whole years in wants for ever after?
>
> II, ii, 380–86

The pair go off together, perhaps arm in arm. Meanwhile the chess game below reaches a climax; it is not surprising that Livia should be victorious:

LIVIA: Did not I say my duke would fetch you o'er, widow?
MOTHER: I think you spoke in earnest when you said it, madam.
LIVIA: And my black king makes all the haste he can too. . . .
MOTHER: You may see, madam,
　　　　My eyes begin to fail.
LIVIA: I'll swear they do, wench. . . .
　　　　Has not my duke bestirr'd himself?
MOTHER: Yes, faith, madam;
　　　　Has done me all the mischief in this game.
LIVIA: Has show'd himself in's kind.
MOTHER: In's kind, call you it?
　　　　I may swear that.
LIVIA: Yes, faith, and keep your oath.

II, ii, 393–95, 397–98, 420–23

When Bianca returns, her veneer of innocence has already disappeared. The new hardness is reflected in her confrontation of Guardiano. "I'm made bold now," she says,

> I thank thy treachery; sin and I'm acquainted,
> No couple greater; and I'm like that great one,
> Who, making politic use of a base villain,
> He likes the treason well, but hates the traitor;
> So I hate thee, slave!　　　II, ii, 444–49

To Livia she is equally bitter, equally direct. "You're a damn'd bawd," she whispers, and her remark stings, for Livia soon echoes it:

> Is't so? *damn'd bawd!*
> Are you so bitter? tis but want of use:
> Her tender modesty is sea-sick a little,
> Being not accustom'd to the breaking billow
> Of woman's wavering faith blown with temptations:
> 'Tis but a qualm of honour, 'twill away;
> A little bitter for the time, but lasts not:
> Sin tastes at the first draught like wormwood-water,
> But drunk again, 'tis nectar ever after.

II, ii, 474–82

VI

Weak and lecherous from the very beginning, the characters continue to deteriorate as the play progresses. Bianca's defiance does, indeed, prove to be a qualm of honor. She is soon reconciled to the loss of virtue—reconciled before her husband's return. When Leantio arrives he does not enter the house immediately, but pauses to apostrophize the institution of marriage:

> I scent the air
> Of blessings when I come but near the house:
> What a delicious breath marriage sends forth!
> The violet-bed's not sweeter. Honest wedlock
> Is like a banqueting-house built in a garden,
> On which the spring's chaste flowers take delight
> To cast their modest odours; when base lust,
> With all her powders, paintings, and best pride,
> Is but a fair house built by a ditch-side.
>
> III, i, 86–94

He goes on to compare the "beautified body" of "a glorious dangerous strumpet" with "a goodly temple/ That's built on vaults where carcasses lie rotting." His transition to Bianca is perhaps inevitable. "After a five days' fast," he says, "She'll be so greedy now, and cling about me,/ I take care how I shall be rid of her." But Bianca does not cling. She greets her husband with a sullenness that verges upon scorn, and soon runs off to attend a banquet with the Duke. By now awakening to the truth, Leantio apostrophizes marriage once again:

> O thou, the ripe time of man's misery, wedlock,
> When all his thoughts, like overladen trees,
> Crack with the fruits they bear, in cares, in
> jealousies! . . .
> What a peace
> Has he that never marries! . . .

Nay, what a quietness has he 'bove mine
That wears his youth out in a strumpet's arms,
And never spends more care upon a woman
Than at the time of lust; but walks away.

III, i, 271–73, 280–81, 285–89

The artificial manner in which the set speeches are juxta-
posed does not detract from their effectiveness—an effectiveness which is perhaps more comic than tragic.

Leantio solaces himself quickly enough. He is taken up by
Livia, who is willing to support him handsomely in return
for his love. Degradation is the destiny of all the principal
characters and, in the case of Leantio and Bianca, it is fulfilled when husband and wife—now stallion and concubine
—confront each other with the finery that is the reward for
their prostitution:

LEANTIO: You're richly plac'd.
 BIANCA: Methinks you're wondrous brave, sir.
LEANTIO: A sumptuous lodging.
 BIANCA: You've an excellent suit there.
LEANTIO: A chair of velvet.
 BIANCA: Is your cloak lin'd through, sir? . . .
 I could ne'er see you in such good clothes
 In my time.
LEANTIO: In your time?
 BIANCA: Sure I think, sir,
 We both thrive best asunder.

IV, i, 52–54, 60–62

Both have become coarsened and hardened by sin, but
Leantio, always the weaker, finally breaks down. "You're a
whore!" he shouts.

 BIANCA: Fear nothing, sir.
 LEANTIO: An impudent, spiteful strumpet!
 BIANCA: O, sir, you give me thanks for your captainship!
 I thought you had forgot all your good manners.

IV, i, 63–65

The spectacle of their collapse, revealed here in its final stage, excites terror perhaps, but never arouses pity. Bianca and Leantio have become too base.

no sentiment

VII

Middleton's own, unsparing detachment, maintained throughout the play, is largely responsible for the chilling effect of *Women Beware Women*.[11] His characters are moral idiots whose utter inability to comprehend the sinfulness of their own careers makes them ultimately repulsive. To Lamb the bawd Livia is a " 'good neighbour,' . . . as real a creature as one of Chaucer's characters. She is such another jolly housewife as the Wife of Bath." [12] He fails to perceive that beneath the amiability and enormous vitality lies a nature almost completely amoral, a disposition sinister in its capacity for evil. When Livia discovers Hippolito's incestuous passion for his own niece, she is prompted—prompted by her very genuine affection for her brother—to lavish all her ingenuity upon his cause. " 'Tis but a hazarding/ Of grace and virtue," she declares, "and I can bring forth

> As pleasant fruit as sensuality wishes
> In all her teeming longings; this I can do.
>
> II, i, 29–32

The other characters are not so much amoral as caught in moral paradoxes and ambiguities. They may, as in the case of Leantio, indulge in sanctimonious moralizing and soon afterward slip easily into sin. Or they may engage in elaborate ethical casuistry, as Bianca does before the Cardinal, urging clever but specious reasonings in behalf of an evil course. Isabella never evidences any qualms about marrying a revolting fool in order to conceal a guilty amour, but when she

Morals

learns that her lover is her uncle, she cries out with all the accents of self-pity and injured innocence:

> Was ever maid so cruelly beguil'd,
> To the confusion of life, soul, and honour,
> All of one woman's murdering!
>
> IV, ii, 130-32

Hippolito enters into an incestuous relationship with his niece and makes no effort to free himself; yet, at the same time, he shows the greatest concern for the honor of his family: "The reputation of his sister's honour's," remarks the Duke, "As dear to him as life-blood to his heart." To preserve her precious reputation Hippolito does not hesitate to slay her lover. When Livia responds ungratefully—so ungratefully that she immediately unmasks him—Hippolito is astonished:

> Here's a care
> Of reputation and a sister's fortune
> Sweetly rewarded by her! . . .
> My love to her has made mine miserable.
>
> IV, ii, 151-53, 156

The Duke is conscience-stricken after being reprimanded for his sinful life by his brother the Cardinal. But Francesco has an odd formula for cleansing his soul: it involves marrying his strumpet after he has brought about the death of her husband. Murder, however indirect, is at best a tortuous road to salvation, and the absurdity of the Duke's morality is nowhere revealed more clearly than in his own soliloquy:

> She lies alone to-night for't, and must still,
> Though it be hard to conquer; but I've vow'd
> Never to know her as a strumpet more,
> And I must save my oath: if fury fail not,
> Her husband dies to-night, or, at the most,
> Lives not to see the morning spent to-morrow;
> Then will I make her lawfully mine own,
> Without this sin and horror. Now I'm chidden,

For what I shall enjoy then unforbidden;
And I'll not freeze in stoves: 'tis but a while;
Live like a hopeful bridegroom, chaste from flesh,
And pleasure then will seem new, fair, and fresh.

                                        IV, i, 268–79

Having only the faintest or most outrageous notions of
good and evil, these personages fail to understand that the
universe is governed by an inexorable moral order, that
someday they will be called to judgment. And so they
stumble on, lost in a maze of pleasure, rationalizing away any
passing doubts, reveling in their momentary triumphs—ignorant of the futility of their projects, unaware that the only
certainty is their own destruction. They take part in elaborate intrigues, only to find themselves the victims of intrigue; they betray their fellows to lust, only to be themselves
betrayed by the same passion. It is the dying Hippolito,
pierced by Cupid's envenomed arrows, who alone seems to
grasp his tragedy and the tragedy of the others. "Lust and
forgetfulness has been amongst us," he says, "And we are
brought to nothing." But his awakening has taken place too
late.

   As must be apparent, the view of life expressed here bears
a striking resemblance to the outlook embodied, many years
previously, in *The Revenger's Tragedy* and the City comedies. There is, furthermore, a structural similarity as well
between *Women Beware Women*, on the one hand, and *The
Phoenix* and *Your Five Gallants*, on the other. In the two
earlier plays Middleton assembles a number of rogues engaged in folly and crime, and places among them his own
spokesman—Prince Phoenix in *The Phoenix*, Fitsgrave in
Your Five Gallants—to uphold virtue and inveigh against
the prevalence of sin. The Cardinal in *Women Beware
Women* serves very much the same function: he represents
moral sanity in the midst of moral anarchy. It is he who survives to pronounce the final judgment:

Sin, what thou art, these ruins show too piteously:
Two kings on one throne cannot sit together,
But one must needs down, for his title's wrong;
So where lust reigns, that prince cannot reign long.

v, i, 264–67

But the mood of *Women Beware Women* is cooler than the mood of *The Revenger's Tragedy* or *The Phoenix.* The speeches of denunciation lack force; the verse no longer blazes. Energy and passion have been superseded by smoothness and complexity. Sin is now regarded with the frigid impassiveness of cynical maturity, rather than the fiery resentment of impressionable youth. The dramatist has recovered from the shock, if not the effects, of disillusionment.

The author's mood of detachment and the absence of elevation in his characters—they lack even heroic pretensions—set *Women Beware Women* apart from the earlier Italianate melodramas. The play has none of the raging bloodlust of *Antonio's Revenge* or the horrified revulsion of *The Revenger's Tragedy*. The romantic sweep of *The White Devil*, the brooding compassion of *The Duchess of Malfi*, are not to be found here. On the surface *Women Beware Women* appears indeed to be, in Eliot's words, "a conventional picture-palace Italian melodrama of the time." [13] Dukes and cardinals and courtiers figure prominently in the action; much of the intrigue takes place against the background of court life. There is the usual tangled net of plot and counterplot. There is, finally, the sensational piling up of horrors as ruin overtakes all the principal characters. But these features are, after all, externals—conventions inherited from previous experiments in the same genre. In spirit, however, *Women Beware Women* is quite different from the earlier tragedies. Livia's dwelling rarely impresses us as being the palace of powerful Florentine aristocrats; it is, rather, the elegantly furnished home of a well-to-do London citizen. Character and incident are depicted with a total absence of romantic heightening.

The tone is conversational, the pace leisurely. There is an abundance of realistic detail, and the imagery has an unpretentious, homespun quality. The sentiments and aspirations of the characters—their pretty speeches and smug platitudes, their yearning for position and preoccupation with material values—are perfectly in keeping with those standards so frequently regarded as middle class. Typical is Bianca's outburst of dissatisfaction:

> Wives do not give away themselves to husbands
> To the end to be quite cast away; they look
> To be the better us'd and tender'd rather,
> Highlier respected, and maintain'd the richer;
> They're well rewarded else for the free gift
> Of their whole life to a husband! I ask less now
> Than what I had at home when I was a maid,
> And at my father's house; kept short of that
> Which a wife knows she must have, nay, and will—
> Will, mother, if she be not a fool born.
>
> III, i, 47–56

The evolution from *The Revenger's Tragedy* is remarkable indeed. Renaissance Italy has ceased to be the embodiment of a poet's fantastic nightmare vision, and princely Florence, once a symbol of opulent decay, is now merely another name for bourgeois London. *Women Beware Women* marks the close of a full cycle in Middleton's development. *The Revenger's Tragedy* was the most subjective and extreme of Elizabethan tragedies having a foreign court as setting. In *The Second Maiden's Tragedy* the dramatist had attempted to blend, within the framework of a double action, courtly melodrama and domestic tragedy. With *Women Beware Women* the court milieu becomes synonymous with the domestic milieu, and the fall of princes no different from the tragic lot of ordinary men and women.

Along with the lowering of the social tone of tragedy there takes place a blurring of the distinction between tragedy and comedy.[14] The cynical and realistic sex intrigue of the first half of *Women Beware Women* is, in its effect, not unlike the sex intrigue of such scabrous comedies of London life as *Northward Ho* and *Westward Ho.* There is, indeed, comedy in Middleton's play. But it is comedy of a particularly brutal and sardonic kind, which requires, on the part of the audience, an attitude of unconcern or disdain toward the characters involved. One cannot help recalling Bergson's theory of laughter:

The comic . . . appeals to the intelligence pure and simple; laughter is incompatible with emotion. . . . Take a downright vice,—even one that is, generally speaking, of an odious nature, —you may make it ludicrous if, by some suitable contrivance, you arrange so that it leaves our emotions unaffected. Not that the vice *must* then be ludicrous, but it *may*, from that time forth, become so. *It must not arouse our feelings;* that is the sole condition really necessary, though assuredly it is not sufficient.[15]

If it is the dramatist's frigid indifference to the fate of his creations that permits bitter laughter to accompany the spectacle of human degradation, it is his masterful use of irony which actually produces that laughter. Not since *The Revenger's Tragedy* has Middleton relied so persistently on irony or used it to such brilliant advantage. Nowhere else does he employ so many ironic images; nowhere else does he elaborate them with such scrupulous care. A number of instances have been already cited; [16] one may, however, be permitted a single further illustration:

> Like a young waiting-gentlewoman in service,
> For she feeds commonly as her lady does,
> No good bit passes her but she gets a taste on't;
> But when she comes to keep house for herself,
> She's glad of some choice cates then once a-week,
> Or twice at most, and glad if she can get 'em;
> So must affection learn to fare with thankfulness.
>
> II, i, 219-25

Irony is apparent in the chess episode and in the arrangement of Leantio's soliloquies on marriage. Irony pervades the careers of the principal characters and embroiders almost every scene. Ironic in the extreme are, for example, Leantio's puzzled remarks as Livia hovers lasciviously near him:

> This [the loss of Bianca] cannot be but of some close
> bawd's working.— [*Aside.*
> Cry mercy, lady! what would you say to me?
> My sorrow makes me so unmannerly,
> So comfort bless me, I had quite forgot you.
>
> III, ii, 267–70

Irony is, of course, the method of tragedy as well as comedy, and the irony of *Women Beware Women* is at times quite terrible. But more often it serves to dispel any incipient compassion, to stir instead derisive laughter.

In *Women Beware Women* Middleton appears to be on the verge of creating a novel kind of drama—a drama that occupies a middle ground between comedy and tragedy; one that places a premium on objectivity rather than passion, clinical insight rather than sympathetic concern. In much the same fashion as in *The Second Maiden's Tragedy*, the playwright charts the gradual disintegration of his characters. He shows how greed and lechery can turn a naïve girl into an impudent harlot; he shows how a cunning and sophisticated woman can be undone, ultimately destroyed, by lust. But, as is the case in the earlier play, the final transformations have taken place long before the last scene is reached. Once again the dramatist is unable to break fully with the melodramatic tradition of his age. Resorting to the worn device of a masque, he suddenly plunges his characters into an indiscriminate carnage in which miscalculation follows miscalculation and murder is huddled upon murder. "Vengeance met vengeance,/ Like a set match," comments the expiring Hippolito,

> as if the plague[s] of sin
> Had been agreed to meet here altogether.
>
> v, i, 198–200

All kinds of machinery—arrows and trap doors, swords and caltrops—are called into service. Occasionally the slaughter is interrupted by a few lines of memorable verse:

> some blest charity
> Lend me the speeding pity of his sword,
> To quench this fire in blood!
>
> v, i, 188–90

But no amount of forced ingenuity or brilliant verse could save so preposterous a denouement. The last act is a failure, and with it the play collapses.

There are other faults as well, faults that are obvious enough. If far too much happens in the last act, not quite enough takes place in the earlier scenes: the exposition is drawn out at needless, occasionally tedious, length. The scenes involving the idiot Ward have all the dullness of obscenity unrelieved by humor or wit. After Hippolito's incestuous affair with Isabella has been initiated, subsequent events afford few opportunities for effective drama. "She can only discover that her sin is incest after all," remarks Barker, "can only vow revenge against Livia, and to accomplish it take part in the frigid intrigue of the final act." [17] Yet *Women Beware Women* has so much to recommend it in the way of characterization and technique, poetry and irony, that one can easily overlook the defects.

The play was received with enthusiasm when it first appeared, if one can trust the praises of Nathaniel Richards, whose commendatory poem is affixed to the first edition:

> I that have seen't can say, having just cause,
> Never came tragedy off with more applause.[18]

In more recent times *Women Beware Women* has been consistently accorded a high place in Middleton's serious work, a place possibly second only to that of *The Changeling*. Symons' final verdict may seem unduly severe; one might, conceivably, object that it is unreasonable to censure a work simply because it differs from one of the author's other writings. Yet perhaps Symons, of all commentators, has balanced most judiciously the excellences and defects of the play:

> in *Women beware Women*, we find much of Middleton's finest and ripest work, together with his most rancid "comic relief"; a stern and pitiless "criticism of life" is interrupted by foul and foolish clowning; and a tragedy of the finest comic savour ends in a mere heap of corpses. . . . There is no finer comedy of its kind in the whole of Elizabethan drama than the scene between Livia, Bianca and the widow. . . . And these vile people are alive, and the vices in them work with a bewildering and convincing certainty. . . . All the meaner passions are seen in probable action, speaking without emphasis, in a language never too far from daily speech for the complete illusion of reality. . . . But the heights of *The Changeling*, the nobility of even what was evil in the passions of that play, are no longer attained. Middleton, left to himself, has returned, with new experience and new capacity, to his own level.[19]

And, one might add (although Symons surely would not approve), that level was high indeed.

VIII

In 1621 appeared the first edition of a work destined to enjoy enormous popularity. Its author was John Reynolds and his book a ponderous collection of grimly sensational tales of crime and retribution bearing an equally ponderous and sensational title, *The Triumphs of God's Revenge against the Crying and Execrable Sin of Murther*. Middleton must have had access to a copy soon after publication, for early in the following year he was collaborating with Rowley on a play based upon one of Reynolds' stories. The fourth history of the first book, the account of Alsemero, Beatrice-Joanna and De Flores, constitutes the principal source of *The Changeling*.[20]

There dwelt in Valencia, according to Reynolds, one Don Pedro de Alsemero, a "noble young Cauallier" whose father had been slain by Hollanders in a sea fight. Alsemero's only ambition was to win glory in the wars, and so he set out for Malta, where he might fill a post of honor on the Island or win fame in the galleys. His first stop was Alicant. There he hoped to book passage to Naples and then proceed, via the Neapolitan galleys, to Malta. But his departure was postponed by an adverse wind—a wind that was, indeed, to prove far more unfavorable than Alsemero could possibly imagine at the time.

For it was owing to his unexpected detainment that he came to know Dona Beatrice-Joanna, daughter of Don Diego de Vermandero, captain of the castle of Alicant:

comming one morning to our Ladies Church at *Masse*, and being on his knees in his deuotion, hee espies a young Gentlewoman likewise on hers next to him, who being young, tender and faire, he thorow her thinne vaile discouered all the perfections of a delicate and sweet beautie, she espies him feasting on the daynties of her pure and fresh cheekes; and tilting with the inuisible lances of his eyes, to hers, he is instantly rauished and vanquished with the pleasing obiect of this Angelicall countenance, and now he can no more resist either the power or passion of loue.[21]

Beatrice could not help noticing the young man alongside her, nor could she hold back the blushes which reddened her cheeks. When, the very next morning, Alsemero declared his love in Our Lady's Church, Beatrice allowed him to escort her back to the castle. There he was received handsomely and shown the sights.

So far, everything had apparently gone well, but there

was one formidable problem: Don Diego had already chosen a husband for his daughter—Don Alonso Piracquo, "a rich Cauallier of the Cittie," the most sought-after bachelor in Alicant. It mattered little to Don Diego that the girl found Alonso repugnant or that she had given her heart to another. The warnings of Thomaso, Alonso's brother, passed unheeded. Beatrice was spirited away to Briamata, ten leagues off, so that the match might be immediately concluded without interference.

But the authority of a parent could scarcely restrain Beatrice once she had determined that none but Alsemero should be her husband. She corresponded with him secretly, confessed her love, summoned him to Briamata. Arriving under the cover of darkness, he was admitted at the postern door by a waiting-gentlewoman, Diaphanta, and conducted through a private gallery to Beatrice's chamber, where the girl ran into his arms. "Againe, after shee hath alleadged and shewne him the intireness of her affection to himselfe, with whom shee is resolued to liue and dye, shee lets fall some darke and ambiguous speeches, tending to this effect, that before *Piracquo* be in another World, there is no hope for *Alsemero* to inioy her for his wife in this." Alsemero vowed to challenge his rival at once, but Beatrice would hear none of it: her beloved must not hazard his life. She might prevail upon her father after all; in the meantime it would be best if Alsemero were to return for a while to Valencia.

With her lover safely away Beatrice felt free to work out a course of action which, some time earlier, had suggested itself to her. Alonso must die—so much was certain—but she would require help. In her need she turned to "a Gallant young Gentleman, of the Garison of the Castle," Antonio de Flores, a family retainer deeply enamoured of Beatrice. She knew of his love, knew also that he could be trusted. And so, with "many promises of kindenesse and courtesies, if

hee will performe it," she commissioned him to murder Piracquo. Together they devised what they hoped would be
the perfect crime.

De Flores insinuated himself into Alonso's confidence and
enticed him into a tour of the castle. The two men viewed
the walls and ravelins, the sconces and bulwarks, then proceeded through a postern that opened upon the ditches, only
to return once more to see the last "rarity"—the eastern case-
mate. At the descent, which was narrow and craggy, first De
Flores and then Piracquo cast aside his dagger, and the guide
led his guest into the vault. While Alonso stooped to look
through a porthole, De Flores reached behind the door for a
poniard he had hidden there, and stabbed the defenseless man
again and again through the back, until at last he lay dead at
De Flores' feet. Without going farther De Flores buried
him "vnder the ruines of an old wall, whereof that *Casamate*
was built," and ran off to tell Beatrice. Her joy was bound-
less. She thanked De Flores—as well she might—with many
kisses, and reminded him to spread the rumor that Piracquo
was last seen entering a boat "to take the ayre of the sea."
It was believed that Alonso had drowned, and not long
afterward Alsemero returned, at Beatrice's bidding, to Alicant. Their marriage was solemnized in the castle.

Within three months an odd change took place in Alsemero. He was transformed, quite inexplicably, from a doting
husband into a jealous wretch. He put curbs on his wife's
liberty, forbade her indeed to see any man. Still not satisfied,
he set spies upon Beatrice, and then accused her, without
any justification whatsoever, of entertaining not one but a
number of lovers. Eventually Beatrice was cured of her
love. When at last she complained to her father, Alsemero
promptly carried her off by coach to Valencia. Don Diego
was so distraught that he dispatched his retainer after them
with letters. The only person who could take pleasure in the

situation was De Flores; he welcomed the opportunity to see once more the woman he loved.

When De Flores arrived in Valencia, Beatrice was alone and so starved for affection that she did not hesitate to accept his kisses and embraces. At first she was unaware that spies were reporting her every step; but even after her husband had warned her, at sword point, to avoid De Flores, she refused to give him up. She became impudent, leaving the chamber doors open while she lay with her paramour. It is scarcely surprising that word about her doings should reach Alsemero, or that he should resolve to take drastic steps. First he had Diaphanta lie in wait to inform him of De Flores' next visit to Valencia. Then, at the appropriate time, Alsemero told his wife that he was setting out on a journey into the country—but instead he hastened to a study adjoining the bedchamber. There, armed with rapier, poniard, and pistols, he awaited the lover's arrival. His preparations were not in vain. He heard De Flores enter and Beatrice greet him. He listened as the pair kissed and embraced, as Beatrice deplored her husband's cruelty, as the lovers fell to their "beastly pleasures." No longer able to control himself, he burst open the door, "when finding them on his bed, in the middest off their adultery, he first dischargeth his Pistols on them, and then with his Sword and Ponyard runnes them thorow, and stabs them with so many deepe and wide wounds, that they haue not so much power, or time to speake a word, but there lye weltring and wallowing in their blood." There could scarcely be any doubt as to the lovers' guilt, and so Alsemero was acquitted by the criminal judge of Valencia.

The deaths of Beatrice-Joanna and De Flores would seem to afford a likely conclusion to the story—*The Changeling* ends at this point—but Reynolds feels obliged to relate further wonders. He must go on to show Alsemero treacherously slaying Thomaso de Piracquo in a duel and, shortly afterward, himself meeting death upon the scaffold. He must show how murder will out; how the circumstances of Alonso's killing are revealed at the last possible moment, how the bodies of Beatrice and De Flores are exhumed and burned and their ashes thrown to the wind. And, of course, he must point a moral. "Loe," Reynolds sums up, "here the iust punishment of God against these deuillish and bloody murtherers! at the sight of whose executions, all that infinite number of people that were Spectators, vniuersally laude and prayse the Maiesty of God, for purging the earth of such vnnaturall and bloodie Monsters."

The moral may be sound enough, but one would be hard pressed to find another feature of the narrative to commend. For Reynolds' story is as preposterous as it is lurid. Told without insight or irony, its complete disregard for human motivation is matched only by its utter lack of artistry. An innocent girl suddenly becomes a cold-blooded murderess; a generous cavalier is transformed almost overnight into a jealous madman, and later into a heartless Machiavellian. The most dreadful of crimes is rewarded with a kiss—and the adequacy of the compensation is never questioned. Blood-guiltiness is concealed by an honorable man who is entirely innocent. A wife makes a public spectacle of her adultery, even though she has every reason to believe that the penalty for discovery will be death. There are, indeed, few plausible episodes or convincing figures in the entire account. Yet this is the story which Middleton follows—follows rather closely in the early scenes—in what is perhaps his greatest play. It is, however, perfectly clear that Middleton is indebted to his source for only the naked outline of the plot. The terrible irony and searing verse are his own, as are the delineations of the two principal characters: the remorseless portrait of Beatrice-Joanna and the penetrating study of De Flores. *The Changeling* is, indeed, a striking illustration of how the genius of a great dramatist can transform the most unpromising melodrama into the subject matter of a memorable and harrowing psychological tragedy.

I X

Unlike the puppet of Reynolds' primitive *exemplum*, Middleton's Beatrice is realized perfectly. She is a pampered, irresponsible child who has been deluded into regarding herself as an adult. She believes that she is capable of love—indeed she becomes attracted, successively, to three different men—but it is evident that her selfishness prevents her from experiencing anything that might be described as normal affection. Her dominant trait, and tragic defect, is willfulness: she tries to order not only her own life but the lives of those around her. But, even though she does manage to cause a good deal of mischief, her projects never work out quite according to plan. For she is too ingenuous to understand the pathology of a man like De Flores, too amoral to know that murder is a nasty business, too immature to realize that acts have consequences.

When the play opens Beatrice has already seen Alsemero in the temple, has already become giddy with love for him. She finds it disagreeable to think of her betrothal to Alonzo de Piracquo, or of the marriage that is to take place so shortly. "For five days past/ To be recall'd!" she sighs,

> sure mine eyes were mistaken;
> This was the man was meant me: that he should come
> So near his time, and miss it!   I, i, 85–88

It is true that a week ago Beatrice adored the very Alonzo she now regards with such distaste. But then she was still an adolescent girl swayed by immediate physical attraction. Since that time, she fancies, a miraculous transformation has occurred within her: the passion she now feels is the intellectual passion of a mature woman. "Methinks I love now with the eyes of judgment," she declares, "And see the way to merit, clearly see it."

Beatrice has yet another admirer, De Flores, an impoverished gentleman serving as the family retainer. But he is scarcely to be regarded as an acceptable suitor. Indeed, his dreadful countenance inspires in Beatrice a horror which seems at times capable of overriding all her other emotions. In her eyes he is a "serpent," a "basilisk," an "ominous ill-fac'd fellow" whose hideously pimpled visage leaves her trembling an hour after she has beheld it. De Flores is indeed repellent—"so foul," remarks an observer,

> One would scarce touch [him] with a sword he lov'd
> And made account of; so most deadly venomous,
> He would go near to poison any weapon
> That should draw blood on him; one must resolve
> Never to use that sword again in fight
> In way of honest manhood that strikes him;
> Some river must devour it; 'twere not fit
> That any man should find it.   v, ii, 15–23

"Deflores is constantly referred to as a 'poison,'" writes Bradbrook, "implying I think the natural antipathy which the good people in the play feel for him, marking him out as opposed to the healthful and life-giving associations of food and feasts."[22] The poisonous face of De Flores serves as an outward manifestation—perhaps the symbol—of an equally poisonous mind: a remarkably subtle and alert intelligence channeled into the pursuit of wholly morbid objectives.

It would no doubt be misleading to describe De Flores' feeling for Beatrice as love, but one cannot overestimate the intensity of his passion. To possess her he will suffer any indignity, stoop to any crime; he will sacrifice his own soul and never regret the loss. De Flores realizes—realizes fully—that the loathing he arouses in Beatrice is as fundamental as his

own lust. When she throws down one of her gloves merely
because the other has been touched by his detested hand, De
Flores rushes to pick it up. "Here's a favour come with a
mischief now!" he declares,

> I know
> She had rather wear my pelt tann'd in a pair
> Of dancing pumps, than I should thrust my fingers
> Into her sockets here: I know she hates me,
> Yet cannot choose but love her.   I, i, 234–38

He can sooner endure Beatrice's curses and taunts than bear
the anxiety of forgoing, even for an hour, the excitement of
her company. Indeed, he has no alternative:

> I can as well be hanged as refrain seeing her;
> Some twenty times a-day, nay, not so little,
> Do I force errands, frame ways and excuses,
> To come into her sight; and I've small reason for't,
> And less encouragement, for she baits me still
> Every time worse than other.   II, i, 28–33

Although his condition appears desperate, he still has hopes
that his

> foul chops
> May come into favour one day 'mongst their fellows:
> Wrangling has prov'd the mistress of good pastime;
> As children cry themselves asleep, I ha' seen
> Women have chid themselves a-bed to men.
>
>   II, i, 84–88

Governed by a morbid, overmastering passion, De Flores is
clearly a pathological type, a study in abnormal sexuality.

In the early scenes Beatrice has no consciousness of the
nature of De Flores' feelings toward her, and so there is no
rational basis for her aversion. Perhaps it is, as she imagines,
the spontaneous antipathy of beauty to ugliness; perhaps—
and more likely—it is a deeply instinctual response to the
force of De Flores' obsession.

Meanwhile preparations for the wedding have been under

way, and in three days' time Beatrice is to be married—to
the wrong man. "How well were I now," she murmurs to
Alsemero at a secret meeting,

> If there were none such name known as Piracquo,
> Nor no such tie as the command of parents!
> I should be but too much bless'd.
>
> II, ii, 18–21

Alsemero immediately proposes a duel, but just as quickly
the project is rejected by Beatrice: her beloved might be
killed or—should Alonzo die—forced into prison or exile.
"I'm glad these thoughts come forth," she says,

> here was a course
> Found to bring sorrow on her way to death;
> The tears would ne'er ha' dried, till dust had chok'd
> 'em.
> Blood-guiltiness becomes a fouler visage;—
>
> II, ii, 36–40

"A fouler visage"—no sooner does she say the words than
De Flores comes to mind, and no sooner does she think of
De Flores than she resolves to charge him with the murder
of Alonzo:

> the ugliest creature
> Creation fram'd for some use; yet to see
> I could not mark so much where it should be!
> [*Aside.*

ALSEMERO: Lady—
BEATRICE: Why, men of art make much of poison,
> Keep one to expel another; where was my art?
> [*Aside.*
>
> II, ii, 43–47

Her decision is made instantly, and she does not pause to
reconsider. There is, however, no indication that Beatrice
regards herself as having embarked upon a criminal career;
it never seems to occur to her that murder is immoral, or
even that it is socially unacceptable. But this one act of

willfulness and irresponsibility, undertaken so casually, is to involve the amoral girl in a moral labyrinth from which she can never escape.

Beatrice is ready now to hide her revulsion. She will address the hideous creature by his name; she will even play the coquette and stroke his pimpled cheek. "What ha' you done/ To your face a' late?" she asks:

> you've met with some good physician;
> You've prun'd yourself, methinks: you were not wont
> To look so amorously.   II, ii, 72–75

De Flores is beside himself. " 'Tis half an act of pleasure," he whispers to himself, "To hear her talk thus to me" (II, ii, 86–87).

His response is so encouraging that Beatrice goes on at once to suggest, with all the skill at her command, that Alonzo is expendable. De Flores understands immediately—understands all—and kneels at her feet in his eagerness to be made the instrument of murder. Beatrice is delighted. She feels that her triumph is soon to be complete, that her ingenuity will lead to the removal of the two impediments to her perfect happiness. For Alonzo will die—there is no doubt of that—and she will pay De Flores to fly the country. Beatrice does not for a moment realize that she has actually outwitted herself. It is still too early for her to know that De Flores is her superior, that he has her already within his power, that he foresees the future much more clearly than she. "O my blood!" his thoughts race ahead after Beatrice has gone,

> Methinks I feel her in mine arms already;
> Her wanton fingers combing out this beard,
> And, being pleasèd, praising this bad face.
> Hunger and pleasure, they'll commend sometimes
> Slovenly dishes, and feed heartily on 'em.

Nay, which is stranger, refuse daintier for 'em:
Some women are odd feeders.   II, ii, 148–55

Piracquo is slain in a vault of the castle, and De Flores returns with a token: the murdered man's ring, along with the
finger from which he was unable to remove it. Beatrice re-
coils, stunned. "Bless me, what hast thou done?" she cries,
for she had not anticipated that murder might involve bloodshed. But she recovers instantly—it is perhaps not surprising
that she has been startled rather than moved. De Flores is told
to keep the stone but bury the finger, and is then presented
with a handsome reward: three thousand golden florins.
Again Beatrice is taken aback, for it is apparent that the
compensation falls short of De Flores' expectations. "What!
salary? now you move me," he shouts,

> Do you place me in the rank of verminous fellows,
> To destroy things for wages? offer gold
> [For] the life-blood of man? is anything
> Valued too precious for my recompense?
>   III, iv, 64–68

Beatrice fails to comprehend her situation, still cannot grasp
what the man is driving at. But she is disturbed enough to
double the reward immediately; indeed, De Flores may name
the sum, so long as he will "make away with all speed possible." It is the measure of her shallowness and naïveté that
for a moment she attributes his scorn to modesty. But De
Flores now declares his price:

> I have eas'd you
> Of your trouble, think on it; I am in pain,
> And must be eas'd of you; 'tis a charity,
> Justice invites your blood to understand me.
>   III, iv, 98–101

This is clear enough, and Beatrice begins to realize that she is
involved as deeply as De Flores, that as a consequence of her

crime she has been trapped. It is in vain that she appeals to him, pleading her innocence, reminding him of the distance between their births. For De Flores relentlessly counters every plea:

> Look but into your conscience, read me there;
> 'Tis a true book, you'll find me there your equal:
> Push! fly not to your birth, but settle you
> In what the act has made you; you're no more now.
> You must forget your parentage to me;
> You are the deed's creature; by that name
> You lost your first condition, and I challenge you,
> As peace and innocency has turn'd you out,
> And made you one with me.   III, iv, 133–41

Beatrice has become, indeed, the deed's creature. It is now her turn to kneel; she makes a last desperate supplication, offering up all her gold and jewels. "Let me go poor unto my bed with honour," she implores him, "And I am rich in all things!" But her effort proves futile: De Flores has become her Nemesis:

> Can you weep Fate from its determin'd purpose?
> So soon may [you] weep me.   III, iv, 162–63

He raises her up, folds the trembling girl in his arms, just as the Duke had embraced the trembling Bianca. De Flores uses the same tone, indeed almost the same words.[23] "Come," he soothes her,

> Come, rise and shroud your blushes in my bosom;
> Silence is one of pleasure's best receipts:
> Thy peace is wrought for ever in this yielding.
> 'Las! how the turtle pants! thou'lt love anon
> What thou so fear'st and faint'st to venture on.
>   III, iv, 167–71

There can be little question that this scene is the greatest in the play; it may also be the greatest scene in Middleton's entire work.

Act 3 Sc 4

x

Beatrice marries Alsemero, but whatever pleasurable anticipation she might once have experienced has since given way to anxiety and misery. For she has already become the mistress of De Flores, and she fears—as well she might—that her husband will discover her shame. There is, indeed, a hurdle to overcome even before the marriage is to be consummated. Alsemero is an amateur chemist, and his book of experiments includes a test of *"How to know whether a woman be a maid or not."* In a preposterous scene Beatrice submits to the trial. She gapes, then is seized with a sudden fit of sneezing; she bursts into hysterical laughter and, finally, falls into a melancholy. Her reactions are all quite proper, because she has learned beforehand how to counterfeit the appropriate signs.

It would, however, be more risky to attempt to dissemble on the bridal bed, and so Beatrice turns to Diaphanta, who is a virgin, and hires her to lie with Alsemero until midnight. But once more Beatrice's planning has consequences she fails to foresee. Diaphanta, it seems, enjoys the bridegroom's embraces so much that she forgets to leave, even though the clock has already struck two. Beatrice is frantic. "O me, not yet!" she complains, "this whore forgets herself." For a second time she is wholly unable to cope with a situation of her own devising; it is De Flores who immediately maps out a practical course of action. He will set Diaphanta's apartment on fire and murder her in the ensuing confusion. It has already occurred to Beatrice that it might be best to do away with the girl, and so she accepts De Flores' project without hesitation or qualm, just as she accepted the murder of Piracquo. "I'm forc'd to love thee now," she tells her hideous paramour, " 'Cause thou provid'st so carefully for my honour." De Flores goes, and almost at once voices can be heard sounding the alarm. "Already?" Beatrice asks herself, incredulously,

> Already? how rare is that man's speed!
> How heartily he serves me! his face loathes one;
> But look upon his care, who would not love him?
> The east is not more beauteous than his service.
>
> v, i, 68–71

Now, as the fire bell rings and De Flores returns, shouting orders to the servants who pass over the stage with their hooks, buckets, and ladders, Beatrice is entranced with his efficiency, his mastery. "Here's a man worth loving!" she exclaims in wonder and admiration. Her remarks reflect a subtle but profound change in her personality. De Flores' earlier words have turned out to be prophetic: Beatrice has, indeed, grown to love him. "What constitutes the essence of the tragedy," writes Eliot,

is the *habituation* of Beatrice to her sin; it becomes no longer sin but merely custom. . . . And in the end Beatrice, having been so long the enforced conspirator of De Flores, becomes . . . more *his* partner, *his* mate, than the mate and partner of the man for the love of whom she consented to the crime. Her lover disappears not only from the scene but from her own imagination. . . . and at the end she belongs far more to De Flores—towards whom, at the beginning, she felt strong physical repulsion—than to her lover Alsemero. . . . The tragedy of Beatrice is not that she has lost Alsemero, for whose possession she played; it is that she has won De Flores.[24]

Beatrice has now fulfilled her destiny—a destiny quite similar to that of the principal figures in *Women Beware Women*. She has been degraded, transformed from a proud girl into a strangely perverted woman. "O, thou art all deform'd!" cries Alsemero toward the end, and he is right. Yet —and once again there is a resemblance to *Women Beware Women*—the play does not end at this point. In a violent final scene, apparently written entirely by Rowley, Beatrice

suddenly confesses the murder of Alonzo and her whoredom
is revealed by De Flores. She is stabbed by her lover and then
dragged out from a closet to die; De Flores, in turn, kills
himself. But, in spite of the bloodshed and rhetoric, one is
scarcely able to forget that the tragedy lies essentially within
Beatrice herself.

XI

The Changeling no doubt has serious weaknesses. There is
the ridiculous episode of the test for virginity; there is the
superfluous sensationalism of the conclusion. The scenes
leading up to the death of Alonzo (ii, ii, 158–67; iii, i–ii) are
perhaps too perfunctory, while no subsequent scene can
touch the heights of the colloquy between Beatrice and De
Flores just after the murder of Piracquo. But the worst
blemish is Rowley's comic underplot concerning the efforts
of two disguised servants to seduce the wife of a madhouse
physician. It is stupid and tedious, and the treatment of in-
sanity is offensive to the modern reader.
　The defects of the play are, indeed, of an obvious sort, and
they have for the most part been recognized by critics and
commentators. But its virtues are equally apparent: *The
Changeling* has always—and deservedly—been accorded the
first place among Middleton's serious works, and a very high
position in the whole body of Elizabethan tragedy. The
dramatist's ability to create scenes of harrowing power is displayed unmistakably in the confrontation scene; there is no
more striking evidence of Middleton's mastery of dramatic
irony than the career of Beatrice; the play as a whole constitutes the most powerful statement of the playwright's thesis
of the self-destructive nature of evil.
　For *The Changeling* Middleton created two unforgettable

figures. Beatrice, the amoral woman, is the brilliant culmination of a whole series of character studies. She is the mature product of the same skill, the same conception of character, that made possible the Wife of *The Second Maiden's Tragedy*, Roxena, and Bianca. De Flores is at once Middleton's most compelling study in evil and his most remarkable exploration in abnormal psychology. Although the entire action centers upon Beatrice and De Flores, one must not overlook the dramatist's skill in delineating the subsidiary characters. Only a few lines of dialogue are needed for the portraits of the lovesick Alsemero, the lecherous Diaphanta, and the somewhat sinister Tomaso; yet these figures emerge quite clearly, quite convincingly.

And of course there is the language. There are passages which one does not easily forget, lines which linger mysteriously in the memory. Several of these have already been quoted, but one may point also to such lines as:

> My joys start at mine eyes; our sweet'st delights
> Are evermore born weeping.   III, iv, 26–27

or:

> I was as greedy on't
> As the parch'd earth of moisture, when the clouds
> weep:
> III, iv, 108–9

or:

> A woman dipp'd in blood, and talk of modesty!
> III, iv, 127

Here is De Flores when he sees for a moment the Ghost of Alonzo:

> Ha! what art thou that tak'st away the light
> Betwixt that star and me? I dread thee not:
> 'Twas but a mist of conscience.
> v, i, 58–60

"The dialogue," writes Wells, "especially in the first three acts, becomes amazingly real and convincing. True poetry is achieved in an almost colloquial idiom. In the rapid and un-rhetorical manner here employed, a single word or gesture carries immense weight." [25]

But it may be unnecessary, perhaps even misleading, to isolate and draw attention to any single feature of *The Changeling*. "The real power and genius of the work," Swinburne writes, "cannot be shown by extracts." [26] The concentration that is so strikingly evident in the language of *The Changeling* is equally apparent in the portrayal of the minor figures and, more important, in the entire conduct of the rather complicated main action. Nowhere else in Middleton are action and dialogue, character and theme blended together into such powerful harmony. "In some respects in which Elizabethan tragedy can be compared to French or to Greek tragedy," says Eliot, "*The Changeling* stands above every tragic play of its time, except those of Shakespeare." [27] It is the poetic and dramatic masterpiece of Middleton's mature style, just as *The Revenger's Tragedy* is the poetic and dramatic masterpiece of his earlier manner.

XII

It is difficult—perhaps even impossible—to summarize in a few paragraphs the contribution of a major Jacobean dramatist to the literature of tragedy. Yet one may be permitted to make the attempt.

Middleton, as has been noted in these pages, was an innovator endeavoring to create a type of drama essentially different from the romantic and heroic drama of his contemporaries. It is a drama that is psychological and realistic, cynical and dispassionate; it often arouses terror, rarely pity. In his tragedies Middleton portrays a somber and disturbing world, yet one in which the workings of an irresistible moral order can be discerned. Driven by impulses and passions which they are unable to master, which indeed they can scarcely understand, Middleton's men and women gradually disintegrate as moral beings, discovering too late that they wear destruction within their own bosoms. For, in their quest after pleasure and gratification, they find themselves entangled—entangled inextricably—in a web of sin. The dramatist expresses his point of view largely through his irony, which pervades every aspect of his art. Irony is implicit in almost every situation, informs the career of almost every character. Irony permeates the imagery and asides, the juxtaposition of speeches. The appeal of such plays as these is to the intelligence rather than to the emotions, and, perhaps for this reason, they have never achieved the widest popularity.

That Middleton did not fully succeed in formulating the kind of drama toward which his genius inclined was possibly as much the fault of his age as the result of his own limitations. He had to compete with, at times imitate, more fashionable dramatists whose methods were different from his own. It was necessary for him to make use of stage traditions and conventions unsuited to his deepest artistic impulses. As a writer of tragedy Middleton was, nevertheless, able to compose three masterpieces—*The Revenger's Tragedy, Women Beware Women*, and *The Changeling*—and one play that is almost a masterpiece—*Hengist*. It is true, as Middleton's critics have pointed out, that his best plays are marred by serious defects, that they are great not so much by reason of their total effect as for striking individual scenes. And yet, for all their defects, these five tragedies have, I feel, sufficient merit to entitle Middleton to the foremost place after Shakespeare in the hierarchy of Jacobean writers of tragedy—a place superior to that of Ford and Chapman, and also of Webster, the author of two great plays.

PART TWO
The Canon

V. Authorship Problems: The Revenger's Tragedy

OF THE FIVE PLAYS discussed in Part One of this study, only *Women Beware Women* has been regarded always as solely by Middleton. For the dramatist collaborated with Rowley on *The Changeling*, and the latter's hand has been sought in *Hengist* as well. The status of *The Revenger's Tragedy* and *The Second Maiden's Tragedy* is highly controversial. So much has already been written on these authorship problems, and especially with regard to *The Revenger's Tragedy*, that it is unlikely that further research will lead to any very remarkable discoveries. But there is a very real need for an assembling and evaluation of the evidence that has been already advanced: The material is often scattered and conflicting; some investigators have relied on questionable methods; others have based their findings on one particular test only, instead of considering all the possibilities. Inasmuch as the procedures used to determine authorship have at times themselves been the subject of controversy, something should perhaps be said at the outset concerning methodology.

I

The best evidence is, of course, external: the testimony of title pages, diaries, the Stationers' Register, the office-book of

the Master of the Revels.[1] Occasionally, however, not a bit
of such proof survives, and scholars must rely almost exclusively on internal tests—on an examination of diction, metrics, imagery, parallels of thought and expression, and other
stylistic peculiarities. Such investigations have been attacked
as untrustworthy. Allardyce Nicoll, for example, in his
edition of Tourneur, apparently dismisses authorship evidence simply because it is stylistic.[2] "Collier and Fleay and
Sykes and Lawrence and Wilson have flitted about among
the lonely orphans," writes Bentley, "assigning parents
here and putative parents there, and Fleay even going so
far as to grant on some occasions temporary custody later
to be revoked."[3] Skepticism is, indeed, often warranted,
but the difficulty is owing not so much to any inherent
defect in principle as to the slipshod manner in which
the material has at times been collected or presented. Much
of the work along these lines has been careless or inadequate—the investigator at times depending upon an unreliable reprint of a play as the basis for the most detailed
textual study.[4] It is true, one may add, that in any instance a
single piece of *reliable* external evidence would outweigh a
heap of statistics, for it is notorious that statistics can be made
to prove anything. But it is precisely the lack of such external
proofs that makes necessary inquiries of the other type. And,
when applied discreetly, internal tests can provide much useful information. Indeed, much of our knowledge of the
Chaucer and Rolle canons derives from stylistic evidence, as
does our knowledge of the respective shares of Beaumont
and Fletcher (and other collaborators) in the plays that go
under their names.

The most convincing attribution discussions "present the
evidence for and against the attribution in a conscientious
attempt to approach the truth."[5] The researcher recognizes

the limitations of his method; he realizes that some tests may
not be valid under all circumstances,[6] that others may prove
to be totally unreliable.[7] He makes use of as many tests as
possible, for they act as a check upon one another and contribute to the cumulative impression which is the ultimate
basis for judgment. His tests will approach, as nearly as can
be expected, complete objectivity; negative checks will be
applied wherever they seem desirable. Literary factors—
similarities of technique, characterization, and point of view
—are more difficult to evaluate objectively, but they are important; they will not be neglected when there is general
agreement on these matters, or when the findings can be expressed concretely, with direct illustrations from the texts.
The investigator is aware also of the possibility that the work
in question may have influenced the proposed author to
adopt certain of his traits, or conversely, that it may itself be
an imitation. He knows that a writer's style often undergoes
change in the course of time, and that the work of a later
period will perhaps bear little resemblance to the earlier manner. He takes into consideration the possibility that similarities between works may be coincidental.

On the whole, the tests are of greater usefulness when the
possibilities are limited. Then the investigator may analyze
the style of each author and apply the results to the work
under consideration. But when there is no such convenient
restriction, as in the case of anonymous plays, the chance
remains that someone has been overlooked, or that the piece
was written by an author who produced nothing else, or
whose other writings have perished.[8]

In the present study we are dealing, at best, with proba-
bilities rather than certainties. But we are fortunate in that a
fair body of writing generally accepted as Middleton's survives; that he does have a distinctive style, although it does

change in the course of his development; that his work is very different from that of his most important collaborator, Rowley. We are fortunate also in that so many able scholars have in the past been stimulated to try to solve the very same problems.

II

On October 7, 1607, *The Revenger's Tragedy* was entered upon the Stationers' books together with a comedy by Middleton:

> George Elde   Entred for his copies under th[e h]andes of Sir GEORGE BUCK and th[e] wardens. Twoo plaies th[e] one called *the revengers tragedie* th[e] other. *A trick to catche the old one* . . . . . xij[d] [9]

In the same year the original quarto was issued.[10] The author's name did not appear on the title page, and the play remained anonymous until the middle of the seventeenth century. In 1656 Archer attributed *The Revenger's Tragedy* to Tourneur in his list appended to *The Old Law*.[11] Five years later Kirkman ascribed the play to the same author in his playlist following *Tom Tyler and His Wife*, and in 1671 he made the same ascription in a catalogue attached to *Nicomede*.[12] Tourneur's claim to authorship remained unchallenged until just before the beginning of the present century, when the striking differences between *The Revenger's Tragedy* and *The Atheist's Tragedy* (*ca.* 1610–11),[13] the only extant play published under Tourneur's name, attracted the attention of scholars interested in stylistic tests of authorship. The views of the various modern authorities may be summarized most conveniently in a table:

Date	Authority	Attribution
1891	Fleay	Webster [14]
1911	Oliphant	Middleton [15]
1918	Wenzel	Marston [16]
1919	Sykes	Tourneur [17]
1929	Nicoll	Tourneur [18]
1930	Eliot	Tourneur [19]
1931	Wagner	Middleton [20]
1931	Dunkel	Middleton [21]
1931	Jones	Middleton [22]
1935	Ellis-Fermor	Tourneur [23]
1939	Mincoff	Middleton [24]
1943	Parrott and Ball	Tourneur [25]
1945	Barker	Middleton [26]
1949	Adams	Tourneur [27]
1951	Schoenbaum	Middleton [28]
1953	Foakes	Tourneur [29]

The case for Tourneur rests chiefly on three types of evidence: the testimony of the playlists, stylistic data, and more general literary characteristics. Nicoll speaks of the Archer and Kirkman attributions as "almost contemporary," [30] but a lapse of half a century is involved, a considerable length of time for an era which lacked the apparatus for scientific bibliography and did not take problems of dramatic authorship quite so seriously as modern scholars do. Errors in these early catalogues are not uncommon. Archer gives *A Trick to Catch the Old One* to Shakespeare and Kirkman attributes *Lust's Dominion* to Marlowe; both compilers ascribe *Mucedorus* to Shakespeare.[31] If any importance may be attached to evidence based on these listings, it is owing to Tourneur's obscurity. To err in ascribing plays to as popular and prolific a dramatist as Shakespeare is easily understandable, but there is less likelihood of employing mistakenly the name of an almost forgotten writer. Perhaps, as Mincoff suggests, the parallelism of the titles:

The Atheist's Tragedy   *The Revenger's Tragedy*

may have influenced the compiler, making him associate the name of Tourneur with both plays.[32] At any rate, evidence derived from the old playlists is not reliable enough to be regarded as conclusive.

Sykes points out similarities of diction between *The Revenger's Tragedy* and *The Atheist's Tragedy*. He notes that both plays contain numerous colloquial contractions of the smaller parts of speech, especially *'t* for *it*, that both contain the expressions "tis oracle" and "serious business," that both show a preference for antithetical couplets. He finds one striking parallel passage, an exclamation to "patient Heaven." T. S. Eliot rests much of his case for Tourneur on the material presented by Sykes, whom he regards as "perhaps our greatest authority on the texts of Tourneur and Middleton." [33] But Sykes' evidence has serious weaknesses. Middleton shows an even greater fondness than Tourneur for the contraction *'t* and antithetical couplets. "Serious business" appears twice in *Women Beware Women* (II, ii, 18 and IV, i, 182), while "you speak oracle," which is not unlike "tis oracle," turns up in *The Ant and the Nightingale*.[34] Oliphant observes that the invocation to "patient Heaven" in both *The Revenger's Tragedy* and *The Atheist's Tragedy* shows an indebtedness to Marston.[35] Sykes' methods have been seriously challenged by M. St. C. Byrne. Writing on Sykes' work on two Chettle collaborations, she remarks: "If we take Mr. Sykes's parallels one by one they are either cancelled by the negative test, or else their significance is so whittled away as to make them practically valueless." [36] The objection applies equally well to Sykes' findings on *The Revenger's Tragedy*. But perhaps the most curious circumstance concerning Sykes' work is that he ultimately felt his case to be weak and, Oliphant reports, deliberately excluded his "Cyril Tourneur: 'The Revenger's Tragedy': 'The Second Maiden's Tragedy' " from *Sidelights on Elizabethan*

Drama. Not only did Sykes abandon his earlier views, but as Oliphant was informed by a mutual friend shortly before Sykes' death, he came to believe that Middleton was the actual author.[37] This reversal undermines much of Eliot's argument.

Ellis-Fermor advances technical data of a different sort. She catalogues and classifies the images used in *The Revenger's Tragedy* and *The Atheist's Tragedy*. From these categories she draws conclusions about the dramatist's childhood and mentality. Feeling that both plays point to a similar background and temperament, she infers that the same man wrote them—although, as Barker points out, "She might quite as well infer that the plays were written at the same time by different men." [38] Her classifications are at times rather arbitrary; she apparently regards the figure of the grinding of the executioner's axe (*Revenger's Tragedy*, III, i, 29–30) as an image "peculiar to the running of a large Elizabethan farm or manor house." [39] The dangers of drawing biographical conclusions from such fragmentary and often misleading evidence are perhaps too well known to require comment, but they are amusingly illustrated in this instance. For, using the same method—the classification of images—but unaware that Ellis-Fermor was engaged on a similar project, another scholar, Mincoff, arrived at a different conclusion; he confidently declared that Middleton is the author of *The Revenger's Tragedy*.[40] Mincoff, it is true, stresses the poet's own imaginative use of imagery rather than possible biographical implications. But any method that can permit such contradictory results may be regarded with a certain degree of skepticism.

Allardyce Nicoll feels that *The Atheist's Tragedy* parallels *The Revenger's Tragedy* in attitude if not in style, and that the two plays have "something of the same spirit, something of the same dark and ironical attitude towards life." [41]

Nicoll's point is too vague to be of much value. Both plays are indeed "dark," but so are most Jacobean tragedies. *The Atheist's Tragedy* may reflect an "ironical attitude" in that several characters undergo reversals of fortune, but that in itself is scarcely noteworthy. The play certainly does not have the conscious ironic pointing, the ingenious variations on the biter bit theme so conspicuous in *The Revenger's Tragedy*.

Parrott and Ball find similarities of thought between Tourneur's early poem, *The Transformed Metamorphosis*, and *The Revenger's Tragedy*. They notice in both a "curious juxtaposition—it cannot be called a blend—of Marston's obsession with vice, specifically with sexual vice, and Spenser's worship of chaste beauty." [42] But, as Barker comments, "they exaggerate: there is not much sex in the poem and not much Spenser in the play." [43]

Henry Hitch Adams feels that "he can detect . . . a development from one play to the other, and that together they present a single mind's ordered view of the universe." [44] He believes that a criticism of the concept of personal revenge is implicit in both *The Revenger's Tragedy* and *The Atheist's Tragedy*, that the essential theme underlying the two plays is that "Heaven will aid the honest man who suffers his wrongs in patience and faith." [45] This message is clearly set forth in *The Atheist's Tragedy* [46] but can be derived from the earlier work only by distorting the structure of the play. For it involves attributing to Antonio—who metes out punishment to the avengers even though his own wife has been ravished by the Duchess' youngest son—an importance out of all proportion to his actual position in the play. The author of *The Revenger's Tragedy* is not interested primarily in the fortunes of patient or even honest men. He concerns himself not with how the good man prospers, but with how the wicked man inadvertently sets in motion the forces that will eventually destroy him. Such a pattern cannot be derived from *The Atheist's Tragedy*.

T. S. Eliot offers a negative argument; he suggests that *The Revenger's Tragedy* is very different from Middleton's other tragedies.[47] This is correct; but Eliot does not allow for the fact that *Women Beware Women* and *The Changeling* were written some fifteen years later, and that *The Revenger's Tragedy* does resemble Middleton's early comedies. The figures in *The Phoenix* (1602–4) and *Your Five Gallants* (1605–7) are indeed, like those of *The Revenger's Tragedy*, "distortions, grotesques, almost childish caricatures of humanity."[48]

The case for Tourneur is certainly not conclusive. Possibly it is owing to a tradition that goes back to the seventeenth century, possibly to the tendency to accept without question *any* external evidence no matter how insubstantial, that Tourneur's claim remained so long unchallenged. And now that *The Revenger's Tragedy* has been enshrined in two critical editions of Tourneur's works, both prepared by eminent authorities, there is perhaps a very natural reluctance to regard the play as another man's work—although a whole body of evidence pointing to such a conclusion has been gradually assembled.

It is Collins, Tourneur's earliest editor, who first indicates that a problem exists. He comments on the curious disparity of quality between *The Atheist's Tragedy* and *The Revenger's Tragedy*. The latter is a tour de force, an elaborate and ingenious tapestry of plot and counterplot, executed with skill and sophistication. But "the plot of the 'Atheist's Tragedy' . . . is disconnected, outrageous, and improbable; the action is systematically interrupted by irrelevant episode: the catastrophe is melodramatic and absurd."[49] Not only is there a lack of artistic development, but more important, a pronounced deterioration from a singularly powerful dramatic expression to a naïve and at times quite crude theatricalism. "Mere inequality in relative merit," Collins continues, "goes of course for nothing—the one may have been a hurried, the other an elaborate work; but the immaturity of the 'Atheist's Tragedy' is of such a kind as would have been impossible in a man who had produced the 'Revenger's Tragedy.' There is as much difference between the crudities and imperfections of an experienced and an inexperienced artist as there is between the bad handwriting of a schoolboy and the bad handwriting of an old man." [50] Collins solves the problem by discarding the testimony of the Stationers' Register and the title pages, and by assuming that *The Atheist's Tragedy* was, in actuality, composed earlier.[51] Moreover, in order to account for the technical brilliance of *The Revenger's Tragedy*, he suggests as "very probable" that Tourneur produced much more of which we have no record.[52] But there is no evidence to support either hypothesis. We know definitely of only one other play by Tourneur, a tragicomedy entitled *The Nobleman*, the sole manuscript of which was destroyed by Warburton's servant; [53] it is idle to suppose that there are others. And, although Ward and Fleay follow Collins in accepting the priority of *The Atheist's Tragedy*,[54] modern scholarship rejects it. Sykes points out similarities in diction —notably a preference for polysyllabic nouns ending in *tion* —between *The Atheist's Tragedy* and the elegy for Sir Francis Vere (1609), and concludes that both works were written at approximately the same time.[55] Oliphant feels that the style is advanced even for 1611: it offers "a foretaste of the class of verse that was to come into vogue something like a quarter of a century later." [56] Nicoll, Tourneur's most recent editor, agrees that no real evidence exists for an earlier assignment; *The Atheist's Tragedy* probably first "appeared on the stage about 1610 or 1611." [57] The problem of artistic development thus remains unexplained.[58]

Not only do *The Revenger's Tragedy* and *The Atheist's Tragedy* differ in quality; they are also written in different poetic styles. Since in matters of this nature the best evidence is the text itself, one may be permitted to reproduce passages characteristic of the verse of the two plays—passages which constitute as well the most memorable expressions of both techniques. The following is an excerpt from Vindice's famous speech on the skull of Gloriana:

> Do's the Silke-worme expend her yellow labours
> For thee? for thee dos she vndoe herselfe?
> Are Lord-ships sold to maintaine Lady-ships
> For the poore benefit of a bewitching minute? . . . .
> Dos euery proud and selfe-affecting Dame
> Camphire her face for this? and grieue her Maker
> In sinfull baths of milke,—when many an infant starues,
> For her superfluous out-side, all for this?
> Who now bids twenty pound a night, prepares
> Musick, perfumes, and sweete-meates? all are husht,
> Thou maist lie chast now! it were fine me thinkes,
> To haue thee seene at Reuells, forgetfull feasts,
> And vncleane Brothells; sure twould fright the sinner
> And make him a good coward, put a Reueller
> Out off his Antick amble
> And cloye an Epicure with empty dishes.
>
> III, v, 75–78, 87–98

Here is the well-known description of Charlemont's supposed drowning:

> Hee lay in's Armour; as if that had beene
> His Coffine, and the weeping Sea, (like one;
> Whose milder temper doth lament the death
> Of him whom in his rage he slew) runnes vp
> The Shoare; embraces him; kisses his cheeke,
> Goes backe againe and forces vp the Sandes
> To burie him; and eu'rie time it parts,
> Sheds teares vpon him; till at last (as if
> It could no longer endure to see the man
> Whom it had slaine, yet loath to leaue him;) with

A kinde of vnresolu'd vnwilling pace,
Winding her waues one in another, like
A man that foldes his armes, or wrings his hands
For griefe; ebb'd from the body and descends:
As if it would sinke downe into the earth,
And hide it selfe for shame of such a deede.

ii, i, 91–106

In the verse of *The Atheist's Tragedy* concentration has given away to discursiveness, metaphor to simile, intensity to slackness. Not only is this verse unlike that of *The Revenger's Tragedy;* it is difficult also to see it as developing out of the style of the earlier play. A number of scholars have preferred to regard *The Revenger's Tragedy* as more probably the work of a different author.

III

Webster and Marston have been proposed as the possible dramatist, but it is unlikely that either was connected with the play. Fleay sees similarities between *The Revenger's Tragedy* and *The White Devil:* "The manner of poisoning, Sc. 4; the 'discovery' of Lodovico and Gasparo, Sc. 13; the 'behind and before,' Sc. 14 (compare *R. T.*, ii, 2); the treading on him, Sc. 16 (compare *R. T.*, iii, 5, 'stamping on him') in the stage directions; and the procuring a brother to debauch a sister (compare the mother in *R. T.* . . . .) are all salient to understanding eyes. Still more so is the metre of *R. T.*, which is purely Websterian, and quite unlike that of *The Atheist's Tragedy*." [59] But Fleay attaches undue importance to situations that may easily pass into the common repertory of dramatic effects; he fails to recognize the possibility that Webster may have been imitating, consciously or unconsciously, the sensational material of an earlier work.

Webster has really little in common with the author of *The Revenger's Tragedy*, aside from the fact that both wrote lurid melodramas. As Eliot remarks, "if we assigned his [Tourneur's] plays to any other known dramatist, Webster would be the last choice. For Webster is a slow, deliberate, careful writer, very much the conscious artist. He was incapable of writing so badly or so tastelessly as Tourneur sometimes did, but he is never quite so surprising as Tourneur sometimes is. Moreover, Webster, in his greatest tragedies, has a kind of pity for *all* of his characters, an attitude towards good and bad alike which helps to unify the Webster pattern. Tourneur has no such feeling for any of his characters." [60]

Resemblances between Marston's plays and *The Revenger's Tragedy* also are superficial. Marston, it is true, established the vogue of bitter dramas of intrigue set in corrupt Italian courts; but he lacks both the poetry and the coherence shown in *The Revenger's Tragedy*. He writes, moreover, in a manner peculiarly his own—a style marked by a highly individualized imagery, chiefly physiological, and by that perverse diction which Jonson satirized so well in *The Poetaster*. It is not the style of *The Revenger's Tragedy*.

The chance of course remains that the play may be the sole—or only surviving—work of a writer now completely forgotten. The technical adroitness evident throughout would indicate, however, that the dramatist was no novice, but a man who had some acquaintance with the stage. Today scholars who reject Tourneur tend to regard *The Revenger's Tragedy* as the work of Thomas Middleton, and enough evidence has, I feel, been gathered connecting the play with his name to discount the possibility that it is the work of another, unknown writer.

IV

The data for Middleton are almost entirely stylistic, but there is one bit of possible external evidence. We now know that in Trinity Term, 1609, Middleton was involved in a law suit with Robert Keysar, who had become manager of the Queen's Revels at Blackfriars in 1605-6. The issue was a debt, which the dramatist claims he satisfied by delivering to Keysar on May 7, 1606, a tragedy, *The Viper and Her Brood*.[61] No other allusions to such a play survive; but, as Dunkel suggests, the date is appropriate for *The Revenger's Tragedy*, and the title describes plausibly the contents of the minor plot—the "viper" signifying the Duchess, and the "brood" her three sons and two step-sons.[62] Indeed, Symonds, who did not know that Middleton had written a play called *The Viper and Her Brood*, characterizes the ducal family of *The Revenger's Tragedy* as "a brood of flatheaded asps." [63] However, Foakes challenges the identification on the grounds that, first, the *Viper* may never have been written and, secondly, if the play actually existed it would have been owned by a private theater—while the quarto states that *The Revenger's Tragedy* was acted by the King's Men.[64] But we have Middleton's testimony that the play was written, and he was surely in a position to know; there are no grounds for questioning the dramatist's word, and we have no reason to believe that he was irregular in his professional dealings. It is, furthermore, possible that *The Revenger's Tragedy* was originally commissioned by the Children of the Revels but ultimately became the property of the King's Men. The play, as Harbage observes, would appear to be more in keeping with the tastes of the select clientele than with those of the popular audiences.[65] Harbage notes that after 1603 the King's Men, whose theater was easily accessible to the more fashionable London circles, made efforts to win the patronage of the select audience.[66] In 1604 the company appropriated Marston's *Malcontent* from Blackfriars, and it is entirely likely that other private theater plays passed by one method or another into the repertory. That *The Revenger's Tragedy* and *The Viper and Her Brood* are the same play cannot, of course, be shown conclusively, but the possibility remains.

The Revenger's Tragedy is like Middleton's work in its point of view, and like his work—especially the earlier examples—in dramatic technique, which is an expression of that point of view. In the City comedies Middleton interests himself not so much in folly as in vice, not so much in fopperies and affectations as in rackets and cheats. The characters involved are often singularly unpleasant—sordid creatures without any moral sense. The rogues in *Your Five Gallants* are typical; others, like Proditor and the Captain in *The Phoenix*, are even worse, more grotesquely depraved. "What monstrous days are these!" comments Prince Phoenix bitterly:

> Not only to be vicious most men study,
> But in it to be ugly; strive to exceed
> Each other in the most deformed deed.
>   I, iv, 267–70

Middleton depicts a world predominantly vicious and venal, where men always cheat and deceive each other, while at the same time professing undying friendship. There are few virtuous characters; the best are generally disinterested rather than good. Prince Phoenix and Fitsgrave are notable exceptions, but they serve primarily as spokesmen for the author.

If evil predominates it is not, however, in the end victorious. A Phoenix or Fitsgrave may be on hand to expose the rogues, but he is not strictly necessary. For evil destroys itself. Even as early as in the City comedies Middleton sees sin as blind, sinners as groping through a universe they cannot understand, unaware that the universe has a moral order. His evildoers are supremely self-confident, sure of their brightness and foresight; but in reality they are not nearly so clever as they think they are. Ignorant of their predicaments, they become their own agents of retribution, bring about their own downfall. When—as in the case of a Hoard, a Follywit, a Quomodo—they feel that they have triumphed most completely, they have actually set in motion the forces that will eventually destroy them. The pattern is not, perhaps, essentially novel, but Middleton uses it more consciously and more persistently than any other Elizabethan dramatist. And he takes pains to point the moral:

> wit destroys wit,   *Michaelmas Term*, v, i, 46

> for craft once known
> Does teach fools wit, leaves the deceiver none.
> v, iii, 94–95

> for craft recoils in the end, like an overcharged musket, and maims the very hand that puts fire to't.
> *Mad World*, iii, iii, 11–13

> Who lives by cunning, mark it, his fate's cast;
> When he has gull'd all, then is himself the last.
> v, ii, 298–99

> Who seem most crafty prove ofttimes most fools.
> *Trick*, v, ii, 207

Since there are few virtuous figures and since the demands of morality must be satisfied, to be destroyed evil must destroy itself.

Ethical judgment is expressed, therefore, through the instrument of irony, which is as notable a feature of Middleton's technique in his early City comedies as in the later tragedies. Irony is utilized in specific situations, in asides and

in commentaries, in wordplay and in the juxtaposition of
speeches. Examples of irony can, of course, be found in the
work of almost every other dramatist of the age. But the
irony, even in these youthful plays, is so pervasive and used
so pointedly as to amount almost to an artistic preoccupation. Thus, Quomodo, in *Michaelmas Term*, basks in his
wife's grief over his supposed death, not realizing that she
has already remarried. In *A Trick to Catch the Old One*
Hoard exults in his fortunate matrimonial choice:

> she's rich, she's young, she's fair, she's wise: when I
> wake, I think of her lands—that revives me; when I
> go to bed, I dream of her beauty—and that's enough
> for me: she's worth four hundred a-year in her very
> smock, if a man knew how to use it.
>
> IV, iv, 6–10

—although his wife is a penniless cast mistress. Sir Bounteous,
in *A Mad World, My Masters*, insists upon redeeming the
"losses" suffered by the man who has just robbed him; Follywit goes on to woo a young lady whom he presumes to be a
virtuous gentlewoman, and manages to marry his grandfather's whore. Harebrain, in the same play, worries inces-
santly about his wife's constancy. He hires constables to
watch his house, gives his wife a bare allowance, conveys
away erotic poems, makes her read pious works on hellfire
and the punishments for lust—but unwittingly he engages a
courtesan to urge her on to virtue and is convinced of his
wife's chastity only after she has lost it.

Disguise, employed in so many Elizabethan plays, is used
by Middleton characteristically to achieve ironic effects.
The disguised Prince Phoenix listens to Tangle's boasting of
legal trickery and to Proditor's traitorous plottings. In *Your
Five Gallants* the scheming rogues, eager to win the wealthy
Katherine's hand, determine to outdo their common rival,
Fitsgrave, by preparing an elaborate entertainment for her

amusement. Not realizing that Master Bouser, an apparently unsuspecting scholar, is really Fitsgrave in disguise, they humbly beg his aid; they plead with the very man resolved to unmask them, are overjoyed when he seizes upon the perfect opportunity to bring about their downfall and assure his own success. Witgood's whore represents herself as a wealthy widow; Follywit poses, successively, as a rich lord, a courtesan, and a strolling player—and these deceptions contribute greatly to the ironic innuendo which is one of the chief delights of the City comedies. Multiple disguise becomes most complex in *Michaelmas Term;* Shortyard and Falselight each pose three times as different fictitious persons, the ironic effect culminating in Easy's search of London for "master Blastfield," his cosigner in a bond that has fallen due. For Easy does not realize that Blastfield is really Shortyard, who now accompanies him in the guise of a wealthy London citizen.

The ironic effect may be implicit in the contrast between a rogue's cleverness and his victim's simplicity. Or it may result from a play on words:

> FIDELIO: So, captain, you deliver this as your deed? [for the sale of his wife]
> CAPTAIN: As my deed; what else, sir?
> PHOENIX: The ugliest deed that e'er mine eye did witness.
> [*Aside.*
> *Phoenix,* II, ii, 222–24

Irony may lurk in a seemingly innocent remark, as when Follywit informs the courtesan's mother that his grandfather keeps a whore:

> FOLLYWIT: Do not tell my wife on't.
> MOTHER: That were needless, i'faith.
> *Mad World,* IV, v, 128–29

It may consist merely of a confirmatory aside, such as "Spoke truer than you think for" (*Phoenix,* v, i, 46), or "He

speaks truer than he thinks" (*Michaelmas Term*, III, iv, 203).
Again, the aside may serve to emphasize an ironic point:

LETHE:　　　　　she for a stranger pleads,
　　　Whose name I ha' not learn'd.
REARAGE:　And e'en now he called me by it.　[*Aside.*
　　　　　　　Michaelmas Term, III, i, 237–39

But it hardly seems necessary to multiply illustrations of a
technique which is the most striking feature of every phase
of the dramatist's career.

　The ironic method utilized with such striking effect in
The Revenger's Tragedy has already been discussed in Chapter I, pages 17–22. It is perhaps superfluous to add here that
the irony which is so pronounced in *The Revenger's Tragedy* is exactly the same as the irony of the City comedies.
There are, however, a few parallels that may be worth not-
ing. The scene in which Lussurioso consults Vindice about
the seduction of Castiza [67] (I, iii) is similar, as Barker points
out, to an episode in *The Phoenix*.[68] Proditor plans to murder the Duke of Ferrara, but he makes the mistake of seeking
aid from Fidelio, the best friend of the Duke's son. Prince
Phoenix himself is proposed and, like Vindice, accepted
without question. Proditor then commissions a son to murder
his father and, like Lussurioso, congratulates himself on his
superior cunning at the very instant he is being outwitted:

PRODITOR:　Nay, give my words honour; hear me.
　　　I'll strive to bring this act into such form
　　　And credit amongst men, they shall suppose,
　　　Nay, verily believe, the prince, his son,
　　　To be the plotter of his father's murder.
PHOENIX:　O that were infinitely admirable!
PRODITOR:　Were't not? it pleaseth me beyond my bliss.
　　　Then if his son meet death as he returns,
　　　Or by my hired instruments turn up,
　　　The general voice will cry, O happy vengeance!
PHOENIX:　O blessed vengeance!　　　　　IV, i, 5–15

In a later scene (III, vi) Ambitioso and Supervacuo argue over who deserves credit for the execution of Lussurioso, an execution which has never taken place. As Barker has shown,[69] irony is used in a like manner in *A Trick to Catch the Old One*, when Hoard's three followers quarrel among themselves over who was most helpful in the winning of the "Dutch widow":

FIRST GENTLEMAN: Did not I use most art to win the widow?

SECOND GENTLEMAN: You shall pardon me for that, sir; master Hoard knows I took her at best 'vantage.

HOARD: What's that, sweet gentlemen, what's that?

SECOND GENTLEMAN: He will needs bear me down, that his art only wrought with the widow most.

HOARD: O, you did both well, gentlemen, you did both well, I thank you.

FIRST GENTLEMAN: I was the first that moved her.

HOARD: You were, i'faith.

SECOND GENTLEMAN: But it was I that took her at the bound.

HOARD: Ay, that was you: faith, gentlemen, 'tis right.

THIRD GENTLEMAN: I boasted least, but 'twas I join'd their hands.
                                                    III, iii, 21-31

Vindice's position as agent of Nemesis parallels the parts played by the Prince in *The Phoenix* and Fitsgrave in *Your Five Gallants*. And, as in the case of Fitsgrave, Vindice's role is not too well integrated with the rest of the action; in both plays the rogues seem capable of outwitting themselves without the assistance of an unmasker. Vindice's use of multiple disguise (he poses as pander, malcontent, and masquer) to outwit Lussurioso resembles Follywit's deceptions of Sir Bounteous.[70] And, like Follywit, Vindice is the dupe of his own cleverness. The tainted Revenger seals his own doom, and what Hippolito had said earlier of the gulled Lussurioso applies with equal point to Vindice himself: "How strangely does himselfe worke to vndo him" (IV, i, 71). The theme of *The Revenger's Tragedy*—the sinner works against his own interests—is then precisely the same as that of the City comedies, and it is conveyed in precisely the same way: by means of dramatic irony. The presence of such a pattern appears to answer what Oliphant regards as "the most telling argument" against the case for Middleton: the assumption that "Middleton never shows any concern whatever with moral problems," whereas the author of *The Revenger's Tragedy* is a moralist.[71] It seems to me that Middleton's plays reveal very much the same sort of moral awareness as that shown in *The Revenger's Tragedy*.

The lesser manifestations of irony are also present, and they are handled in Middleton's manner. There are the characteristic ironic plays on words (e.g., the punning on *brook* in the scene of the Duke's murder) and the seemingly forthright lines which have undercurrents of irony. The tendency to juxtapose seemingly antithetical words and ideas to form curiously inverted lines [72] is paralleled in *The Phoenix*:

> one that would sell
> His lordship if he lik'd her ladyship?
> II, ii, 237–38 [73]

> Call you him dear that has sold you so cheap?
> II, ii, 300

There are the ironic asides ("'Tis a good child, he calls his Father slaue," v, i, 37; "O good deceite, he quits him with like tearmes," v, i, 107); there is the ironic confirmation ("Spoke truer then you ment it," II, i, 152; "Most right ifaith," II, i, 189). The aside serves also to underscore an ironic point, as in Vindice's remarks to the audience when he stands alongside the Duke's body:

> Thus much by wit a deepe Reuenger can:
> When murders knowne, to be the cleerest man.
> We're fordest off, and with as bould an eye,
> Suruay his body as the standers by.
> v, i, 96–99

It is Oliphant who first pointed out Middleton's use of confirmatory asides, and he cites as well several other distinctive mannerisms held in common by Middleton and the author of *The Revenger's Tragedy:* 1. The practice of characterizing units of time (e.g., "one false minute," I, ii, 188; "a whispring and with-drawing houre," I, ii, 207; "a bewitching minute," III, v, 78). 2. The habit of using *faith* or *troth* together with the word *true* (e.g., "Troth he sayes true," II, i, 256; "In troth tis true too," III, i, 9; "Faith thou sayst true," v, i, 82). 3. A fondness for making one character express agreement with another (e.g., "Brother y'aue truly spoke him," I, i, 99; "Brother y'aue spoke that right," III, v, 69; "You haue my voice in that," III, v, 120.). 4. A preference for the idiom "give . . . due" (e.g., "giue Reuenge her due/ Sha's kept touch hetherto," I, i, 46–47; "giue 'em their due, men are not comparable to 'em," II, ii, 75–76; "He showd himselfe a Gentleman in that: giue him his due," III, vi, 57).[74]

On the basis of an examination of 172 plays by thirty-three dramatists, F. L. Jones finds considerable variation in the use of the insignificant words *of* and *to* at the ends of lines. He finds also that the playwright will tend to be consistent from play to play, having approximately the same number of *to*'s and *of*'s in each work. In *The Atheist's Tragedy*, *of* is used twenty-seven times and *to* nine times, for a total of thirty-six, but *of* is found only seven times in *The Revenger's Tragedy* and *to* just once, for a total of eight. The figures for *Women Beware Women*—five *of*'s and three *to*'s, totaling eight—are virtually the same.[75]

Wagner furnishes a bit of negative evidence. He points out that the spellings *hable* and *habilitie(s)*, recognized as characteristic of Tourneur, occur twelve times in his works, while no such addition of an initial *h* appears in *The Revenger's Tragedy*. "If Middleton was the author," writes Wagner, "and the 'copy' used by the printer was autograph, no *h* should appear, if we may judge from the spellings in the holograph manuscript of 'A Game at Chesse.' " [76]

Oliphant cites several unusual words and usages that appear in *The Revenger's Tragedy* and elsewhere in Middleton. These include *unbribed* ("that vnbribed euerlasting law," I, ii, 184); *hereafter* used as an adjective ("hereafter times," v, i, 21); and *covetous* in the context of "Ime couetuous/ To know the villayne" (IV, ii, 133–34).[77] Bullen points out that *sasarara* (IV, ii, 68), a corruption of *certiorari*, is paralleled by *sursurrara* in *The Phoenix* (I, iv, 121; II, iii, 238; IV, i, 82).[78] To these peculiarities Barker adds *luxur* (I, i, 12; II, ii, 129), which may be an original coinage.[79] The only other instances of this rare word cited by the *New English Dictionary* occur in two Middleton pamphlets—once in *The Black Book* and once in *The Ant and the Nightingale*, both published in 1604. Barker also points to Middleton's fondness for the word *slave* as a term of abuse, and counts twenty-six instances of its use in *The Revenger's Tragedy*, but none at all in *The Atheist's Tragedy*. *Slave* appears thirteen times in *Your Five Gallants*, and five times in *A Trick to Catch the Old One*. *Comfort*, a recognized favorite of Middleton,[80] is used fifteen times, but only twice in *The Atheist's Tragedy*.

Middleton's favorite oaths, *in faith* (or *faith* or *by my faith*) and *troth* (or *a' my troth* or *by my troth*) appear in about the same proportion of the total number of oaths as in Middleton's other early plays:

	Total Number of Oaths	Number of *faith*	Number of *troth*	Percentage of *faith*	Percentage of *troth*
Revenger's Tragedy	107	45	12	42.1	11.2
Phoenix	88	35	17	39.8	19.3
Mad World	147	88	17	59.9	11.6
Your Five Gallants	206	109	23	52.9	11.2
Michaelmas Term	93	58	17	62.4	18.3
Trick	123	80	19	65	15.4

Faith appears only eight times in *The Atheist's Tragedy* and
troth four times. *S'foot*, which occurs eight times in *The Revenger's Tragedy*, appears nine times in *The Phoenix*, thirteen times in *Mad World*, and seventeen times in *Your Five
Gallants*. Tourneur does not use this oath in *The Atheist's
Tragedy*.

Middleton is fond of the interjection *push*, a relatively in-
frequent variant of *pish*, while Tourneur favors *tush*:

	Push	Tush
Revenger's Tragedy	6	0
Mad World	7	0
Your Five Gallants	6	0
Michaelmas Term	3	0
Trick	4	0
Atheist's Tragedy	0	8

It would be absurd, of course, to rely too much on any single
verbal test, but these results can scarcely be dismissed with a
tush or a push, or even a pish.

"The danger of metrical evidence," writes Lucas, "is that
it is too often believed." [81] But Lucas uses such data himself,
as valuable in the confirmation of an hypothesis already
likely on other grounds. It is apparent that the verse of *The
Revenger's Tragedy* is unlike that of *The Atheist's Tragedy*,
and in several ways it is similar to Middleton's verse. The
bitter concentration and searing metaphor of *The Revenger's Tragedy* are duplicated in such lines as these, from
The Phoenix—lines which might well have a place in *The
Revenger's Tragedy*:

—This lord sticks in my stomach.
—How? take one of thy feathers down, and fetch him
     up.   II, ii, 277–79

Monster, to sea! spit thy abhorred foam
Where it may do least harm; there's air and room;
Thou'rt dangerous in a chamber, virulent venom
Unto a lady's name and her chaste breath.
                                  II, ii, 319–22

He the disease of justice, these of honour,
And this of loyalty and reverence,
The unswept venom of the palace.
v, i, 159–61

Oliphant notes several traits common to Middleton and the
author of *The Revenger's Tragedy*,[82] but perhaps the sim-
plest and most reliable of metrical tests is the count of feminine endings; it is certainly the most objective and mechan-
ical. I give Barker's figures below,[83] which the results of my
own checks approximate:

	Number of Lines Tested	Number of Feminine Endings	Percentage of Feminine Endings
Revenger's Tragedy	400	110	27.5
Phoenix	250	67	26.8
Michaelmas Term	150	36	24
Atheist's Tragedy	500	37	7.4

Several scholars—Oliphant, Dunkel, Barker, and Bullen
—have pointed out parallels of expression between passages in *The Revenger's Tragedy* and lines in Middleton's
acknowledged works. Many of these parallels are suspect.
Some have been taken from collaborate works and cannot
definitely be shown to be by Middleton; others are not sufficiently striking; still others fail to withstand the negative
test. But even when all these are eliminated, the remaining
parallels are numerous and impressive enough to reinforce
the case for Middleton. A list of selected parallels follows:

I, i, 18: My studies ornament,
Oliphant compares *More Dissemblers*, I, ii, 4:
My study's ornaments.

I, i, 56–57: —What comfort bringst thou? how go things
at Court?
—In silke and siluer brother:
Barker compares *Michaelmas Term*, induction, l. 35:
Crept up in three terms, wrapt in silk and silver,

I, iii, 23: *Hipolito?*—be absent leaue vs.

II, ii, 16: Your absence, leaue vs.

Oliphant compares *Women Beware Women*, II, i, 61:

> Your absence, gentle brother;

I, iii, 129–31:   honesty
> Is like a stock of money layd to sleepe,
> Which nere so little broke, do's neuer keep.

Barker compares *Phoenix*, II, ii, 20–21, where Castiza speaks of "chaste credit" and goes on to say:

> Well may I call it chaste; for, like a maid,
> Once falsely broke, it ever lives decay'd.

II, i, 19–20: Why say so mad-man, and cut of a great deale of durty way;

Barker compares *Mad World*, I, i, 74–75:

> to be short, and cut off a great deal of dirty way,

II, i, 122: my spirit turnes edge.

Barker compares *Phoenix*, v, i, 205:

> Our duties shall turn edge upon our crimes.

II, i, 140: the comfortable shine of you,

Oliphant compares *No Wit*, I, iii, 36:

> the comfortable shine of joy

II, i, 157: troupes of celestiall Soldiers gard her heart.

Barker compares *Mad World*, IV, i, 31:

> Celestial soldiers guard me!

II, i, 176–78: Virginity is paradice, lockt vp.
> You cannot come by your selues without fee.
> And twas decreed that man should keepe the
> key!

Barker compares *No Wit*, II, i, 16–17, 19–20:

> You must think, sweet widow, if a man keep
> maids, they're under his subjection. . . . They
> have no reason to have a lock but the master
> must have a key to't.

II, ii, 31–32: A right good woman in these dayes is changde
                Into white money with lesse labour farre,
Barker compares *Phoenix*, I, iv, 245–46:
                he does determine to turn her into white money;

II, ii, 53–54: But set spurs to the Mother; golden spurs
                Will put her to a false gallop in a trice.
Barker compares *No Wit*, III, i, 35–36:
                I know the least touch of a spur in this
                Will now put your desires to a false gallop,

II, ii, 91–92: and all the farthingales that fal plumpe about
                twelue a clock at night vpon the Rushes.
Oliphant compares *Hengist*, I, ii, 29–31:
                                        —twill
                throbb at the very falle of a farthingale
                —Not if it fall on the rushes

II, ii, 121: The pen of his bastard writes him Cuckold!
II, ii, 147: This their second meeting writes the Duke
                                                Cuckold

Barker compares *Phoenix*, I, ii, 100:
                he'll one day write me cuckold;

II, ii, 151: To Grace those sins that haue no grace at all.
Barker compares *Michaelmas Term*, II, iii, 453–54:
                —A very good grace to make a lawyer.
                —For indeed he has no grace at all.

II, ii, 291–92: A Dukes soft hand stroakes the rough head of
                                                law,
                And makes it lye smooth.
Barker compares *Triumphs of Truth* (Vol. VII, p. 260):
                I was not made to fawn or stroke sin smooth;

III, v, 4–5: O tis able to make a man spring vp, & knock his
                                                for-head
                Against yon siluar seeling.

Oliphant compares *No Wit*, v, i, 455–56:

> Methinks I could spring up and knock my head
> Against yon silver ceiling now for joy!

III, v, 100–101:   see Ladies, with false formes
> You deceiue men, but cannot deceiue wormes.

Oliphant compares *Your Five Gallants*, ii, i, 332–35:

> Whose clothes
> E'en stand upright in silver, when their bodie[s]
> Are ready to drop through 'em; such there be;
> They may deceive the world, they ne'er shall
>   me.

III, v, 147: Giue me that sin thats rob'd in Holines.

Barker compares *Game at Chess*, ii, ii, 141, 143:

>   but to finde Sin . . .
> Under a Robe of Sanctitie,

IV, ii, 52–53: —Tell me, what has made thee so melancholy?
> —Why, going to Law.

Compare *Phoenix*, IV, i, 175:

> Going to law, i'faith, it made me mad.

IV, ii, 99–100: And thou hast put my meaning in the pockets,
> And canst not draw that out;

Barker compares *No Wit*, ii, ii, 96–97:

> Deal plainly, heaven will bless thee; turn out all,
> And shake your pockets after it;

IV, ii, 138: All this is I.
I, iii, 159: That's I my Lord.

Oliphant compares *No Wit*, v, i, 127:

> That's I still;

But the expression is really very common in Middleton: see
Phoenix, IV, i, 64, *Michaelmas Term*, v, i, 75, etc.

IV, ii, 255: Nay doubt not tis in graine, I warrant it hold
>   collour.

Vindice is saying that his scheme is good; Barker compares

Mad World, III, iii, 81–82, where Follywit expresses approval of a plan:

> nay, 'tis in grain; I warrant it hold colour.

IV, iii, 22: Most women haue small waste the world
through-out,

Dunkel compares *Phoenix*, I, vi, 135:

> How small are women's waists to their expenses!

IV, iv, 16–17: —A bawde? O name far loathsomer then hell.
—It should be so knewst thou thy Office well.

Dunkel compares *Michaelmas Term*. IV, ii, 2–3:

> To be bawd!
> Hell has not such an office.

IV, iv, 143–44: In three houres reading, to vntwist so much
Of the black serpent, as you wound about me?

Barker compares *Game at Chess*, IV, iv, 9–10:

> When they haue woond about our constant
> Courages
> The glitteringst Serpent that ere falshood
> fashiond

V, i, 17–18: how quaintly hee died like a Polititian in
hugger-mugger, made no man acquainted with
it,

Bullen compares *Phoenix*, I, vi, 71–72:

> Would he die so like a politician and not once
> write his mind to me?

V, ii, 7: Winde vp your soules to their full height agen.

Barker compares *Mad World*, I, i, 161:

> To have our wits wound up to their stretch'd
> height!

Thus it can be seen that *The Revenger's Tragedy* conforms to Middleton's acknowledged early writings in diction and in verse, in idiom and in mannerism. The play is very similar to the City comedies in point of view, characterization, and dramatic technique. It affords also striking examples of phraseology paralleled closely in works accepted as Middleton's. Several of the stylistic peculiarities of *The Revenger's Tragedy* can perhaps be detected elsewhere among the dramatists of the period, but the cumulative effect of all the Middleton characteristics to be found in the play is unmistakable. The case for Middleton's authorship is, I believe, sufficiently strong to warrant including *The Revenger's Tragedy*—at least tentatively—among the acknowledged plays in the canon of his works.

VI. *The Authorship of*
The Second Maiden's Tragedy

The Second Maiden's Tragedy survives in a unique copy at the British Museum, in MS Lansdowne 807, a volume preserving the remnants of the priceless Warburton collection. The manuscript is in the hand of a highly skilled scribe who was apparently commissioned to make a fair copy of the author's rough draft.[1] On the last leaf appears Sir George Buc's licensing note: [2]

> *This second Maydens tragedy (for it hath*
> *no name inscribed) may with the reformati-*
> *ons bee acted publikely.* 31. *october.*
> *1611* /. *G. Buc.*

When he named the work before him, Buc was presumably recollecting Beaumont and Fletcher's *Maid's Tragedy* which, as censor, he must have seen not long previously.[3] The designation reappears in a later hand on the margin of the first leaf; it occurs also on the verso of the last page. On September 9, 1653, the following entry was inserted in the Stationers' books: [4]

> Master Mosely. Entred also . . . the severall playes
> following . . xx^s vj^d

This heading precedes a lengthy enumeration of titles, among which "*The Maids Tragedie,* 2d part" is listed, after several plays by Massinger. As it is unlikely that a sequel followed Beaumont and Fletcher's play, the present work is probably meant. The identification is further confirmed by an item in Warburton's list referring to the manuscript as "2d. pt. Maidens Trag. Geo. Chapman," for the listing shows many points of contact with the Moseley entry.[5] We know that the play was written for the King's Men because the names of two actors in that company, Robert Gough and Richard Robinson, appear in the stage directions (ll. 1723–24, 1928–29).

At least four different hands have been distinguished in the text of the manuscript. One belongs to the scrivener, another probably to the prompter, and the third presumably to the official censor, Sir George Buc. The fourth hand is described by Greg as "almost certainly" that of the author,[6] but proof is lacking for such an assertion. The evidences of this hand consist of minor alterations: slight changes of punctuation, spelling, and diction. A comma or question mark is added; an apostrophe is inserted or deleted. *Hath* becomes *have, one* is changed to *owne*, while *waie* is replaced by *pathe* and *honest* by *virtuous*.[7] A few words are added—"AND I MUST THOROW," for example, is inserted at line 2208—but these additions are of a neutral type. The revisions are in all instances trivial, and it is questionable whether all are in the same hand.[8] Not one alteration is striking enough to be regarded as characteristic of the style of the play. The changes, it is true, are of a literary nature, but that would hardly appear to constitute sufficient evidence to assume that the author was responsible for them. It seems sounder to refer to the reviser merely as the "literary corrector," a label which Greg uses several times.

I

Several attributions occur in the manuscript itself. On the verso of the last leaf the play is ascribed to Thomas Goff, or Gouff, in what is apparently a mid-seventeenth-century handwriting. This name has been scored through and re-placed by "George Chapman," which in turn has been crossed out for "Will Shakspear." Both entries probably be-long to the eighteenth century.[9] None of these ascriptions merits serious consideration. The play is utterly unlike Chap-man's work; Thomas Goff, whose surviving plays are of a very different nature, first entered Christ Church in 1609 and did not receive his B.A. degree until 1613.[10] It scarcely seems necessary to account for the presence of Shakespeare's name.

The Second Maiden's Tragedy was edited anonymously in 1824, and since then several scholars have expressed views concerning the authorship of the play. But inasmuch as *The Second Maiden's Tragedy* has usually been regarded as in-ferior to *The Revenger's Tragedy*, the question of who wrote it has prompted less controversy in recent years than the authorship of the earlier play. A sufficient number of readers have, however, devoted their attention to the prob-lem to warrant the presentation of their findings in the form of a table:

Date	Authority	Attribution
1829	Tieck	Massinger [11]
1830	Beddoes	Tourneur [12]
1874	Bullen	Tourneur [13]
1875	Swinburne	Middleton [14]
1891	Fleay	Author of *The Revenger's Tragedy* [15]
1894	Boyle	Massinger and Tourneur [16]
1902	Rosenbach	Tourneur [17]
1911	Oliphant	Middleton [18]
1919	Sykes	Tourneur [19]
1929	Nicoll	Tourneur(?) [20]
1945	Barker	Middleton [21]

Tieck identifies *The Second Maiden's Tragedy* with one of Massinger's lost plays, *The Tyrant*, entered by Moseley on the Stationers' Register in 1660; Boyle ascribes the first two acts to Massinger and the rest to Tourneur. One of the chief characters is labeled only as "Tyrant" in the manuscript, but there is no evidence that Massinger was writing for the stage as early as 1611, and *The Tyrant* is entered as a separate item in both the Stationers' Register and Warburton's list. Boyle gives no data to support his opinion; Massinger has, indeed, little in common with the author of *The Second Maiden's Tragedy*. The remaining authorities are not so far apart as they may appear to be, for those who favor Tourneur assume that he wrote *The Revenger's Tragedy* and base their findings primarily on the resemblances between that play and *The Second Maiden's Tragedy*.

The two works obviously have some relation to one another. Sykes points to verbal parallels: [22]

> thy once crackt honestie
> is like the breaking of whole monye
> it neuer comes to good but wastes awaie
> ll. 945–47

Sykes compares *Revenger's Tragedy*, I, iii, 129–31:

> for honesty
> Is like a stock of money layd to sleepe,
> Which nere so little broke, do's neuer keep.

> heare take this Iewell beare it as a token
> to our hearts Sainct, twill doe thy wordes no harme
> speech may do much, but wealths a greater charme
> then any made of wordes,   ll. 1150–53

Sykes compares *Revenger's Tragedy*, I, iii, 31–32:

> yet words are but great-mens blanckes.
> Gold tho it be dum do's vtter the best thankes.

But the parallels of situation are certainly more impressive; they have, indeed, been noted by a number of readers in the course of over a century. Govianus paints the corpse of his mistress with poison to kill the Tyrant (ll. 2319 ff.); Vindice poisons the lips of his mistress' skull to murder the Duke

(III, v, 105–8, 154–59).[23] Helvetius entreats his daughter to become the Tyrant's whore (ll. 645 ff.); similarly, Gratiana urges her daughter, Castiza, to submit to Lussurioso (II, i, 153 ff.).[24] The Lady pretends not to recognize her father (ll. 738–49); Castiza makes believe she does not know her own mother (II, i, 180–82, 260–62).[25] Helvetius is converted by Govianus (ll. 750 ff.), just as Gratiana is reformed by her sons (IV, iv, 38 ff.).[26] Anselmus, dying, learns of his wife's unfaithfulness (l. 2188 1–16); the Duke is told of the infidelity of his Duchess just before his death (III, v, 185–234).[27] The Lady commits suicide rather than yield to the Tyrant's lust (ll. 1294 ff.), while Antonio's wife kills herself after she has been raped by Junior (I, iv, 30–53).[28] Govianus, in an effort to avoid suspicion of murder, props up Sophonirus' body against a door to make him appear alive (ll. 1374 ff.); Vindice and Hippolito, for the same purpose, place the Duke's corpse, presumably in an upright position, against a post or wall (IV, ii, 238–53; v, i, 1 ff.).[29]

Some of these resemblances can, no doubt, be paralleled in other plays of the period, but it is unusual to find so many correspondences. The similarities can be explained, it would seem, in only two ways: either (1) the author of *The Second Maiden's Tragedy* imitated the writer of *The Revenger's Tragedy*, or (2) the same man wrote both plays. In order to discount the first possibility, one must provide data exclusive of similarities between the two works. Thus, efforts have been made by some scholars to relate *The Second Maiden's Tragedy* to Tourneur's one undisputed play, *The Atheist's Tragedy*, while other authorities have compared *The Second Maiden's Tragedy* with Middleton plays of the same period. I feel that no substantial proof has been set forth for Tourneur, but that a convincing case can be made for Middleton's authorship. Such a finding would, clearly, strengthen as well Middleton's title to *The Revenger's*

Tragedy. But first we must review the evidence for Tourneur.

Nicoll points to similarities of characterization and plot between *The Second Maiden's Tragedy* and *The Atheist's Tragedy;* Sykes offers parallels of phraseology. The evidence of both investigators is, however, very tenuous. Nicoll feels that "the deaths of Anselmus, Votarius, and the Wife remind us of the deaths of Sebastian, Belforest, and Levidulcia in *The Atheist's Tragedie*." [30] Perhaps they do, but, as Barker replies, "the principal characters of domestic tragedies often die in the final scene." [31] Nicoll finds also a "general likeness" between Govianus and the Lady in *The Second Maiden's Tragedy* and the lovers Charlemont and Castabella in *The Atheist's Tragedy*. Such a remark is too vague to have value as evidence. Sykes' parallels are hardly more impressive. The phrases themselves lack distinction; points of resemblance are at times difficult to perceive.[32] If we regard *The Atheist's Tragedy* as the only important source of uncontroversial data for Tourneur, as I think we must, we are tempted to conclude that there is no evidence at all favoring his authorship of *The Second Maiden's Tragedy*.

II

Swinburne first suggested Middleton; Fleay objected: "It could not be by Middleton, *q. v.*, who did not attain a connexion with the King's men (who performed it) until 1622." [33] But Fleay's unequivocal statement distorts the facts. It is true that we have no document to show that Middleton was writing for the King's Men as early as 1611. But that is all we can say. The dramatic records for the period are far from complete; our knowledge of Middleton's career is especially inadequate. "The details of his biography remain for the most part unexplored," writes Adams. "The history of his long connection with the stage and of his labors for various theatrical companies is, in spite of the efforts of Dyce and Bullen, distressingly obscure." [34] Fleay's assertion cannot, therefore, be regarded as a serious objection. There is, on the other hand, a good deal that may be said for Middleton.

The author of *The Second Maiden's Tragedy* appears to follow Middleton's usual practice in his reliance upon a profoundly ironic pattern—a reliance that is quite conscious. In the most characteristic plays of his mature period, Middleton is concerned with how men and women betray themselves by succumbing to their own passions. His characters are for the most part weak or impulsive figures lacking in insight, without enough strength of will to govern their emotions. And so they manage to become involved in emotional entanglements that are usually illicit, inevitably degrading, and ultimately self-destructive. The impulses which lead Middleton's characters astray center almost exclusively in the sexual sphere; the dramatist is preoccupied with sex, particularly when it leads to guilty, at times even perverse, relationships. To Middleton sexuality is a source of anguish, driving men and women to sin and degradation. His personages are sinful creatures who delude themselves with expectations of pleasure, only to find out too late that sin has a high price, higher than they are able to afford. Although Middleton's tragedies terminate in melodramatic bloodshed, such scenes are in reality extraneous: a more terrible retribution has already taken place within the character structure of the individual himself. This pattern has, I trust, been discussed adequately in Chapters II–IV; it is perhaps unnecessary to note here that the pattern is most clearly evident in such plays as *More Dissemblers Besides Women*, *Hengist*, *Women Beware Women*, and *The Changeling*.

In the Tyrant-Lady-Govianus sections of *The Second Maiden's Tragedy*, the dramatist repeats situations from *The Revenger's Tragedy*, handling them in the manner of Fletcherian melodrama, a manner which Middleton found especially attractive during his period of tragicomedies. As it is derivative material treated in a borrowed vein, one cannot expect an individualized pattern in these elements of the play. But such a pattern, revealing Middleton's characteristic preoccupation with sexual transgression and its essentially ironic consequences, is apparent in the Anselmus-Wife-Votarius scenes. These three characters are very similar to the sexually obsessed figures who people Middleton's later plays, and they undergo very much the same kind of deterioration.[35] Their tragedy lies, indeed, not so much in the customary retributive justice at the hands of other characters, as in the perversion of their own characters:

> man has some ennemy still that keepes him back
> in all his fortunes, and his mynde is his,
> and thats a mightie adversarie. ll. 435–37

Much the same point is made in *Women Beware Women*, when Livia asks Hippolito how he came by his incestuous passion for his niece. "Even as easily," Hippolito replies,

> As man comes by destruction, which ofttimes
> He wears in his own bosom. II, i, 2–4

It is precisely the same theme as that expressed in the City comedies; only, in *The Second Maiden's Tragedy* and in Middleton's mature plays, it is developed more through character than action.

The particular situations and devices used to set forth this message are at times closely paralleled in the plays of Middleton. By neglecting his wife and then making Votarius approach her, Anselmus sets up the very situation which undoes him. "Man in thease daies," comments Votarius,

is not content to haue his ladie honest
and so rest pleazd with her without more toile,
but he must haue her tride forsooth, and tempted
and when she proues a Queane then he lies quiet.

ll. 827–31

Anselmus recalls Harebrain in *A Mad World, My Masters*. Harebrain also dwells morbidly on the problem of his wife's faithfulness and manages, through his care, to bring about the very occurrence he wishes most to avoid. Only after she has fallen does he feel assured of her chastity. "Welcome, sweet wife," he greets Mistress Harebrain after she has returned from her first assignation, "alight upon my lip!/ Never was hour spent better" (iii, ii, 251–52).

"Tis a fine life to marrie! no states like it" (l. 899), says Anselmus, who has not yet discovered that he is a cuckold. His words suggest, as Barker points out, Leantio's eulogy to marriage, which begins:

How near am I now to a happiness
That earth exceeds not! not another like it.
Women Beware Women, iii, i, 82–83

Leantio does not know that his wife has become the Duke's mistress. Anselmus' words also bring to mind Hoard's delight in marrying the "Dutch widow" who later proves to be a courtesan:

Who would not wed? the most delicous life!
No joys are like the comforts of a wife.
Trick, v, ii, 41–42

The minor features of Middleton's irony are also to be found in *The Second Maiden's Tragedy*. There is the ironic word-play—word-play which in one instance is carefully underscored and explained by the dramatist. Votarius instructs Anselmus on how to eavesdrop at a "test," prepared beforehand, of his wife's virtue. "Tis a matche Sir" (l. 1998),

Anselmus agrees, and then leaves. "Troth he saies true ther," Votarius comments,

> tis a matche indeed
> he does not knowe the strengthe of his owne wordes.
>
> ll. 1999–2000

There is the ironic aside, also involving at times a play on words. "Pray watche the door," the Wife tells her servant, aware that Anselmus listens,

> and suffer none to troble vs
> vnless it be my lord
> LEONELA: twas finely spoke that
> my lord indeed is the most troble to her.   [*Aside*
>
> ll. 2066–69

A few moments later the Wife pretends to be outraged by the approaches of Votarius:

> whers modesty and honour? haue I not thrice
> answerd thy lust
> LEONELA: birladie I thinck oftner.   [*Aside*
>
> ll. 2103–5

There is the ostensibly innocent remark concealing a bitter irony. Anselmus goes off in order to provide Votarius with a better opportunity to tempt the Wife. She yields easily and, when her husband returns, kisses him with dissembled love. Anselmus next embraces his friend, who remarks simply, "You neuer come to soone sir" (l. 879). When asked how he has fared, Votarius replies that the Wife is a woman of ice. But Anselmus is still not satisfied:

> ANSELMUS: I see by this thow didst not try her throughlie
> VOTARIUS: how sir not throughlie, by this light he liues not
> that could make triall of a woman better
> ANSELMUS: I feare thow wast to slack
> VOTARIUS: good faith you wronge me sir
> she neuer found it soe.   ll. 888–93

In the later plays Middleton's ironic point of view also finds expression through his imagery. As has been remarked pre-

viously in another section, a number of ironic images are to
be found scattered through the verse of *The Second Maid-
en's Tragedy*,[36] and these are quite similar to the ironic images in Middleton's acknowledged works. Indeed, the use of
such figures to reinforce the ironic pattern of the play itself
is a peculiarity of Middleton's technique. No images of this
type appear in *The Atheist's Tragedy*.

Since Middleton's verse has an individuality which sets it
apart from the work of his fellow dramatists, evidence based
upon a consideration of the verse technique may be of value.
And, certainly, the verse of *The Second Maiden's Tragedy*
and the verse of Middleton's later plays leave, as Swinburne
first noted, a very similar impression.[37] It hardly seems profit-
able, however, to cite mannerisms or analyze imagery here,
for the characteristics of Middleton's mature verse have been
discussed along with the verse of *The Second Maiden's
Tragedy* in a previous chapter.[38] Still one may be permitted
the quotation of a single illustrative passage—a passage of
some length:

> I pittie you madame
> y'aue an vnpleasing lord, would twere not so
> I should reioice with you,
> you'r younger, the very Springes vpon you now
> the Roses on your cheekes are but new blowne,
> take you together y'are a pleasaunt garden
> wher all the sweetnes of mans comfort breathes,
> but what is it to be a worke of beautie
> and want the heart that should delight in you,
> you still retaine your goodnes in your selues
> but then you loose your glorie, which is all,
> the grace of euery benifit is the vse
> and ist not pittie you should want your grace?
> looke you like one whose lord should walke in groues
> about the peace of midnight Alas madame
> tis to me wondrous how you should spare the daie
> from amorous clips, much less the generall season
> when all the worldes a gamster,

that face deserues a frend of heart and spirrit
discourse, and motion, indeed such a one
that should obserue you (madam) without ceasinge,
and not a wearie lord.   ll. 466–87

There can be little question, it seems to me, that the figures
and rhythms are entirely in Middleton's manner.

The speech, already reproduced, in which Helvetius re-
bukes his daughter for not submitting to the Tyrant's lust is
cited by Barker as characteristic of Middleton's later verse.
He points especially to the lines "when Glorie is set for thee
and thy seed" and "pursued allmost to my eternall hazard."
They are, he feels, unmistakably Middleton's,[39] and one is
inclined to agree. Barker notes also the similarity in image
and language between the lines containing the figure of the
seasons:

<blockquote>
ioye
able to make a latter springe in me
in this my fowrescore sommer,
                    ll. 660–62
</blockquote>

and a passage in *No Wit, No Help Like a Woman's:* [40]

<blockquote>
O my reviving joy! thy quickening presence
Makes the sad night of threescore and ten years
Sit like a youthful spring upon my blood.
                    IV, i, 1–3
</blockquote>

The count of feminine endings provides further evidence.
I give Barker's figures for *The Second Maiden's Tragedy*
and Middleton plays of approximately the same period: [41]

	Number of Lines Tested	Number of Feminine Endings	Percentage of Feminine Endings
Second Maiden's Tragedy	500	210	42
Chaste Maid	400	185	46.3
No Wit	500	226	45.2
Atheist's Tragedy	500	37	7.4

My own checks have yielded similar results.

When Jones' test of the frequency with which *of* and *to*

are used at the ends of lines [42] is applied to *The Second Maiden's Tragedy* the results favor Middleton; the totals are, indeed, strikingly similar to the figures for *The Revenger's Tragedy* and Middleton's accepted works, but significantly different from the totals for *The Atheist's Tragedy*:

	Of	To	Total
Second Maiden's Tragedy	2	3	5
Revenger's Tragedy	7	1	8
Chaste Maid	2	2	4
No Wit	2	3	5
Witch	3	1	4
Hengist	1	2	3
More Dissemblers	3	5	8
Women Beware Women	5	3	8
Atheist's Tragedy	27	9	36

The oaths a playwright uses will vary considerably from play to play in both number and kind, depending, among other things, upon legal prohibitions, the social status of the characters, the seriousness of tone or degree of elevation of the work itself, and—it scarcely needs mentioning—the length of the play. But the totals do provide a rough check. Middleton most favors *faith*. Recurring with extreme frequency in the City comedies, the oath appears somewhat less often in the later tragicomedies and tragedies, but remains nevertheless his unquestionable favorite. Middleton relies less upon *troth*, but his use of it is perhaps even more consistent. The figures for *The Second Maiden's Tragedy*, a comparatively short play, are in accordance with Middleton's usual practice:

	Total Number of Oaths	Number of *faith*	Number of *troth*	Percentage of *faith*	Percentage of *troth*
Second Maiden's Tragedy [43]	65	25	9	38.5	13.8
Chaste Maid	121	58	9	47.9	7.4
No Wit	107	54	11	50.5	10.3
More Dissemblers	49	15	7	30.6	14.3
Women Beware Women	74	36	15	48.6	20.3

Faith appears nine times in *The Atheist's Tragedy* and *troth* four times. When *The Second Maiden's Tragedy* was written, Middleton apparently had a fondness for the oath *life* (or *'slife*), as it turns up fairly often in two plays of that period—*Chaste Maid* (twelve times) and *No Wit* (eight times). *Life* occurs ten times in *The Second Maiden's Tragedy*, but not at all in *The Atheist's Tragedy*. It may be remarked that the not very common oath *cuds me* is used in *The Second Maiden's Tragedy* (l. 1625). The only instance of it cited by *The New English Dictionary* is from *Michaelmas Term* (ii, iii, 303), but it appears also in *No Wit* (i, iii, 208 and iv, i, 204).

Middleton favors the ejaculation *push* (or *pish*), while Tourneur uses *tush*. The totals for *The Second Maiden's Tragedy* are in full accordance with the figures for Middleton, but quite different from Tourneur's practice:

	Push (or Pish)	Tush
Second Maiden's Tragedy	5	0
Chaste Maid	4	1
No Wit	8	0
More Dissemblers	2	0
Hengist	5	0
Women Beware Women	5	0
Atheist's Tragedy	0	9

Barker lists, without totaling, several abstract words used in *The Second Maiden's Tragedy*—words of which Middleton is fond:

	Number of Times Used		Number of Times Used
blessing	6	joy	8
comfort	7	peace	14
glory	9	sin	16
grace	10		

To nouns of this type, rich in associations, may be added two others: *destruction* (eight times) and *treasure* (eight times). The author shares Middleton's fondness for the word *slave* used as a term of abuse (seven times) and for the modifiers *strange* or *strangely* (twenty times) and *precious* (four times). Barker notes the unusual usage of *mystical* in the sense of "secret" or "unavowed." It appears in the phrase *misticall Pandaress* (l. 993) and elsewhere in Middleton: *Mystical quean* (*Your Five Gallants*, v, i, 5–6), *mystical bawdy-house* (*Roaring Girl*, preface), *mystical baggage* (*Chaste Maid*, III, i, 20), and *mysticall harlott* (*Hengist*, v, ii, 199). One may cite also the use of *troth* in conjunction with *true* ("troth he saies true," l. 1999), which Oliphant cites as a Middleton mannerism.[44]

The most impressive evidence favoring Middleton consists, however, of the numerous and striking parallels of thought and expression which have been assembled by Barker. I give all, with the exception of those from collaborate works:

> and laye vsurpers svnnynge in their glories
> like *Adders* in warme beames   ll. 13–14

Barker compares *Game at Chess*, IV, iv, 10, 13:

> —The glitteringst Serpent . . .
> —Looke, would you see distruction lye a sunning

Also *Women Beware Women*, III, ii, 292–93:

> From many beggars, that had lain a-sunning
> In thy beams only else,

> tis but the syn of Ioye, ther is no gladnes
> but has a pride it liues by,—thats the oyle
> that feedes it into flames;   ll. 29–31

Barker compares *No Wit*, II, ii, 35:

> When joy, the oil that feeds it, is dried up?

>   one whose heart is lockt
> vp in anothers bosome¿   ll. 75–76

Barker compares *Women Beware Women*, III, i, 85–86:

>   the conceal'd comforts of a man
> Lock'd up in woman's love.

> as poore as *Vertue*,   l. 182

Barker compares *Women Beware Women*, I, i, 128:

> And I'm as rich as virtue can be poor,

fortunes are but the outsides of true worth   l. 189
Barker compares *Mad World*, IV, iii, 41:
Some have fair outsides that are nothing worth.

your grace hath hapned
vpon a straung waie, yet it proues the neerest:
ll. 247–48
Helvetius is expressing approval of the Tyrant's scheme for
seducing the Lady. Barker compares *No Wit*, I, ii, 104–5,
where Mistress Low-Water comments on Sir Gilbert Lamb-
stone, who plans to seduce her:
What a strange path he takes to my affection,
And thinks 't the nearest way!

The only enemmye that my life can showe me   l. 623
Bellarius is revealing his hatred for Votarius—a hatred which
is never explained by the dramatist. Barker compares *More
Dissemblers*, III, ii, 59–60, where Lactantio reveals a hatred
—which Middleton never clarifies—for Andrugio:
The only enemy that my vengeance points to

Yet could you be more pretious then a father
which next a husband is the ritchest treasure
mortalitie can show vs,   ll. 694–96
Barker compares *Hengist*, I, ii, 180–81:
You Chaste Lampe of eternitye, tis a treasure
Too pretious for deaths moment to pertake,

aboue the flight of twentie fetherd mistresses
[that glister in the Svnne of Princes fauours,
ll. 714–15
Barker compares *Women Beware Women*, IV, ii, 21–22:
I'll see that glistering whore, shines like a serpent
Now the court sun's upon her.

does thy scorne cast
so thick an ignoraunce before thine eyes
ll. 746–47

Barker compares *More Dissemblers*, iv, i, 2–5:
>   cast all their eyes
>   That guard the castle
>   Into a thicker blindness than thine own,
>   Darker than ignorance or idolatry,

>   —and maye it proue
>   the first asscent of your ymortall risinge
>   neuer to fall agen;
>   —a springe of blessinges
>   keep euer with thee,   ll. 813–17

The Lady here raises her kneeling father from the ground;
he blesses her. Barker compares *No Wit*, ii, ii, 53, where
Lady Twilight addresses her kneeling son:
>   Rise, and a thousand blessings spring up with thee!

>   like one that has a watche of curious makinge,
>   thinckinge to be more cvnnynge then the workeman
>   neuer giues ouer tampringe with the wheeles
>   till either springe be weakned, ballance bowde
>   or some wrong pin put in, and so spoiles all;
>   ll. 832–36

Barker compares *Women Beware Women*, iv, i, 11–15:
>   If I should set my watch, as some girls do,
>   By every clock i' the town, 'twould ne'er go true;
>   And too much turning of the dial's point,
>   Or tampering with the spring, might in small time
>   Spoil the whole work too;

>   his eye offendes me,   l. 914

Barker compares *Michaelmas Term*, iv, iv, 80:
>   No eye offends us:

>   I haue lockt my self
>   from myne owne libertie with that key,
>   ll. 986–87

Barker compares *Mad World*, i, ii, 111–14:
>   And as a keeper that locks prisoners up
>   Is himself prison'd under his own key,

Even so my husband, in restraining me,
With the same ward bars his own liberty.

one that knowes how to imploye thee, and scornes
death
as much as some [great] men feare it,   ll. 1353–54

that he became as hatefull to our myndes
as death's vnwellcome to a howse of ritches
ll. 2432–33

Barker compares *More Dissemblers*, i, iii, 99:
Hates him as deeply as a rich man death;
Also *Women Beware Women*, iii, i, 111–12:
Why, this is dreadful now as sudden death
To some rich man,

like some man
in tyme of sicknes that would rather wish
(to please his fearefull flesh) his former health
restord to him then death, when after triall,
if it were possible ten thowsand worldes
could not entice him to returne agen
and walke vpon the earth from whence he flew;
ll. 1441–47

Barker compares *Hengist*, i, i, 76–78:
A gloryfied soule departed from the Bodye,
Wold to that loathsom gaole returne againe,
With such greate paine,

o the wronges
that ladies do their honors when they make
their slaues familier with their weaknesses
thei'r euer thus rewarded for that deed,
they stand in feare eene of the groomes they feed;
ll. 1566–70

Barker compares *Your Five Gallants*, iv, ii, 85–88:
she's a fool
That makes her servant fellow to her heart;
It robs her of respect, dams up all duty,
Keeps her in awe e'en of the slave she keeps:

> she trustes me now to cast a mist forsooth
> before the servauntes eyes,   ll. 1636–37

Barker compares *No Wit*, II, ii, 136:

> And to cast mists before my father's eyes,

Also *Black Book* (Vol. VIII, p. 35):

> to cast a cuckold's mist before the eyes of her husband,

Also *Triumphs of Truth* (Vol. VII, p. 242):

> to cast mists to blind the plain
> And simple eye of man;

> in that pale parte
> which drawes so many pitties from these springes
> ll. 2308–9
> what slowe springes haue I? . . .
> how pittie strikes een throughe inscensible thinges
> ll. 1738, 1740

Barker compares *Mad World*, I, i, 177–78:

> a fool that truly pities
> The false springs of thine eyes,

Also *Game at Chess*, I, i, 15:

> Rayse the least Spring of pittie in her Eye,

> wellcome to myne eyes
> as is the daye-springe from the morninges woombe
> ll. 2388–89

Barker compares *Triumphs of Truth* (Vol. VII, p. 258):

> Before the day sprang from the morning's womb

> Ime like a man pluckt vp from many waters
> that neuer lookt for help, and am here plac'te
> vpon this cheerfull mowtaine wher prosperitie
> shootes forth her ritchest beame   ll. 2422–25

Barker compares *No Wit*, II, iii, 252–54:

> I feel a hand of mercy lift me up
> Out of a world of waters, and now sets me
> Upon a mountain, where the sun plays most,

The parallels between *The Second Maiden's Tragedy* and Middleton's acknowledged plays are too numerous and the turns of phrase too individual to be the result of coincidence. Such close resemblances between an anonymous play and the works of a prominent dramatist can perhaps be accounted for in three possible ways:

1. The author of *The Second Maiden's Tragedy* examined and patterned himself after the writings of Middleton.

2. Middleton studied and imitated the style of *The Second Maiden's Tragedy*.

3. Middleton wrote *The Second Maiden's Tragedy*. The first explanation is ruled out by the circumstance that a number of the parallels concern plays written after 1611. The second possibility is also unlikely; Middleton would hardly pattern his writing minutely after a lesser work which did not stimulate enough interest to warrant publication in the dramatist's own time. When the parallel passages are considered along with the other evidence—the similarities between *The Second Maiden's Tragedy* and Middleton's plays with regard to characterization, theme, irony, diction, and verse—only one conclusion would appear plausible: Thomas Middleton wrote *The Second Maiden's Tragedy*.

VII. *Collaboration with Rowley:*
Doubtful Attributions

COLLABORATIONS present problems of even greater complexity than anonymous plays, for dramatists may work together in several different ways. It is quite possible that: 1) collaboration was close, extending to individual speeches and even to lines; or 2) the collaborators allocated the acts and scenes among themselves and wrote their respective shares independently; or 3) one participant supplied the central idea, major characters, or chief incidents, while another did the bulk of the actual composition; or 4) a section, or perhaps the entire work, was written by one author and then revised by another. All of these approaches were undoubtedly used at one time or another by Elizabethan dramatists, and in some instances perhaps more than one method was employed in a single play. One can only admire the ingenuity of Morris in dividing *The Spanish Gypsy* line by line between Middleton and Rowley [1]—especially since the tragicomedy may very well have been the unaided work of Ford.[2]

I

The principal issues involved in determining the literary relations of Middleton and Rowley have, fortunately, been settled to the satisfaction of most scholars, although doubt as to certain individual lines and isolated passages will probably always remain. The verdict with regard to *The Changeling*, the only tragedy known definitely to be the work of both writers, has been virtually unanimous. Wiggin's excellent *Inquiry into the Authorship of the Middleton-Rowley Plays* first appeared in 1897, and her findings have never been seriously challenged—a remarkable record for a study based entirely upon internal evidence.[3] After an interval of more than half a century, Dewar M. Robb has made a new and complete study of the data;[4] his work serves to confirm the high quality of the Wiggin monograph. Robb's analysis of *The Changeling*, for example, corresponds exactly with Wiggin's division. Since *The Changeling* is the sole Middleton-Rowley play treated here, and since the case is so clear-cut, it is necessary only to summarize the characteristics of Rowley's style and to present the evidence.

Rowley's technique—as shown in his pamphlet, *A Search for Money* (1609), and his plays, *A Shoemaker, a Gentleman* (*ca.* 1607–9), *A New Wonder, a Woman Never Vext* (*ca.* 1610), and *All's Lost by Lust* (*ca.* 1619)[5]—differs from Middleton's in almost every respect. Although, in Robb's words, "eclectic, opportunist, and even to the last somewhat imitative,"[6] Rowley does tend toward the romantic rather than the realistic view of life; he can create "noble, consistent and unswervingly virtuous characters, who can win and keep the sympathy of the audience."[7] But there is a lack of subtlety in his delineations, a tendency to exaggerate and oversimplify motivation. "They [his personages] seem each to be moved by one passion, of which they are somewhat conventionalized and extravagant exponents, and the passions are the universal ones of love, revenge, honor."[8] At times, indeed, motivation is discarded entirely: Stephen, in *A New Wonder*, marries the wealthy Widow and is transformed suddenly and inexplicably from an indigent wastrel into a staid and thrifty husband. Rowley's plots are amorphous and confused, the incidents piled up with little discretion or sense of proportion, for he is not capable of sustained quality. His humor tends to be whimsical and droll, broad and exaggerated; he seeks not intellectual appreciation, but a hearty laugh, and this he obtains through buffoonery and vigorous action. In his serious work, Rowley is given to melodramatic violence: "His characters say too much; they foam at the mouth, beat each other and hurl invectives with astonishing freedom." [9] The Queen in *A Shoemaker, a Gentleman* spits defiantly at her captor, Maximinus, Emperor of Rome (i, i, 183).[10] Indeed, Rowley's heroines indulge on more than one occasion in unfeminine behavior. "O that I could spit out the spiders bladder,/ Or the toads intrals into thee," cries the ravished Jacinta at her jailor in *All's Lost by Lust* (iii, i, 15–16); [11] Mrs. Foster, in *A New Wonder*, flies out at the factor who has brought her husband bad news: "Oh, thou fatal raven! let me pull thine eyes out/ For this sad croak." [12] But perhaps the essential difference between Rowley and Middleton is, aside from matters of quality, the distinction between the romantic and the realist, between the humble man who views humanity with sympathetic, if naïve, optimism, and the sophisticate who looks primarily upon the weaknesses of mankind and regards them with irony and cynical detachment. It is, of course, also the difference between the clumsy actor-playwright relying on stock figures and the finished craftsman interested in psychological analysis.

Unfortunately, Rowley's plays have come down to us in untrustworthy texts with misdivided lines, with verse printed as prose and prose as verse. In the modern editions of Morris and Stork attempts are made at recension and restoration, but the editors have not been entirely successful; they have, indeed, managed to corrupt the text with serious errors of their own.[13] Under such circumstances statements about metrics may well have an insecure foundation. But we do have enough of Rowley's verse to form an idea of what it is like, and since his style is almost the complete antithesis of Middleton's, a few obvious generalizations may be permitted. Rowley's verse is, as all critics have noted, rough and irregular. He has no conception of the long verse-paragraph unit. "When he attempts eloquence," writes Robb, "he builds his paragraph uncertainly, in a style staccato, of short breaths, as if composing phrase by phrase rather than with fluency. Even so he abandons his ideas before they are exhausted; he as totally lacks, for example, Heywood's device of amplifying one idea by various statement as he lacks Massinger's habit of viewing a paragraph as a whole before beginning to write it down." [14] Robb goes on to cite several other features of Rowley's verse: the haphazard use of feminine endings, light endings, and alexandrines—introduced, apparently, for convenience only; the omission of a metrical beat, usually at the caesura or at the beginning of the line, to permit the actor to pause, gesture, or perform an action; the presence of extra syllables just after a caesura; the ignoring in scansion of such words as *sir* and *madam*, interruptions, and parenthetical exclamations; the tendency to use alexandrines in blank verse passages of the earlier plays; the habit of rhyming a line of five iambs with one of three or four.[15] Because of the state of the texts, Wiggin's figure for feminine endings (less than one in four) can no longer be regarded as precise; but one may assert that Rowley uses feminine endings with considerably less frequency than Middleton (approximately one in two). Rowley tends to use run-on lines somewhat more often than Middleton, and he does not share Middleton's habit of employing regular caesuras to break successive run-on lines.[16] Although Rowley's verse may vary greatly from passage to passage, the following selection may be regarded as typical of much of his work:

> Tut, feare frights us not, nor shall hope foole us:
> If neede provoke, wee'le dig supply through hell
> And her enchantments. Who can prefixe us
> A time to see these incantations loosde?
> Perhaps 'twill stay tenne generations more,
> When our bloud royall may want succession,
> If not; what bootes it us (lost in our dust
> And memory 500. yeeres) that then this hidden
> Worke shall be; tush, the weakenesse of our prede-
> cessors
> Shall not fright us, all is not deadly,
> That lookes dangerous.
>
> *All's Lost by Lust*, i, i, 65–75

One may note also several minor characteristics and mannerisms which serve to give Rowley's style its own individuality. Rowley uses the interjection *tush* rather than *push*, Middleton's favorite. He has the unlettered man's fondness for displaying his learning: he uses such inkhorn terms as *altitonant, asterism, augurism, geomantick,* and *gigliotories*; he employs Latin derivatives in their primary sense—*apprehensive* for "quick to apprehend," *cadence* for "fall," *performance* for "the completion of a continued act"; he introduces puns and jests based on Latin and Greek words and on grammatical terminology. Like so many other Elizabethan dramatists, he relies greatly on wordplay, which in his case is often coarse and invariably obvious. Puns as a source of humor appear more frequently than in Middleton's plays; Rowley will play upon the meanings of words in his most serious scenes.[17] Robb points out Rowley's interest in Welsh ways, language, and places; his habit of introducing ideas related to the language of flowers; his use of such proverbial and cant phrases as "far fetched and dear bought for ladies," or "though I say it that should not"; his fondness, as shown by references, for particular songs, such as "Loth to depart"; his tendency to employ certain clichés and pet words and expressions—*enigma, party* in the sense of *person,* "betwixt you and I," "as old as I am"; his way of linking speeches by the repetition of terminal words:

> LORD: There is now some hope.
> HUGH: A promising faire hope.
>
> *A Shoemaker, a Gentleman,* I, iii, 38 [18]

It would seem, indeed, that in almost every respect Rowley's style is individual enough to make possible a reasonably precise estimate of his share in the collaborations with Middleton.

II

The Changeling was "licensed to be acted by the Lady Elizabeth's Servants at the Phoenix, May 7, 1622." [19] It was entered upon the Stationers' Register on October 19, 1652, as "a comedie . . . written by Rowley." [20] Middleton's name appears alongside Rowley's on the title page of the first quarto, which was issued in 1653.[21] The views of the various authorities with regard to the respective shares of the two dramatists may be summarized conveniently in a table:

Date	Authority	Middleton	Rowley
1840	Dyce [22]	"Terribly impressive passages."	
1885	Bullen [23]	"Chief share."	Occasional traces in the opening scenes; underplot; v, iii.
1887	Swinburne [24]	"Main part of the tragic action."	I, i and v, iii.
1891	Fleay [25]	II, i–ii; III, i–ii, iv; IV, i–ii; v, i–ii.	I, i–ii; III, iii; IV, iii; v, iii.
1897	Wiggin [26]	Same as Fleay.	

Date	Authority	Middleton	Rowley
1910	Stork [27]	Same as Fleay, except that v, ii marked doubtful.	
1910	Symons [28]	II, III (though perhaps completed by Rowley).	Underplot; I (but traces of Middleton), IV and V.
1929	Oliphant [29]	Same as Fleay except that Middleton is tentatively assigned some lines in I, i.	Same as Fleay except that Rowley is assigned the first sixteen lines of IV, ii.
1933	Dunkel [30]	Middleton wrote the play;	Rowley revised it.
1945	Barker [31]	Same as Fleay.	
1950	Robb [32]	Same as Fleay.	

The main plot is marked by "the subtlety and relentless realism" (Wiggin), the "cold development and dramatic inevitability" (Stork) characteristic of Middleton's art; the great scenes "are beyond the ability of Rowley" (Dyce). The underplot shows Rowley's "wild extravagance" (Bullen), his "tendency to burlesque and to horseplay" (Wiggin). An important role is taken by Tony, the clown—a character type of which Rowley is fond (Wiggin). The first and last scenes of the principal story display Rowley's "somewhat hard and curt directness of style, his clear and trenchant power of straight-forward presentation or exposition" (Swinburne), and typical of Rowley are "the rapidity of movement and the abundance of stage action" (Stork). When De Flores stoops and returns Beatrice's glove in Act I, scene i, she reacts with a fury similar to that shown on other occasions by Rowley heroines (Wiggin). In Act v, scene iii, "the violence of the language . . . the introduction of ill-timed comic touches . . . and the metrical roughness" (Bullen) are reminiscent of the lesser dramatist. The punning on the title which closes the play reflects Rowley's fondness for introducing wordplay even on the most inappropriate occasions (Wiggin). *Tush* is used in the scenes ascribed to Rowley, while *push* appears in the sections regarded as Middleton's:

	Tush	Push
Rowley scenes	4	0
Middleton scenes	1	5

That *The Changeling* is written in more than one type of verse may be seen clearly when one compares two characteristic passages, both concerned with the main action. Here is Tomaso urging Alsemero not to marry Beatrice:

> Think what a torment 'tis to marry one
> Whose heart is leap'd into another's bosom:
> If ever pleasure she receive from thee,
> It comes not in thy name, or of thy gift;
> She lies but with another in thine arms,
> He the half-father unto all thy children
> In the conception; if he get 'em not,
> She helps to get 'em for him; and how dangerous
> And shameful her restraint may go in time to,
> It is not to be thought on without sufferings.
>
> > II, i, 130–39

Here, in quite different verse, Alsemero thrusts De Flores into the closet to join his weeping mistress:

> Peace, crying crocodile, your sounds are heard;
> Take your prey to you;—get you in to her, sir:
>
> > [*Exit* De Flores *into closet.*
>
> I'll be your pander now; rehearse again
> Your scene of lust, that you may be perfect
> When you shall come to act it to the black audience,
> Where howls and gnashings shall be music to you:
> Clip your adulteress freely, 'tis the pilot
> Will guide you to the *mare mortuum,*
> Where you shall sink to fathoms bottomless.
>
> > v, iii, 113–21

Wiggin, in her metrical examination of the play, summarizes ably the distinguishing features of the two styles:

In Acts II. 1, 2; III. 1, 2, 4; IV. 1, 2; and v. 1, 2 (the scenes in which we have found traces of Middleton), the proportion of feminine endings is approximately one in two; a large number of these endings are double or triple,—ten in the one hundred and seventy lines of III. 4; the end-stopt line prevails, and the verse flows easily and smoothly, showing few lines in which the inversions fall on other than the first foot or the foot immediately following the caesura. On the other hand, in Acts I. 1, 2; III. 3; IV. 3; and v. 3, . . . the proportion of feminine endings is less than one in four,—in I. 1 (205 lines) there are only forty; they are very rarely double or triple,—in I. 1, but two of the forty have double endings; run-on lines and weak endings abound, and the accent is very frequently inverted in the second and the last foot. These are exactly the usual differences between Middleton's rhythm and Rowley's.[33]

Barker has made counts of the feminine endings in a number of scenes: his findings, summarized below, serve to confirm Wiggin's figures: [34]

Scene	Number of Lines Tested	Percentage of Feminine Endings
I, i (Rowley)	50	24
II, i (Middleton)	100	42
II, ii (Middleton)	50	48
III, iii (Rowley)	50	22
III, iv (Middleton)	50	56
IV, i (Middleton)	25	56
IV, ii (Middleton)	50	48
v, i (Middleton)	33	69
v, ii (Middleton)	50	50
v, iii (Rowley)	50	46

Several sets of parallels have been pointed out; these may be regarded as supplementary evidence for the division:

I, i, 116–17: Such to mine eyes is that same fellow there,
The same that report speaks of the basilisk.

Compare *A New Wonder*, IV, i, p. 316:
Hence! thou basilisk,
That kill'st me with mine [*sic*] eyes.

I, ii, 19–20: —I am old, Lollio.
—No, sir, 'tis I am old Lollio.

Wiggin compares *Maid in the Mill*, v, ii, p. 73: [35]

   —Oh, your Wife, *Franio?*

   —'Tis oh my wife indeed, my Lord,

But Middleton uses a similar exchange in *The Widow*, II, i,
33–34.

  I, ii, 70–71: —What hour is't, Lollio?

       —Towards belly-hour, sir.

       —Dinner time? thou mean'st twelve o'clock?

Barker compares *Shoemaker*, I, ii, 182–84:

       —Whats a clocke, Barnaby?

       —The chimes of my belly has gone, it should be
         past twelve.

  II, ii, 6–7: These women are the ladies' cabinets,

       Things of most precious trust are lock'd into 'em.

Barker compares *Women Beware Women*, I, i, 55–56:

       Save that which lies lock'd up in hidden virtues,

       Like jewels kept in cabinets.

Also *Game at Chess*, II, ii, 276–77:

            that Cabinet of Nicenes

       Halfe the Virginities of the earth lockt up

  II, ii, 66–67: Why, put case I loath'd him

       As much as youth and beauty hates a sepulchre,

Barker compares *Women Beware Women*, II, i, 84:

       I loathe him more than beauty can hate death,

Also *More Dissemblers*, I, iii, 99:

       Hates him as deeply as a rich man death;

III, iii, 183–84: Walk through the orchard of th' Hesperides,

       And, cowardly, not dare to pull an apple?

Wiggin compares *Maid in the Mill*, IV, i, p. 50:

       Shall I walk by the tree? desire the fruit,

       Yet be so nice to pull till I ask leave

       Of the churlish Gard'ner, that will deny me?

Also *All's Lost*, I, i, 136:

       Wee'le plucke this apple from th' Hesperides.

III, iv, 91: What makes your lip so strange?
Wiggin compares *Women Beware Women*, III, i, 157–58:
> Speak, what's the humour, sweet,
> You make your lip so strange?

III, iv, 170: 'Las! how the turtle pants!
Wiggin compares *Women Beware Women*, II, ii, 326:
> I feel thy breast shake like a turtle panting
Also *Game at Chess*, III, iii, 6:
> the panting of a Turtle

IV, ii, 150–51: Chaste as the breath of heaven, or morning's
> womb,
> That brings the day forth!
Barker compares *Triumphs of Truth*, Vol. VII, p. 258:
> Before the day sprang from the morning's womb

v, iii, 118: Where howls and gnashings shall be music to
> you;
Barker compares *All's Lost*, II, i, 110:
> Comparde with gnashings, and the howles below.

v, iii, 165–66: Yes, and the while I coupled with your mate
> At barley-break; now we are left in hell.
Barker compares *A New Wonder*, I, i, p. 247:
> If you find my mistress have a mind to this
> coupling at barley-break, let her not be the last
> couple to be left in hell.

Although Stork considers Act v, scene ii doubtful, he gives no evidence to support his opinion. The scene is short —eighty-seven lines—but the frequency of feminine endings (one to two) points to Middleton, and the imagery is in his vein. Barker cites the expression "I thirst for 'em" (l. 85) as a phrase used frequently by Middleton; he notes also that the lines, "I'll rather like a soldier die by th' sword,/ Than like a politician by thy poison" (ll. 28–29), are paralleled in

The Phoenix: "Would he die so like a politician" (I, vi, 71–72).

Oliphant feels that Middleton may be responsible for some of the lines in Act I, scene i; with regard to Act IV, scene ii he states definitely that "Rowley's part ends with the servant's exit," and that "Middleton's begins there"—thus assigning the first sixteen lines of the scene to Rowley.[36] The very first line of *The Changeling*—" 'Twas in the temple where I first beheld her"—does convey the richly ironic implications of which Middleton is so fond. But there is no real evidence to substantiate Oliphant's view; it is essentially a subjective reaction. The opening passage of Act IV, scene ii is in rough verse, and it does concern the underplot rather than the main action. The section is too brief, however, to be regarded as satisfactory material for authorship tests.

Dunkel stresses general similarities between the subplot of *The Changeling* and Middleton's City comedies, and on this basis relegates Rowley's share to that of reviser. Dunkel points to the lack of plot development; to the hurried ending and concluding didactic observation; to the part played by the jealous husband, a type which appears more than once in Middleton's plays. These features are to be found in the City comedies, but they may be paralleled just as easily in other plays of the period. Since Dunkel offers no stylistic data to indicate the presence of Middleton's hand in the scenes usually ascribed to Rowley, his theory may be dismissed as unfounded.

Several commentators have taken a contrary view; they suggest that Rowley exerted a more important influence upon *The Changeling* than the scenes allotted to him would seem to show—that he had, indeed, much to do with the development of the principal figures. Wiggin believes that Rowley's romantic view of life was felt especially in the characterization of Beatrice. In spite of her weakness and cruelty she retains our sympathy, thus reflecting Rowley's belief in "the essential dignity and beauty of human nature." [37] As Symons states most persuasively the case for allowing Rowley greater credit for his share in the collaborations with Middleton, one may feel justified in quoting him at some length:

Now, if we begin to look for the influence of Rowley upon Middleton, we shall find it not so much in the set scenes of low comedy which he inserted among Middleton's verse, as in a new capacity for the rendering of great passions and a loftiness in good and evil which is not to be recognised as an element in Middleton's brilliant and showy genius, and which hardly survives the end of his collaboration with Rowley. The whole range of subject suddenly lifts; a new, more real and more romantic world (more real and more romantic because imagination, rather than memory, is at work) is seen upon the stage; and, by some transformation which could hardly have been mere natural growth, Middleton finds himself to be a poet.[38]

"The play is De Flores," Symons goes on to remark, "and De Flores seems to grow greater as he passes from one to the other of the two playwrights, as they collaborate visibly at his creation. This great creation is the final result and justification of Middleton and Rowley's work in common; for it is certain that De Flores as he is would never have been possible either to Rowley or to Middleton alone." [39]

Such a view can be justified, it seems to me, neither by an examination of the text of *The Changeling*, nor by a comparison of the play with Rowley's independent work. It is true that *The Changeling* deals with great passions; but great passions serve also as the material for several of Middleton's earlier plays—notably *More Dissemblers* and *Hengist*. I find little "loftiness in good and evil" in *The Changeling*. The principal characters are conspicuously lacking in nobility; the dramatist is preoccupied with sin and deterioration, interested only indirectly in virtue. Beatrice and De Flores belong to the succession of sexually obsessed and morally perverse figures which fascinated Middleton from the time of *The Second Maiden's Tragedy*, and the irony which invests their relationship is entirely in keeping with Middleton's technique and point of view.

De Flores resembles Horsus more closely than any character created by Rowley. Both personages are driven by lust for their mistresses, and both permit their mistresses to marry —with the understanding that their relationship will afterwards continue. Beatrice is more akin to Bianca than to any of Rowley's heroines. Like Bianca she is a moral idiot, devoid of any conception of honor, completely lacking in any understanding of the meaning of human relationships. It is sentimental to regard her as not forfeiting our sympathy; she has never earned it. When first we see her she has already cast aside her first love—"and that's a kind/ Of whoredom in the heart" (III, iv, 144–45). De Flores and Beatrice are too subtly delineated to be the creations of Rowley, whose approach is essentially nonpsychological. Their behavior, when they appear in Rowley scenes, is marked by the physical violence to which he so often resorts, a violence not in harmony with the action of the great scenes, which depend for their effect almost exclusively upon the interplay of emotions.

Insofar as the main plot is concerned, *The Changeling* is certainly superior to anything that Middleton had written previously, but it seems more just to attribute this preeminence to Middleton's attainment of maturity as an artist rather than to the influence of a third-rate dramatist who never in his independent work gave any indication of exceptional talent. One may, then, reasonably conclude that Middleton is responsible for the characterization of the principal figures and the general conduct of the main action, and that he wrote the following scenes: II, i–ii; III, i–ii, iv; IV, i–ii; v, i–ii. Rowley was entrusted with the composition of the first and last scenes and the minor plot—I, i–ii; III, iii; IV, iii; v, iii.

III

Hengist, King of Kent, or the Mayor of Queenborough survives in three separate texts—two scribal transcriptions and a late quarto edition. One manuscript is included in the Lambarde volume of seventeenth-century plays; the other belongs to the library of the Duke of Portland at Welbeck Abbey. Both manuscripts, apparently private transcripts derived from annotated prompt-copy, were composed by the same scrivener, in a hand which belongs, presumably, to the second quarter of the seventeenth century.[40] The earliest reference to Middleton as author of the play occurs in the 1661 Stationers' Register entry; his name appears also on the title page of the original quarto, which was issued in the same year.[41]

Although Middleton is given sole credit for *Hengist* in the early edition, several commentators have, in more recent times, suggested the possibility of a collaborator. Swinburne feels that "we find a note so dissonant and discordant in the lighter parts of the dramatic concert that we seem at once to recognise the harsher and hoarser instrument of Rowley."[42] Stork goes further: he detects Rowley's hand not only in the comic sections, but also, "less distinctly," in several of the serious scenes.[43] Simon, the Mayor of Queenborough, does perhaps bear some resemblance to Rowley's clowns; and a few passages, notably Act IV, scene i and the fourth chorus, seem too primitive for Middleton. But there is no real evidence of Rowley's hand. "The spirit of Rowley's comedy is," as Bald remarks, "cruder, clumsier, and grosser than the spirit of these scenes [the comic underplot], and one has only to compare them with the comic scenes in *The Birth of Merlin* to detect the difference." [44] One incident in the sub-plot of *Hengist*, the gulling of Simon by the traveling players (Act v, scene i), is paralleled in Middleton's *A Mad World, My Masters*, in which Follywit and his cohorts, disguised as strollers, cheat Sir Bounteous by means of a theatrical performance (Act v, scene ii). Stork's analysis of the play cannot be regarded as reliable, for he conjectures that Middleton made his contribution to *Hengist* about 1606 [45] —some time before he had achieved the maturity so evident in the greater part of the tragedy. The presence in *Hengist* of elements in a cruder style may be the result of Middleton having used as the foundation of his work an old chronicle play, perhaps the "valteger" or "henges" listed by Henslowe as new on December 4, 1596. [46]

IV

Scholars have formulated several theories of composition to account for the unsatisfactory state of *Timon of Athens*. [47] It has been suggested that *Timon*, as it has come down to us, is 1) an incomplete version of a play started by Shakespeare and then abandoned; 2) an adaptation by Shakespeare of an earlier work, now lost, by a different playwright; or 3) a revision of a Shakespearian play by some other dramatist. A number of possible collaborators—Heywood, Tourneur, Wilkins, Chapman, and Field—have been proposed, but the most elaborate case has been made for Middleton. In 1920 William Wells speculated that *Timon* was an early Middleton tragedy revised by Shakespeare five or six years after its original composition, which was not later than 1607; he assigned Middleton seven scenes—I, ii; III, i–v, vi (except

Timon's outburst at the banquet)—and traced his hand in several others: II, ii; IV, ii, iii; V, i.[48] Sykes, in 1921, arrived at a similar conclusion, except that he found Middleton touches also in I, i and evidence of a third author, John Day, in I, i, II, ii, and IV, iii.[49] The data assembled by Wells and Sykes are entirely stylistic, their most interesting material consisting of parallels of phraseology between *Timon* and acknowledged Middleton works. Some of the parallels are indeed striking:

I, i, 284: He's opposite to humanity.
Sykes compares *Phoenix*, I, ii, 79–80:
> How comes it that you are so opposite
> To love and kindness?

I, ii, 47–50: The fellow that sits next him now, parts bread
with him, pledges the breath of him in a divided draught, is the readiest man to kill him.
Wells compares *No Wit*, I, iii, 78–79:
> And yet ofttimes, sir, what worse knave to a
> man
> Than he that eats his meat?

I, ii, 55: Let it flow this way, my good lord.
The Second Lord is responding to Timon's toast. Sykes compares *Michaelmas Term*, III, i, 216, in which Lethe replies to Shortyard's toast:
> Let it flow this way, dear master Blastfield.

I, ii, 99–103: They [i.e. friends] were the most needless
creatures living . . . and would most resemble sweet instruments hung up in cases, that
keep their sounds to themselves.
Wells compares *More Dissemblers*, I, iii, 22–24:
> I commend
> The virtues highly, as I do an instrument
> When the case hangs by th' wall;

I, ii, 107–8: O, what a precious comfort 'tis
Sykes compares *Phoenix*, I, vi, 81:
> What a precious joy and comfort's this,

Compare also *Trick*, II, i, 213–14:
> more precious comfort than all these widow's
> revenues.

I, ii, 206: his land's put to their books.
Sykes compares *Ant and the Nightingale* (Vol. VIII, p. 72):
> all his land should be put to their book

II, ii, 34: Give me breath.
Timon is being dunned by Isidore's Servant. Sykes compares *Trick*, IV, iii, 32, in which Witgood, when dunned by his creditors, replies:
> Pray, sirs,—you'll give me breath?

III, i, 7–8: you are very respectively welcome, sir.
Wells compares *Your Five Gallants*, II, i, 82–83:
> Gentlemen, you are all most respectively
> welcome.

III, i, 29–30: Every man has his fault, and honesty is his.
Sykes compares *Michaelmas Term*, III, iv, 146–47:
> O, what's a man but his honesty, master Easy?
> and that's a fault amongst most of us all.

III, ii, 49–50: What a wicked beast was I to disfurnish myself against such a good time,
Wells compares *Mad World*, II, v, 12–13:
> Ah, what a beast was I to put out my money
> t'other day!

III, iii, 28–29: The devil knew not what he did when he
made man politic. He crossed himself by't;
Sykes compares *Your Five Gallants*, IV, v, 69–72:
> The devil scarce knew what a portion he

gave his children when he allowed 'em large
impudence to live upon . . . surely he gave
away the third part of the riches of his kingdom;

III, iv, 86–88, 104:

TITUS: My lord, here is my bill.
LUCIUS' SERVANT: Here's mine.
HORTENSIUS: And mine, my lord. . . .
TIMON: They have e'en put my breath from me, the
slaves!

Sykes compares *Trick*, IV, iii, 30–32:

SECOND CREDITOR: Here's mine of forty.
THIRD CREDITOR: Here's mine of fifty.
WITGOOD: Pray, sirs,—you'll give me breath?

III, v, 96: My wounds ache at you.
Wells compares *Chaste Maid*, v, i, 13:
my wound aches at thee,

The remaining evidence for Middleton's hand is, however,
less remarkable. Wells and Sykes point to the indiscriminate
mixture of prose and verse, the frequency of rhyme, the
presence of antithetical couplets and irregular couplets
(those in which one line is shorter than the other). The verse
in the doubtful scenes is very irregular—so rough, indeed,
that if Middleton wrote it he must have done so very early
in his career, perhaps not later than *ca.* 1604. Occasionally
the bitter mood of Prince Phoenix's denunciation of the
iniquity of Ferrara is suggested by the harshness of the lines:

Why, this is the world's soul, and just of the same piece
Is every flatterer's spirit. Who can call him
His friend that dips in the same dish? For in
My knowing Timon has been this lord's father
And kept his credit with his purse,
Supported his estate. Nay, Timon's money
Has paid his men their wages. He ne'er drinks
But Timon's silver treads upon his lip;

And yet—O, see the monstrousness of man
When he looks out in an ungrateful shape!—
He does deny him (in respect of his)
What charitable men afford to beggars.

III, ii, 71–82

Such a line as "thou disease of a friend" (III, i, 56) suggests "he the disease of justice" (*Phoenix*, v, i, 159). But so little of Middleton's immature dramatic verse has been preserved that metrical evidence must be regarded as not at all conclusive.

Sykes notes the appearance, on six occasions, of the common Middleton contractions *has* for *he has* and *had* for *he had*, but these are used as well by other dramatists of the period. Wells and Sykes point also to the occurrence of such words as *apperil*, *comely*, *occasion*, and *rioter*, and to the use of the verbs *to furnish*, *to pleasure*, and *to supply;* none of these is, however, unusual enough to be regarded as evidence. *Push*, cited by both authorities, is a favorite Middleton expletive, but it appears only once. Wells and Sykes have not succeeded in showing that the diction of *Timon* is characteristic of Middleton.

There is, indeed, good reason to doubt that Middleton was concerned with *Timon*. One can scarcely say that the dialogue is clearly in his manner, and the play lacks completely the conscious irony which almost invariably pervades Middleton's work. *Faith*, an oath that Middleton uses with extraordinary frequency in his early plays, occurs but four times, and *troth*, another favorite, does not appear at all. One must conclude that Sykes and Wells have made an ingenious rather than convincing argument for the presence of Middleton's hand in *Timon*. Recent scholarship tends to follow Chambers' theory that the play is one of Shakespeare's unfinished works—the beginning and end having been brought close to completion, while the middle scenes were left in a rough state.[50] "It can hardly be doubted," writes Greg, "that the play was set up from foul papers that had never been reduced to order." [51]

v

In 1639 appeared the first edition of *The Bloody Banquet*, "By T. D."—the only edition, except for a photographic facsimile, ever printed.[52] The play survives in a curtailed and unsatisfactory text which presents interesting problems for the investigator. Relatively little effort has been expended to solve them, however, for *The Bloody Banquet* is distinctly a minor work. The date of composition has never received serious consideration, and the authorship has until recently been a subject for guesswork alone. In 1656 Archer ascribed the play to a Thomas Barker, of whom there is no record; [53] during the nineteenth century Robert Davenport and Thomas Drue were proposed, with little plausibility.[54] "It is now probably too late," wrote Cole in 1919, "to ascertain with any degree of certainty who actually wrote *The Bloody Banquet*." [55] But Oliphant, in 1925, made a serious attempt to determine authorship. He identified the "T.D." on the title page with Thomas Dekker and further suggested, on the basis of stylistic evidence, that Middleton wrote the greater part of the play. Oliphant assigns to Middleton I, i (from the exit of the Tyrant), iv; II, iv; III, i–iii; v, i, ii (although the closing section, after the entry of the Tyrant and the Queen, is marked doubtful, as unlike either Dekker or Middleton). He finds traces of Middleton also in I, ii and iii, and in the Dekker portion of I, i.[56]

The case for Middleton is based upon a survey of the diction, turns of phrase, and metrical technique. Oliphant feels that the vocabulary is "markedly" Middleton's; he points to the use of the word *comfort* (four times), the habit of addressing characters as *sir*, and the presence of Middleton's favorite oaths and ejaculations—with the exception of *push* and *byrlady*. Oliphant lists a number of metrical characteristics which are features as well of Middleton's verse: the occurrence of slurs; a preference for double-ending rhymes; the tendency to add a trochaic address word to a pentameter line; a fondness for successive double-ending lines; the habit of joining a preposition and a contracted *it* to make a double-ending line or a single-ending rhyme; and the use of trochaic lines, lines with a couple of anapaestic feet, triple-endings, and, on one occasion, a quadruple-ending. He quotes passages from *The Bloody Banquet* which remind him of Middleton's phraseology and thought—such lines, for example, as:

> Ile take my leave on purpose in his presence,
> He's jealous, and a kisse runnes through his heart,
> Ile make a thrust at him on your lip.
>
> II, iii

> I thinke they count how the day goes by kissing,
> Tis past foure since I met them.
>
> II, iii

> A leaping spirit; hee'le run through horrors jawes
> To catch a sin; but to oretake a vertue
> He softly paces, like a man that's sent
> Some tedious dark, unprofitable journey.
>
> IV, i

> Perfideously betray'd me to the fury
> Of my tempestuous unappeased Lord.
>
> IV, iii

Furthermore, "the management of the more interesting of the two stories told is (or should be) recognizable as unquestionably Middleton's," for the dramatist is "ingenious and thorough in his conception and execution of an intrigue of lust." [57] Oliphant concludes by remarking that lack of space prevents him from making an even stronger argument for Middleton. The following year, in the course of an article on the authorship of *The Revenger's Tragedy*, Oliphant commented in passing that Middleton's part-authorship of *The Bloody Banquet* is "obvious to anyone acquainted with his style." [58] So certain is he that he includes parallels from the play as evidence that Middleton wrote *The Revenger's Tragedy*.

Although Oliphant writes with great conviction, his findings cannot be regarded as conclusive. He is too often entirely subjective: he fails, for the most part, to provide statistics; he neglects to employ negative checks. A number of Middleton's favorite oaths and several of the abstract nouns of which he is fond do appear, as does one unusual expression associated with his writings: "Mysticall Strumpet" (iv, iii) —yet one would hesitate to agree, on the basis of such data, that the diction is "markedly" his. The metrical evidence which Oliphant supplies is rendered suspect by the fact that rhyme and masculine endings occur too frequently for Middleton's later work, while the verse is not harsh enough to be in his earlier manner. Occasionally one happens upon lines that bring Middleton to mind, but perhaps more often—and in the very same scenes—the dialogue is in a style quite unlike his. Such, for example, is the passage in which the Queen struggles unsuccessfully against her passion for Tymethes:

> It cannot be kept downe with any Argument,
> Tis of aspiring force; sparkes flye not downeward,
> No more this receiv'd fancy of *Tymethes*,
> I threaten it with my Lords Iealousy,
> Yet still it rises against all objections;
> I see my dangers, in what feares I dwell
> There's but a Planke on which I runne to hell,
> Yet were't thrice narrower I should venture on,
> None dares doe more for sinne than woman can.
>
> I, iv

That Middleton was "ingenious" in handling an "intrigue of lust" has little significance: lust is a popular subject in Elizabethan drama. It is conceivable that Middleton was in some way concerned with *The Bloody Banquet*, but Oliphant has failed to make a convincing case,[59] and it is unlikely that any clear-cut proof will be forthcoming.

In summation one may remark that, while the respective shares of Middleton and Rowley in *The Changeling* have been determined satisfactorily, efforts to associate Rowley with *Hengist, King of Kent* and Middleton with *Timon of Athens* and *The Bloody Banquet* have not proved successful.

Notes

1. The Revenger's Tragedy

1. Henslowe's *Diary,* ed. Greg, I, 166–67, 171.

2. *The Phoenix* is set in Ferrara, but the context indicates clearly that London is meant throughout.

3. The date of *The Revenger's Tragedy* cannot be determined precisely, but Middleton was probably influenced by *The Malcontent* (1604?), and he may have derived the name Dondola from *The Fawn* (1604–6). Since the play was entered upon the Stationers' Register in 1607, it was very likely written between 1604 and 1607, with perhaps 1606 the most plausible conjecture.

4. *Cyril Tourneur,* ed. Collins, I, xiii.

5. Lockert, "Greatest of Elizabethan Melodramas," p. 104.

6. Barker, *Thomas Middleton,* unpaged. Mr. Barker has been kind enough to place this study, as yet in manuscript, at my disposal. Completed in 1945, it is the only work on Middleton to include the known facts of his life, a critical survey of all his writings, and a thorough examination of the canon. Mr. Barker's *Thomas Middleton* is a valuable piece of criticism and scholarship; I am pleased to have had the opportunity to refer to it so frequently in my own pages.

7. *Cyril Tourneur,* ed. Collins, I, xlii. Passages dealing with Tourneur are included in this survey of critical opinion only when it is apparent from the context that the remarks are designed to apply to *The Revenger's Tragedy.*

8. Oliphant, *Shakespeare and His Fellow Dramatists,* II, 94.

9. *Webster and Tourneur,* ed. Symonds, pp. x–xi.

10. Oliphant, *Shakespeare and His Fellow Dramatists,* II, 94.

11. Prior, *Language of Tragedy,* p. 144.

12. Parrott and Ball, *Short View,* p. 216.

13. Boyer, *Villain as Hero,* p. 148.

14. Wells, *Elizabethan and Jacobean Playwrights*, p. 34.

15. Oliphant, *Shakespeare and His Fellow Dramatists*, II, 93.

16. Thorndike, *Tragedy*, p. 202.

17. Lee, "Italy of the Elizabethan Dramatists," p. 77.

18. *Cyril Tourneur*, ed. Nicoll, pp. 40–41.

19. Eliot, "Cyril Tourneur," p. 162.

20. Archer, *Old Drama and the New*, p. 74.

21. Prior, *Language of Tragedy*, p. 144.

22. Oliphant, *Shakespeare and His Fellow Dramatists*, II, 95.

23. Nashe, *Pierce Penilesse*, in *Works*, ed. McKerrow, I, 186.

24. *Repentance of Robert Greene*, p. 20.

25. Marston, *Satires*, II, 145–46, in *Works*, ed. Bullen, III.

26. See Roeder, *Man of the Renaissance*, pp. 162, 195; also Moryson, *Shakespeare's Europe*, p. 406.

27. Nashe, *Unfortunate Traveller*, in *Works*, ed. McKerrow, II, 301.

28. Moryson, *Shakespeare's Europe*, p. 408.

29. Nashe, *Pierce Penilesse*, in *Works*, ed. McKerrow, I, 220.

30. Webster, *The White Devil*, V, i, 67–75, in *Works*, ed. Lucas, I.

31. See Symonds, *Renaissance in Italy*, IV, Pt. 2, 118; also Lee, "Italy of the Elizabethan Dramatists," p. 71; Eckert, *Die dramatische Behandlung der Ermordung des Herzogs Alessandro de' Medici*, pp. 20–21; Schoenbaum, " 'The Revenger's Tragedy': a Neglected Source," p. 338. It is curious to note that Symonds, in his volume of Webster and Tourneur plays (1888) which appeared in the Mermaid Series after the first printing of the *Renaissance in Italy* (1875–81), remarks that there is no known source for *The Revenger's Tragedy* (p. 341).

32. Varchi, *Storia Fiorentina*, in *Opera*, I, 368–69.

33. Segni, *Istorie Fiorentine*, ed. Gargani, 275–76.

34. Varchi, *Storia Fiorentina*, I, 409–12; Segni, *Istorie Fiorentine*, pp. 313–15; Napier, *Florentine History*, V, 8–9, 15, 38–47; Young, *The Medici*, I, 506–8.

35. Swinburne, "John Marston," in *Works*, ed. Gosse and Wise, XI, 359.

36. *The Malcontent*, I, vii, p. 159, in *Plays of John Marston*, ed. Wood, I. Lines are not numbered in Wood's text.

37. *Ibid.*, I, i, p. 71.

38. *Ibid.*, V, v, p. 129.

39. Lockert, "Greatest of Elizabethan Melodramas," p. 121.

40. Dates, unless otherwise specified, are the limits given by Harbage in his *Annals*.

41. Bowers, *Elizabethan Revenge Tragedy*, p. 138.

42. *Ibid.*, pp. 133–34.

43. Bradbrook, *Themes and Conventions*, p. 165.

44. Prior, *Language of Tragedy*, p. 138.

45. Bradbrook, *Themes and Conventions*, p. 165.

46. See above, p. 15.

47. Parrott and Ball, *Short View*, p. 218.

48. Collins considers this allusion minute enough to be of biographical value, an indication that Tourneur—whom he regards as the author—may have been a member of the Inns of Court (*Cyril Tourneur*, I, xvii). But Middleton has an identical reference in *Michaelmas Term* (Induction, l. 59).

49. Lockert, "Greatest of Elizabethan Melodramas," p. 119.

50. Wells, *Elizabethan and Jacobean Playwrights*, p. 35.

51. Even those critics who reject the play as a whole praise its language. Ward, repelled by the "stifling atmosphere" and "sewer-like windings" of the plot, nevertheless grants the author to be "a tragic poet of unmistakeable distinction," with "a gift of diction matching itself with extraordinary fitness to demands such as few if any of our dramatists have ever made upon their powers" (*History of English Dramatic Literature*, III, 69 ff.; see also Vaughan, *Cambridge History*, VI, 189, 190). Those who admire the play admire it most for its verse. "What lingers in the memory after reading *The Revenger's Tragedy*," write Parrott and Ball, "is neither the tangled plot nor the repulsive characters but single scenes couched in dramatic poetry of extraordinary power and terrible beauty" (*Short View*, p. 218). According to Eliot, the author (Tourneur, of course, is meant) owes his rank as a "great poet" to "this one play, in which a horror of life, singular in his own or any age, finds exactly the right words and the right rhythms" ("Cyril Tourneur," p. 169).

52. *Cyril Tourneur*, ed. Collins, I, xlviii, 1.

53. Swinburne, "Cyril Tourneur," in *Works*, ed. Gosse and Wise, XI, 473.

54. Barker, *Thomas Middleton*.

55. Wells, *Elizabethan and Jacobean Playwrights*, p. 37.

56. Wilson, *Elizabethan and Jacobean*, p. 101; see also Foakes, "Authorship of 'The Revenger's Tragedy,' " pp. 134–35.

57. Of course, the Phoenix had been Christianized since the Middle Ages, when its strange history came to be regarded as an allegory of the death and resurrection of Christ.

58. Owst, *Preaching in Medieval England*, p. 344.

59. Spencer, *Death and Elizabethan Tragedy*, p. 186.

60. Eliot, "Cyril Tourneur," p. 166.

61. See Ivins, introd., *Dance of Death*, p. ix.

62. Kurtz, *Dance of Death*, pp. 86–87.

63. It is perhaps for this reason that the editors of *The Revenger's Tragedy* have been unable to find a source for the play. (Symonds' suggestion has been overlooked by later commentators.)

64. Eliot, "Cyril Tourneur," p. 166.

65. *Ibid.*, pp. 165–66.

II. *The Second Maiden's Tragedy*

1. Bradbrook, *Themes and Conventions*, p. 213.

2. Ellis-Fermor, *Jacobean Drama*, p. 152.

3. Bradbrook, *Themes and Conventions*, p. 213.

4. The two actions may perhaps be regarded as affording a contrast between two kinds of love—the sensuality of the Wife, as opposed to the highly idealized love of the Lady, who chooses to die rather than sacrifice her virtue. But the two stories are handled so differently that the reader is scarcely aware of the contrast.

5. Cervantes, *Don Quixote*, I, 287. The "Story of the One Who Was Too Curious for His Own Good" appears on pp. 280–314, 318–22.

6. *Ibid.*, pp. 302, 306, 314. "Ah, unfortunate and ill-advised Anselmo! . . . Behold what you are doing to yourself: plotting your own dishonor and bringing about your own ruin" (p. 294); "Anselmo, thoroughly deluded, would by no means hear of this, and thus in a thousand ways he became the creator of his own dishonor in place of what he took to be his happiness" (p. 318).

7. In the play it is Leonela, rather than Votarius, who informs Anselmus of his wife's amour.

8. Cervantes, p. 296.

9. *Ibid.*, p. 313.

10. *Ibid.*, p. 282.

11. *Ibid.*, p. 291.

12. Ellis-Fermor, *Jacobean Drama*, p. 149. Ellis-Fermor may be indebted for her observation to T. S. Eliot: "Middleton understood women in tragedy better than any of the Elizabethans—better than the creator of the Duchess of Malfy, better than Marlowe, better than Tourneur, or Shirley, or Fletcher, better than any of them except Shakespeare alone" ("Thomas Middleton," p. 145).

13. Barker, *Thomas Middleton*.

14. See Chapter VI, pp. 186–87.

15. *Second Maiden's Tragedy*, ed. Greg, p. v.

16. Ward, *History of English Dramatic Literature*, II, 672.

17. Ristine, *English Tragicomedy*, p. xiii.

18. In Beaumont and Fletcher, *Works*, ed. Glover and Waller, X.

19. "Beaumont and Fletcher did not trace out the sequence of emotions which would follow from an actual situation," writes Thorndike; "they sought to contrast as many varying emotions as possible" (*Influence of Beaumont and Fletcher on Shakspere*, p. 112).

20. See, especially, Thorndike, *Influence of Beaumont and Fletcher on Shakspere*, pp. 122–24.

21. "He [Philaster] is at different moments an irresolute prince, a fervent lover, a jealous madman, and a coward who cannot fight; he is never a real individual" (*Ibid.*, p. 120).

22. Bradbrook, *Themes and Conventions*, p. 247.

23. Barker, *Thomas Middleton*.

24. Eliot, "Cyril Tourneur," p. 168.

25. Bradbrook, *Themes and Conventions*, p. 239.

26. And again:

> Our joy breaks at our eyes; the prince is come!
> *The Phoenix*, v, i, 56

> I've a joy weeps to see you, 'tis so full,
> So fairly fruitful.
> *The Old Law*, IV, ii, 35–36

My joys start at mine eyes; our sweet'st delights
Are evermore born weeping.

The Changeling, III, iv, 25–26

27. For these figures and others of the same type see *Chaste Maid*, v, i, 61–64; *No Wit*, I, i, 41–43; I, ii, 73–75, 104–5; II, i, 37–39, 392–93, 416; IV, i, 123–24; *More Dissemblers*, I, iii, 99; II, iii, 58; III, ii, 123–25; *Women Beware Women*, I, iii, 1–3; II, ii, 94–96; III, i, 111–14, 173–75; III, ii, 162–63, 314–17; IV, i, 97–99; IV, ii, 182; *Hengist*, IV, iii, 23–25, 72–74, 78–79; V, ii, 43–44. In *Women Beware Women* Middleton at one point plays quite self-consciously with such figures, exercising his dexterity as image follows image in rapid succession:

all preferment
That springs from sin and lust it shoots up quickly,
As gardeners' crops do in the rotten'st grounds;
So is all means rais'd from base prostitution
Even like a salad growing upon a dunghill.
I'm like a thing that never was yet heard of,
Half merry and half mad; much like a fellow
That eats his meat with a good appetite,
And wears a plague-sore that would fright a country;
Or rather like the barren, harden'd ass,
That feeds on thistles till he bleeds again;
And such is the condition of my misery.

III, ii, 47–58

28. See also lines 229–32, 315–19, 1208–10, 1211, 1249–50, 2123.

29. Hazlitt, *Lectures*, p. 60.

30. Courthope, *History of English Poetry*, IV, 231.

31. "Fletcher is at once a poet and a romanticist, which Middleton scarcely ever is. . . . Middleton's versification—in which again he approaches Fletcher but does not surpass him—is remarkable for its grace and easy swing. Middleton's verse has the pervading qualities of competence for its service, lightness, and artistic restraint" (Schelling, *Elizabethan Drama*, I, 517).

32. Herford, "Thomas Middleton," *DNB*, XXXVII, 360.

33. Eliot, "Thomas Middleton," p. 148. It is always valuable to have for our guidance a judgment on a poet by a critic who is himself a distinguished poet. In this case, however, it is not easy to determine with confidence how much weight should be

given to the critic's evaluation: Eliot cites in support of his view a single passage from *The Changeling*, and there can be little question that that passage is the unaided work of Rowley. The selection is taken from Act v, scene iii, and begins: "I that am of your blood was taken from you / For your better health."

34. Brooke, *Literary History of England*, ed. Baugh, p. 567.

35. Oliphant, *Shakespeare and His Fellow Dramatists*, II, ii.

36. *Hengist*, ed. Bald, p. li.

37. The first edition of *The Second Maiden's Tragedy*—a very poor text—appeared in 1824 as part of the Old English Drama series. In 1829 Tieck included his translation of the play in the second volume of his *Shakspeare's Vorschule*. *The Second Maiden's Tragedy* was reprinted twice in 1875: in Hazlitt's *Dodsley* and in the *Poems and Minor Translations* volume of the Chatto and Windus *Chapman*. Both texts are unsatisfactory. The sole modern reprint, edited by Greg in 1909 for the Malone Society, is excellent but designed primarily for the specialist.

38. Schelling, *Elizabethan Drama*, I, 599.

39. Ward, *History of English Dramatic Literature*, II, 672.

40. Barker, *Thomas Middleton*.

iii. *Hengist, King of Kent*

1. He joined with Rowley on *A Fair Quarrel* (1615–17) and *The World Tossed at Tennis* (1619–20), and with Rowley and Massinger on *The Old Law* (*ca.* 1616–18). He may have had a hand in a Beaumont and Fletcher play, *Wit at Several Weapons* (*ca.* 1609–20), and Fletcher may have participated in *The Widow* (1616).

2. *Hengist* was entered upon the Stationers' Register on September 4, 1646, and again on February 13, 1661 (Eyre, *Transcript of . . . Registers of . . . Company of Stationers; . . . 1640–1708*, I, 245, II, 288). The play is, however, first mentioned much earlier, in a Revels Office slip inserted by Sir George Buc in the manuscript of his *History of the Life and Reign of Richard III* (*King's Office of the Revels*, ed. Marcham, pp. 10–11). This slip, containing a canceled play-list, helps us to date *Hengist*. The list cannot be earlier than 1615, for it includes "The Cambridge Play of Albumazar and Trinculo," written for James I's visit to

the university in March of that year; it is not later than 1620, when Buc went mad. The allusion in *Hengist* to "a great enormitie in wool" (I, ii, 103) would be appropriate, as Bald points out, for 1616 or any date thereafter, with the possible exception of 1618 (*Hengist*, ed. Bald, pp. xiii–xiv). Bald very plausibly suggests *ca.* 1619–20 as a likely date for the composition of *Hengist* (*ibid.*, p. xiii); his view is supported by the style of the play, which is clearly in Middleton's mature manner.

3. See Middleton's *Works*, ed. Bullen, I, xviii; Symons, *Cambridge History*, VI, 69; *Hengist*, ed. Bald, p. xlvi; Boas, *Introduction to Stuart Drama*, p. 233; Schelling, *Elizabethan Drama*, I, 510, and *English Chronicle Play*, pp. 181–83; Barker, *Thomas Middleton*. Bullen, one page later, calls *Hengist* a "chronicle play." Harbage, in his *Annals*, describes the work as a "pseudo-history."

4. See *Hengist*, ed. Bald, pp. xxxvii–xxxix, 127–36.

5. Holinshed, *Historie of England*, in *Chronicles*, I. The accounts of Vortiger and Hengist appear on pp. 551–67.

6. To avoid confusion I adhere to the names as found in *Hengist*, rather than Holinshed's variants. Vortiger, for example, appears in the *Historie of England* as Vortigerus, Vortigernus, and most frequently, Vortigerne.

7. Holinshed, p. 560.

8. Middleton may be thinking of Holinshed when he has Constantius remark:

> Did not great Constantine our noble ffather
> Deeme me vnfitt for gouerment and rule
> And theirfore pressed me into this profession:
>
> I, i, 106–8

but he immediately makes him add: "Which I haue held strict and loue it aboue glorye?" (I, i, 109).

9. Fabyan, *Cronycle*, F. XXXII.

10. Tillyard, *Shakespeare's History Plays*, p. 99.

11. Nashe, *Pierce Penilesse*, in *Works*, ed. McKerrow, I, 212.

12. Heywood, *Apology*, F. 3.

13. *Ibid*.

14. Campbell, *Shakespeare's "Histories,"* p. 74.

15. Holinshed, *Historie of England*, in *Chronicles*, I, 554.

16. *A Game at Chess* (1624) is perhaps the only exception,

but even in this political allegory the sexual interest is great.

17. Harbage, *Shakespeare and the Rival Traditions*, pp. 85, 288.

18. *Ile of Gvls*, A 2.

19. Harbage, *Shakespeare and the Rival Traditions*, p. 71.

20. Holinshed, *Historie of England*, in *Chronicles*, I, 556.

21. Marston's Malevole also expresses this thought; see *Malcontent*, I, iii, pp. 149–50, in *Plays*, ed. Wood, I.

22. Boas, *Introduction to Stuart Drama*, p. 220.

23. Eliot, "Thomas Middleton," p. 145.

24. Barker, *Thomas Middleton*.

25. *Ibid.*

26. *Hengist*, ed. Bald, p. xlvii.

27. *Ibid.*

28. *Ibid.*, p. l.

29. In the manuscript, the name is usually spelled "Hersus" when preceding dialogue.

30. *Hengist*, ed. Bald, p. xliii.

31. Ward, *History of English Dramatic Literature*, II, 500. A number of the earlier critics praise the writing but find the story crude or repulsive (see Middleton's *Works*, ed. Bullen, I, xix–xx; Swinburne, introd. Mermaid *Middleton*, II, xi–xii; Herford, "Thomas Middleton," p. 360; and Schelling, *English Chronicle Play*, p. 182). Symons admires certain passages but regards the play as a whole as "the premature attempt of a man, not naturally equipped for tragic or romantic writing, to do the tragic comedy then in fashion" (*Cambridge History*, VI, 69). To Ellis *Hengist* is so painful that he questions Middleton's responsibility for it and is able to include the play in the Mermaid collection only "after considerable hesitation" (pref. Mermaid *Middleton*, II, xi–xii).

32. Parrott and Ball echo the nineteenth-century commentators: the play is a "curious medley of history, tragedy, and farce," with "occasional flashes of fine poetry" that "reveal the hand of Middleton" (*Short View*, p. 166). Eliot does not mention *Hengist* in his essay on Middleton, and it is not treated in Ellis-Fermor's *Jacobean Drama*, Wells' *Elizabethan and Jacobean Playwrights*, or Bradbrook's *Themes and Conventions of Elizabethan Tragedy*.

33. *Hengist*, ed. Bald, p. xliii.

34. Barker, *Thomas Middleton*.
35. *Hengist*, ed. Bald, p. xlvi.

IV. *Women Beware Women* AND *The Changeling*

1. *Women Beware Women. A Tragedy, By Tho. Middleton, Gent. London: Printed for Humphrey Moseley, 1657*. In *Two New Plays. . . . 1657.* 8 vo. There is some question as to the precise date of composition. The conjectures of Schelling (*ca.* 1612) and Fleay (1613) are too early to be satisfactory (*Elizabethan Drama*, I, 586; *Biographical Chronicle*, II, 97), while Oliphant's guess (1627) seems to be too late (*Shakespeare and His Fellow Dramatists*, II, 948). Oliphant finds a connection between the composition of the play and publication of *The True History of the Tragic Loves of Hippolito and Isabella, Neapolitans*, an English translation of one of the sources. It was not, however, entered upon the Stationers' books until November 9, 1627, four months after Middleton's death. Since *Women Beware Women* is not included in the records of Sir Henry Herbert, it is unlikely that the play was written after 1622, the year in which the records begin. Bald proposes 1621, a date as little removed as possible from *The Changeling* ("Chronology of Middleton's Plays," p. 42). His view is supported by Maxwell, on the basis of Livia's reference to stocking a new-found land (I, ii, 61) and Middleton's changing Francesco's age from twenty-three to fifty-five: "That's no great age in man," Bianca declares; "he's then at best / For wisdom and for judgment" (I, iii, 95–96). The passage, Maxwell suggests, may be intended as flattery of James, who was fifty-five in the summer of 1621 ("Date of Middleton's *Women Beware Women*," pp. 338–42). Although the evidence is not conclusive, the year 1621 would seem to be a plausible conjecture.

2. Bradbrook, *Themes and Conventions*, p. 224.
3. Bradbrook feels that the subplots are closely related to the main actions (*Ibid.*, pp. 213, 225, 234). But her explanations are ingenious rather than convincing. See also Empson on *The Changeling* (*Some Versions of Pastoral*, pp. 48–52).
4. Barker, *Thomas Middleton*.
5. Symons, *Cambridge History*, VI, 86.
6. Malespini, *Dvcento Novelle*, II, 275–80. The source was

pointed out in 1905 by Karl Christ (*Quellenstudien zu den Dramen Thomas Middletons*, pp. 50–63).

7. I follow Malespini in referring to Pietro as Bianca's husband. Actually there is no indication in the narrative that a marriage ceremony ever took place.

8. Moryson, *Shakespeare's England*, pp. 94–95.

9. Barker, *Thomas Middleton*.

10. Lamb, *Specimens*, p. 137.

11. Ellis-Fermor has a different view. To her the characterizations of Bianca and Leantio reveal "the process by which a nature may be dislocated by a sudden jar or shock of evil fate. . . . In every case there is enough indication that the nature is drawn on a generous scale; it is the promise of a fine flowering that is destroyed. Middleton seems to have grasped the principle (as did few of his contemporaries) that the more generously a nature is endowed, especially perhaps a woman's, the more bitter is its corruption if it is thwarted or maimed in the full course of its development" (*Jacobean Stage*, p. 142). But the text would scarcely seem to justify Ellis-Fermor's interpretation.

12. Lamb, *Specimens*, p. 137.

13. Eliot, "Thomas Middleton," p. 144.

14. Swinburne speaks of "the high comedy of the scene between Livia and the Widow" (introd. Mermaid *Middleton*, I, xxix). According to Boas the play is noteworthy primarily for "its lighter and more genial scenes" (*Stuart Drama*, p. 237). Parrott and Ball stress the comic aspects of the work: "*Women Beware Women* shows Middleton's reversion after his collaboration with Rowley to his proper field of satiric comedy, but comedy now tinged with irony and leading to tragic issues. . . . The link between the two actions is the widow Livia, who plays the role of the intriguer in a comedy" (*Short View*, pp. 237–38). See also Symons' comments below, p. 132.

15. Bergson, *Laughter*, p. 139.

16. See Chapter II, n. 27.

17. Barker, *Thomas Middleton*.

18. Middleton, *Works*, VI, 235.

19. Symons, *Cambridge History*, VI, 88–89.

20. Reynolds, *God's Revenge*, pp. 105–46.

21. *Ibid.*, p. 109.

22. Bradbrook, *Themes and Conventions*, p. 234.

23. See *Women Beware Women*, II, ii, 325–28:

Prithee, tremble not;
I feel thy breast shake like a turtle panting
Under a loving hand that makes much on't:
Why art so fearful?

24. Eliot, "Thomas Middleton," p. 143.
25. Wells, *Elizabethan and Jacobean Playwrights*, p. 41.
26. Swinburne, introd. Mermaid *Middleton*, I, xxxvii–xxxviii.
27. Eliot, "Thomas Middleton," p. 144.

v. *Authorship Problems: The Revenger's Tragedy*

1. Even these sources are often inaccurate, misleading, or inadequate; see Bentley, "Authenticity and Attribution," pp. 106–15.
2. *Cyril Tourneur*, ed. Nicoll, pp. 19–20, 49.
3. Bentley, "Authenticity and Attribution," p. 101.
4. Sykes' work, for example, is justly criticized by Byrne, "Bibliographical Clues," pp. 21–48. See also Walter's edition of *Charlemagne*, pp. x–xi, for criticism of Schoell's attempts to establish Chapman's authorship of the play. Sykes, realizing the possibility of error, nevertheless uses the unreliable Mermaid text for his research on *The Revenger's Tragedy* and Hazlitt's "Dodsley," which is notoriously untrustworthy, for his work on *The Second Maiden's Tragedy;* see Sykes, "Cyril Tourneur," pp. 225–29. Oliphant, working on *The Bloody Banquet*, does not take pains to verify the date of the original quarto, although the information is of considerable importance and readily available ("A Dekker-Middleton Play, *The Bloodie Banquet,*" p. 882).
5. Bentley, "Authenticity and Attribution," p. 117.
6. Parallel passages, for example, constitute one of the chief sources of evidence, but they are of little value when derived from disputed or collaborate works. Eberle makes a good case for the presence of Dekker's hand in *The Family of Love*, but he does not strengthen his argument by citing parallels from *Blurt Master Constable* and *The Bloody Banquet*, both of which have been assigned conjecturally to Dekker in recent years, *The*

Bloody Banquet only in part. See Eberle, "Dekker's Part in *The Familie of Love*," pp. 723–38.

7. Data based on the classification of imagery are suspect, see below, p. 159.

8. Collaborations present difficulties of a different nature; see Chapter VII, p. 203.

9. *Transcript of . . . Registers of . . . Stationers of London, 1554–1640*, ed. Arber, III, 360.

10. *The Revengers Tragaedie. As it hath beene sundry times Acted, by the Kings Maiesties Seruants. At London Printed by G. Eld, and are to be sold at his house in Fleete-lane at the signe of the Printers-Presse. 1607*. In some copies the date is 1608.

11. See Greg, *List of English Plays*, App. II, xlii–xliii and cii.

12. *Ibid.*, pp. xliii–xlvi and cii.

13. Nicoll's date. See *Cyril Tourneur*, ed. Nicoll, pp. 22–23, and below, p. 162.

14. Fleay, *Biographical Chronicle*, II, 272.

15. Oliphant, "Problems of Authorship," p. 428; see also "Authorship of 'The Revenger's Tragedy,'" pp. 157–68; *Shakespeare and His Fellow Dramatists*, II, 1–3; "Tourneur and 'The Revenger's Tragedy,'" XXIX, 1087 and XXX, 99; "Cyril Tourneur and T. S. Eliot," pp. 546–52. In the last article Oliphant reports that two English scholars, Bertram Lloyd and William Wells, arrived independently at a similar view (p. 547).

16. Wenzel, *Cyril Tourneurs Stellung*, p. 133.

17. Sykes, "Cyril Tourneur," pp. 225–29.

18. *Cyril Tourneur*, ed. Nicoll, pp. 18–20.

19. Eliot, "Cyril Tourneur," pp. 162–64; "Tourneur and 'The Revenger's Tragedy,'" p. 12.

20. Wagner, "Cyril Tourneur," p. 327.

21. Dunkel, "Authorship of *The Revenger's Tragedy*," pp. 781–85.

22. Jones, "Cyril Tourneur," p. 487.

23. Ellis-Fermor, "Imagery of 'The Revenger's Tragedie' and 'The Atheist's Tragedie,'" pp. 289–301.

24. Mincoff, "Authorship of 'The Revenger's Tragedy,'" pp. 1–87.

25. Parrott and Ball, *Short View*, pp. 215–16.

26. Barker, "Authorship of the *Second Maiden's Tragedy* and *The Revenger's Tragedy*," pp. 51–62, 121–33.

27. Adams, "Cyril Tourneur on Revenge," pp. 72–87.

28. Schoenbaum, " 'Revenger's Tragedy' and Middleton's Moral Outlook," pp. 8–10.

29. Foakes, "Authorship of 'The Revenger's Tragedy,' " pp. 129–38.

30. *Cyril Tourneur*, ed. Nicoll, p. 18.

31. Greg, *List of English Plays*, pp. cxiii, lxxvi, xci.

32. Mincoff, "Authorship of 'The Revenger's Tragedy,' " p. 6.

33. Eliot, "Cyril Tourneur," p. 163.

34. Middleton's *Works*, ed. Bullen, VIII, 101.

35. Oliphant, "Authorship of 'The Revenger's Tragedy,' " p. 158.

36. Byrne, "Bibliographical Clues," p. 28.

37. Oliphant, "Tourneur and Mr. T. S. Eliot," pp. 546–47.

38. Barker, "Authorship of the *Second Maiden's Tragedy* and *The Revenger's Tragedy*," p. 122.

39. Ellis-Fermor, "Imagery of 'The Revenger's Tragedie' and 'The Atheist's Tragedie,' " p. 297.

40. Mincoff, "Authorship of 'The Revenger's Tragedy,' " pp. 1–87.

41. *Cyril Tourneur*, ed. Nicoll, p. 19. Similarly, to Foakes both plays "seem remarkably alike in the more intangible qualities which evade strict analysis, in mood, general temper and moral fervour" ("Authorship of 'The Revenger's Tragedy,' " p. 138). His remark is open to the same objection as Nicoll's.

42. Parrott and Ball, *Short View*, p. 216.

43. Barker, "Authorship of the *Second Maiden's Tragedy* and *The Revenger's Tragedy*," p. 122.

44. Adams, "Cyril Tourneur on Revenge," p. 72.

45. *Ibid.*, p. 79.

46. II, vi, 26–27; III, ii, 44–45; and v, ii, 303.

47. Eliot, "Cyril Tourneur," pp. 163–64, and "Tourneur and 'The Revenger's Tragedy,' " p. 12.

48. Eliot, "Cyril Tourneur," p. 162.

49. *Cyril Tourneur*, ed. Collins, I, xxxvi.

50. *Ibid.*, p. xxxviii.

51. Collins is the first to give this idea currency, although it was suggested as early as 1823, in an anonymous article on Tourneur in *The Retrospective Review* (VII, 345).

52. *Cyril Tourneur*, ed. Collins, I, xxxix.

53. Furthermore, *The Atheist's Tragedy* apparently precedes *The Nobleman*, which was entered on the Stationers' books several months later, on February 15, 1611/12 (*Cyril Tourneur*, ed. Nicoll, p. 24). Oliphant detects Tourneur's hand in *The Honest Man's Fortune* (I; II, i and iii); see *Plays of Beaumont and Fletcher*, pp. 383–91. Bullen felt at one time that Tourneur might have written *Charlemagne or The Distracted Emperor*, but he changed his mind; see *Collection of Old English Plays*, ed. Bullen, II, 442–43, and III, 161.

54. Ward, *History of English Dramatic Literature*, III, 69; Fleay, *Biographical Chronicle*, II, 263.

55. Sykes, "Cyril Tourneur," pp. 225–29.

56. Oliphant, *Plays of Beaumont and Fletcher*, p. 91. See also "Authorship of 'The Revenger's Tragedy,' " p. 168.

57. *Cyril Tourneur*, ed. Nicoll, p. 23.

58. Jenkins feels that *The Atheist's Tragedy* reflects an advance in thought over *The Revenger's Tragedy* ("Cyril Tourneur," pp. 21–36). But the maturity Jenkins finds in *The Atheist's Tragedy* has little to do with poetic ability or command of stage technique.

59. Fleay, *Biographical Chronicle*, II, 272.

60. Eliot, "Cyril Tourneur," p. 161.

61. Hillebrand, "Thomas Middleton's *The Viper's Brood*," pp. 35–38.

62. Dunkel, "Authorship of *The Revenger's Tragedy*," p. 785.

63. *Webster and Tourneur*, ed. Symonds, p. xiv.

64. Foakes, "Authorship of 'The Revenger's Tragedy,' " p. 136.

65. Harbage, *Shakespeare and the Rival Traditions*, p. 88.

66. *Ibid.*, pp. 88–89.

67. It is curious that characters named Lussurioso and Castiza appear also in *The Phoenix*. There is another Castiza in *Hengist*, and a servant named Dondola appears in *More Dissemblers Besides Women*.

68. Barker, "Authorship of the *Second Maiden's Tragedy* and *The Revenger's Tragedy*," p. 123.

69. *Ibid.*, p. 124.

70. It may also be noted that the scene in which the disguised Vindice solicits his mother and sister brings to mind, as Dunkel

suggests, those scenes in *Michaelmas Term* in which Lethe deceives his mother (i, i) and the Country Wench her father (iii, i); Dunkel also points out that both Lethe and Vindice try to make bawds of their mothers ("Authorship of *The Revenger's Tragedy*," p. 784).

71. Oliphant, "Tourneur and 'The Revenger's Tragedy,' " p. 1087. Later Oliphant apparently modified his view slightly, for he excepts *The Phoenix* in a similar statement in "Cyril Tourneur and T. S. Eliot," p. 549.

72. See Chapter I, p. 15.

73. These lines are paralleled very closely in *The Revenger's Tragedy:* "Are Lord-ships sold to maintaine Lady-ships" (iii, v, 77).

74. Oliphant, "The Authorship of 'The Revenger's Tragedy,' " pp. 161–63.

75. Jones, "Cyril Tourneur," p. 487.

76. Wagner, "Cyril Tourneur," p. 327.

77. Oliphant, "Authorship of 'The Revenger's Tragedy,' " pp. 160–61, 164.

78. Middleton's *Works*, ed. Bullen, I, 122. The variants in the 1607 quarto of *The Phoenix* are *Sursurarers* and *Sursararaes*.

79. Barker, "Authorship of the *Second Maiden's Tragedy* and *The Revenger's Tragedy*," p. 126.

80. *Comfort* appears seven times in *The Phoenix*, ten times in *Michaelmas Term*, eight times in *Mad World*, seven times in *Your Five Gallants*, and fifteen times in *Trick*.

81. *John Webster*, ed. Lucas, IV, 250.

82. Oliphant, "Authorship of 'The Revenger's Tragedy,' " p. 159.

83. Barker, "Authorship of the *Second Maiden's Tragedy* and *The Revenger's Tragedy*," p. 127. Foakes attacks the verse statistics on the grounds that they are "based . . . on a verse-structure, on line-endings and irregularities for which editors are to some extent responsible" ("Authorship of 'The Revenger's Tragedy,' " p. 134). Barker's figures are, however, based upon the best available text (Nicoll's); and, allowing all possible margin for error, it can scarcely be denied that the two plays differ widely with regard to frequency of feminine endings and that Middleton's practice is consistent with that found in *The Revenger's Tragedy*. Inasmuch as Foakes apparently does not dis-

tinguish between feminine endings and light or weak endings (see note, *ibid.*), his views on metrical data may be regarded with some skepticism.

VI. *The Authorship of The Second Maiden's Tragedy*

1. *Second Maiden's Tragedy*, ed. Greg, p. vi; see also Greg, *Editorial Problem in Shakespeare*, p. 31.

2. *Ibid.*, p. 78.

3. *The Maid's Tragedy* cannot be dated precisely, but it is usually regarded as belonging to the period between *ca.* 1608 and 1611, with perhaps 1610 as the most likely date. The play was not entered upon the Stationers' Register until April 28, 1619 (Arber, *Transcript of . . . Registers of . . . Company of Stationers . . . 1554–1640*, III, 360), but we know of a court performance given during 1612–13 (Chambers, *Elizabethan Stage*, III, 224).

4. Eyre, *Transcript of . . . Registers of . . . Company of Stationers; . . . 1640–1708*, I, 428.

5. *Second Maiden's Tragedy*, ed. Greg, pp. v–vi.

6. *Ibid.*, p. i.

7. Ll. 5, 42, 804, and 2453.

8. *Ibid.*, p. xii.

9. *Ibid.*, pp. v, 78.

10. *Ibid.*, p. v; see also Chambers, *Elizabethan Stage*, III, 322. Goff was born in 1591.

11. Tieck, *Shakspeare's Vorschule*, II, xliii–xlvii.

12. Postscript to a letter to Thomas Forbes Kelsall dated July 19, 1830; in Beddoes, *Works*, ed. Donner, p. 650.

13. Bullen, "Cyril Tourneur," pp. 465–66.

14. Swinburne, "George Chapman," in *Works*, ed. Gosse and Wise, XII, 182–88; see also XI, 398–99 and XVIII, 153, 375.

15. Fleay, *Biographical Chronicle*, II, 272, 330–31.

16. Boyle, "Massinger," *DNB*, XXXVII, 14–15.

17. Rosenbach, "Curious-Impertinent in English Dramatic Literature," p. 362.

18. Oliphant, "Problems of Authorship in Elizabethan Dramatic Literature," pp. 423–24; "Authorship of 'The Revenger's Tragedy,'" pp. 158–59; *Plays of Beaumont and Fletcher*, p. 443; *Shakespeare and His Fellow Dramatists*, II, 10.

19. Sykes, "Cyril Tourneur," pp. 225–29.

20. *Cyril Tourneur*, ed. Nicoll, pp. 47–49. Nicoll summarizes the case for Tourneur and seems to favor him, but he is not certain enough to include the play in his edition.

21. Barker, "Authorship of the *Second Maiden's Tragedy* and *The Revenger's Tragedy*," pp. 51–62, 121–33. Barker's article constitutes the only really detailed study of the evidence published thus far; it is the basis of much of this chapter.

22. Sykes, "Cyril Tourneur," p. 228.

23. Beddoes, *Works*, ed. Donner, p. 650.

24. Fleay, *Biographical Chronicle*, II, 272.

25. Oliphant, "Authorship of 'The Revenger's Tragedy,'" p. 163.

26. Stoll, *John Webster*, p. 114.

27. *Ibid.*

28. *Cyril Tourneur*, ed. Nicoll, p. 48.

29. Barker, "Authorship of the *Second Maiden's Tragedy* and *The Revenger's Tragedy*," p. 61.

30. *Cyril Tourneur*, ed. Nicoll, p. 48.

31. Barker, "Authorship of the *Second Maiden's Tragedy* and *The Revenger's Tragedy*," p. 52.

32. As Sykes lists only four sets of parallels, they may be reproduced in full so that the reader may judge for himself their quality. Italics marked with an asterisk are Sykes':

> h'as lost the kingdome but his mynde's restorde
> which is the larger empire? pre thee tell me.
> *Domynions* haue their lymitts, the whole earth
> is but a prisoner, nor the sea her Iailor
> that with a siluer hoope lockes in her bodie . . .
> But the vnbounded kingdome of the mynde
> is as vnlymitable as heav'ne,
>
> ll. 266–70, 273–74

Sykes compares *Atheist's Tragedy*, III, iii, 36–37, 41–47:

> I haue a heart aboue the reach
> Of thy most violent maliciousnesse. . . .
> I was a Baron. That thy Father has
> Depriu'd me off. Instead of that, I am
> Created King. I'ue lost a Signiorie,
> That was confin'd within a piece of earth;
> A Wart vpon the body of the world.

But now I am an Emp'rour of a world.
This little world of Man.

ile sooner giue my blessing to a drunkerd
whome the *ridiculous power of wine,** makes humble
as foolish vse makes thee,—   ll. 655–57
Sykes compares *Atheist's Tragedy*, II, ii, 23–25:
    Their *drunkennesse** that seemes *ridiculous,**
    Shall be a serious instrument, to bring
    Our sober purposes to their successe.

tis the first stone that euer I took of
from any ladie, marrie I haue brought em manie
faire diamondes, *Saphires, Rubies;* ll. 1792–94
Sykes compares *Atheist's Tragedy*, II, iv, 111–14:
                     e'er his faltring tongue
    Could vtter double Oo; I knock'd out's braines
    With this faire Rubie. And had another stone
    Iust of this forme and bignesse ready:

thow thief of rest, robber of monuments,
Cannot the bodie after funerall
sleep in the graue for thee? must it be raisde
onlie to pleaze the wickednes of thine eye?
does all thinges end with death and not thy lust?
                          ll. 2359–63
Sykes compares *Atheist's Tragedy*, III, i, 151–54:
    Of all mens griefes must mine be singular?
    Without example? Heere I met my graue.
    And all mens woes are buried i' their graues
    But mine.

33. Fleay, *Biographical Chronicle*, II, 331.
34. Adams, foreword to *Hengist*, ed. Bald, p. vii.
35. For a discussion of characterization in *The Second Maiden's Tragedy*, see Chapter II, pp. 44–49. One may, however, call attention here to the close similarity between Sophonirus, a minor personage in *The Second Maiden's Tragedy*, and Allwit in *A Chaste Maid in Cheapside*—a resemblance which appears to have been first pointed out by Barker ("Authorship of the

Second Maiden's Tragedy and *The Revenger's Tragedy*," pp.
53–54). Sophonirus is a wittol who delights in his unsavory
homelife. He allows his wife a lover "to stop her mowth/ and
keep her quiet" (ll. 42–43), indeed, even provides him with a
lodging and feed for his horse. In return the lover

> getts me all my children, there I saue by'te, . . .
> Tis the right waie to keep a woman honest
> one frend is Baracadoe to a hundred
> & keepes em owte, nay more, a husbands sure
> to haue his children all of one[s] mans getting,
> & he that performes best, can haue no better,
> I'me eene as happie then that saue a labour—
>
> ll. 48, 54–59

Allwit too is, as his name implies, a contented cuckold, and he
defends his peculiar domestic arrangements with the same relish
and, at times, almost exactly the same language:

> He gets me all my children, and pays the nurse
> Monthly or weekly . . . .
> I'm as clear
> From jealousy of a wife as from the charge:
> O, two miraculous blessings! 'tis the knight
> Hath took that labour all out of my hands.
>
> I, ii, 18–19, 48–51

36. See Chapter II, pp. 64–65.
37. Swinburne, "George Chapman," in *Works*, ed. Gosse and
Wise, XII, 186.
38. Chapter II, pp. 59–66.
39. Barker, "Authorship of the *Second Maiden's Tragedy* and
The Revenger's Tragedy," p. 55.
40. See also *Honourable Entertainments* (*Ent. viii*, l. 175): "in
this latter Spring of your graue yeares." But the author of *The
Second Maiden's Tragedy* may also be echoing Falstaff: "Farewell, thou latter spring! farewell, All-hallown summer!" (*I
Henry IV*, I, ii, 177).
41. Barker, "Authorship of the *Second Maiden's Tragedy* and
The Revenger's Tragedy," p. 56.
42. Jones, "Cyril Tourneur," p. 487; see also "An Experiment
with Massinger's Verse," pp. 727–40.

43. The figures for *The Second Maiden's Tragedy* include oaths deleted in the manuscript.

44. Oliphant, "Authorship of 'The Revenger's Tragedy,'" p. 161.

VII. *Collaboration with Rowley: Doubtful Attributions*

1. *Middleton and Rowley's Spanish Gypsie and All's Lost by Lust*, ed. Morris, pp. xlviii–xlix.

2. Sykes, "John Ford the Author of 'The Spanish Gipsy,'" pp. 183–99. This study constitutes one of Sykes' more convincing arguments. Sargeaunt offers further reasons for ascribing the Roderigo-Clara plot to Ford but feels that "the gipsy scenes are undoubtedly not substantially the work of Ford" (*John Ford*, pp. 41–57). In any case it is most unlikely that either Middleton or Rowley was concerned in *The Spanish Gipsy*.

3. Wiggin, *Inquiry*, pp. 1–61. Fleay's division of *The Changeling* is identical with Wiggin's and appeared earlier; yet it is to Wiggin that we must turn, for Fleay gives no evidence to back up his findings.

4. Robb, "Canon of William Rowley's Plays," pp. 129–41.

5. Robb's dates.

6. Robb, p. 130.

7. Wiggin, *Inquiry*, p. 20.

8. *Ibid.*, pp. 15–16.

9. *Ibid.*, p. 18.

10. In *William Rowley*, ed. Stork.

11. These lines are numbered incorrectly in Stork's edition; they should be 20–21.

12. III, i, p. 302, in *Old Plays*, V.

13. Robb, "Canon of William Rowley's Plays," p. 129.

14. *Ibid.*, p. 134.

15. *Ibid.*

16. Wiggin, *Inquiry*, p. 28.

17. *Ibid.*, p. 38; Robb, "Canon of William Rowley's Plays," p. 133; *William Rowley*, ed. Stork, pp. 25, 39.

18. Robb, "Canon of William Rowley's Plays," p. 133.

19. The license appears on the flyleaf of Malone's copy. See Lawrence, "New Facts," p. 820; also Bentley, *Jacobean and Caroline Stage*, I, 183.

20. Eyre, *Transcript of . . . Registers of . . . Company of Stationers; . . . 1640–1708*, I, 403.

21. *The Changeling: As it was Acted (with great Applause) at the Privat house in Drury-Lane, and Salisbury Court. Written by Thomas Midleton, and William Rowley. Gent. Never Printed before. London, Printed for Humphrey Moseley, and are to be sold at his shop at the sign of the Princes-Arms in St Pauls Church-yard, 1653.*

22. Middleton's *Works*, ed. Dyce, I, iv.

23. Middleton's *Works*, ed. Bullen, I, lix–lx.

24. Swinburne, introd. Mermaid *Middleton*, I, xxv.

25. Fleay, *Biographical Chronicle*, II, 101.

26. Wiggin, *Inquiry*, pp. 43–51.

27. *William Rowley*, ed. Stork, pp. 44–45.

28. Symons, *Cambridge History*, VI, 86–87.

29. Oliphant, *Shakespeare and His Fellow Dramatists*, II, 907–45.

30. Dunkel, "Did not Rowley Merely Revise Middleton?" pp. 800–802.

31. Barker, *Thomas Middleton*.

32. Robb, "Canon of William Rowley's Plays," p. 140.

33. Wiggin, *Inquiry*, pp. 49–50.

34. Barker, *Thomas Middleton*. The last percentage is unusually high for Rowley.

35. In Beaumont and Fletcher, *Works*, ed. Glover and Waller, VII. *The Maid in the Mill* was written in collaboration with Fletcher; there is, however, complete agreement among the authorities as to the division of scenes, so that parallels from Rowley sections may be regarded as of value (see Robb, "Canon of William Rowley's Plays," pp. 132, 190).

36. Oliphant, p. 931.

37. Wiggin, *Inquiry*, p. 56. Stork agrees that "Beatrice never quite forfeits our pity even in her most abject state." *The Changeling*, as well as the other Middleton-Rowley plays, resulted from "a close co-operation of the two authors." These works "are all more romantic, more extreme, in conception than anything else of Middleton's except *The Mayor of Queenborough*. And the characters have a greater nobility, awakening a larger sympathy than such depraved women as Livia and Bianca in *Women Beware Women*" (*William Rowley*, pp. 45–46).

38. Symons, *Cambridge History*, VI, 82–83.
39. *Ibid.*, p. 87.
40. *Hengist*, ed. Bald, pp. xxv, xxvii–xxix.
41. *The Mayor of Quinborough: A Comedy. As it hath been often Acted with much Applause at Black-Fryars, By His Majesties Servants. Written by Tho. Middleton. London, Printed for Henry Herringman, and are to be sold at his Shop at the Sign of the Blew-Anchor in the Lower-Walk of the New-Exchange. 1661.* The quarto text differs considerably from the scribal copies, which are virtually identical. The manuscripts contain 175 lines omitted in the quarto, while the quarto has about twenty-five lines not included in the manuscripts. Furthermore, the quarto edition, which may derive from another private transcript, has a different conclusion—one apparently not written by Middleton (Bald, pp. xxxi–xxxv).
42. Swinburne, introd. Mermaid *Middleton*, I, xxii. Parrott and Ball believe also that "Several scenes in the native tradition of low comedy . . . are quite plainly the work of Rowley" (*Short View*, p. 166).
43. *William Rowley*, ed. Stork, *op. cit.*, p. 47.
44. *Hengist*, ed. Bald, p. xxii.
45. *William Rowley*, ed. Stork, p. 46.
46. Henslowe, *Diary*, ed. Greg, I, 50–53; see also *Hengist*, ed. Bald, pp. xvii–xix.
47. *Timon* was first published in the First Folio, where it appears, in a defective text, between *Romeo and Juliet* and *Julius Caesar*. The pagination would indicate that *Timon* occupies the space originally reserved for *Troilus and Cressida*, which was finally printed between the Comedies and Histories and omitted from the table of contents. There survive, indeed, two copies of the Folio with a canceled sheet, of which the recto side contains the conclusion of *Romeo and Juliet* and the verso the beginning of *Timon*. It is possible that the editors of the First Folio did not plan originally to include *Timon* at all.
48. Wells, " 'Timon of Athens,' " pp. 266–69.
49. Sykes, *Sidelights*, pp. 1–43.
50. Chambers, *William Shakespeare*, I, 482–83; see also Ellis-Fermor, "*Timon of Athens;* an Unfinished Play," pp. 270–83.
51. Greg, *Editorial Problem*, p. 149.
52. *The Bloodie Banqvet. A Tragedie. Hector adest secum-*

que Deos in proelia ducit / Nos haec novimus esse nihil. By T. D. London. Printed by Thomas Cotes. 1639. The quarto has presented bibliographical problems which may now be regarded as solved. For a time it seemed that there might have been as many as four editions; 1620, 1629, 1630, and 1639 have been suggested as possible dates of issuance. One encounters 1620 perhaps the most frequently; Greg (*List*), Schelling (*Elizabethan Drama*), Farmer (*Bloody Banquet*, Students' Facsimile Edition), Oliphant ("A Dekker-Middleton Play, *The Bloodie Banquet*"), Harbage (*Annals*), and Wells (Supplement to *Elizabethan and Jacobean Playwrights*) all give 1620 as the date of publication, although Oliphant expresses some skepticism and Greg refers also to a 1639 edition mentioned by Hazlitt. The confusion arose because the line including the date had been trimmed partially away in several copies, leaving visible only the tops of the numerals. The various quartos have, however, been compared by George Watson Cole, who finds that there was only one printing, that of 1639. See "Bibliographical Ghosts," pp. 98–112. There is no basis for Schelling's remark that *The Bloody Banquet* was registered for publication in 1620 (*Elizabethan Drama*, I, 594).

53. See Greg, *List*, App. II, liii.

54. See Baker, *Biographia Dramatica*, II, 61, and Fleay, *Biographical Chronicle*, I, 162.

55. Cole, "Bibliographical Ghosts," p. 103.

56. Oliphant, "A Dekker-Middleton Play, *The Bloodie Banquet*," p. 882. It is likely, however, that Oliphant meant to attribute II, iv to Dekker and II, iii to Middleton. Although Oliphant ascribes II, iii to Dekker alone, he goes on to cite three passages in that scene as characteristic of Middleton; II, iv concerns the Lapirus story, for which, Oliphant believes, Dekker is primarily responsible. It may be noted that, as early as 1911, Oliphant had suggested the possibility of Dekker's authorship ("Problems of Authorship," p. 425). In *Notes and Queries*, January 7, 1922, Oliphant refers to an entry in his notebook assigning *The Bloody Banquet* to Middleton and—hesitantly—Dekker (" 'Anything for a Quiet Life,' " p. 11).

57. Oliphant, "A Dekker-Middleton Play, *The Bloodie Banquet*," p. 882.

58. Oliphant, "Authorship of 'The Revenger's Tragedy,'"
p. 161.

59. "I . . . find in it [*The Bloody Banquet*] no flavour of
Dekker," writes Sykes in 1922. "Nor do I find any evidence to
support Mr. Oliphant's opinion that Middleton was concerned
in it. Whether by Thomas Drue or not . . . it seems to me all
by one hand" ("'Anything for a Quiet Life,'" p. 50).

List of Works Cited

Adams, Henry Hitch. "Cyril Tourneur on Revenge," *Journal of English and Germanic Philology*, XLVIII (January, 1949), 72–87.

Anonymous. "Cyril Tourneur's Plays," *Retrospective Review*, VII (1823), 331–51.

Archer, William. *The Old Drama and the New*. Boston, 1923.

Baker, David Erskine. *Biographia Dramatica; or, a Companion to the Playhouse*. 3 vols. in 4. London, 1812.

Bald, R. C. "The Chronology of Thomas Middleton's Plays," *Modern Language Review*, XXXII (January, 1937), 33–43.

Barker, Richard Hindry. "The Authorship of the *Second Maiden's Tragedy* and *The Revenger's Tragedy*," *Shakespeare Association Bulletin*, XX (April, 1945), 51–62 (July, 1945), 121–33.

——— *Thomas Middleton*. Unpublished manuscript.

Beaumont, Francis, and John Fletcher. *The Works of Francis Beaumont and John Fletcher*. Ed. Arnold Glover and A. R. Waller. 10 vols. Cambridge, 1905–12.

Beddoes, Thomas Lovell. *The Works of Thomas Lovell Beddoes*. Ed. H. W. Donner. London, 1935.

Bentley, G. E. *The Jacobean and Caroline Stage*. 2 vols. Oxford, 1941.

——— "Authenticity and Attribution in the Jacobean and Caroline Drama," *English Institute Annual, 1942*. New York, 1943.

Bergson, Henri. *Laughter; an Essay on the Meaning of the Comic*. Trans. Cloudesley Brereton and Fred Rothwell. New York, 1913.

The Bloody Banquet. ("Old English Drama") Students' Facsimile Edition. London, 1914.

Boas, Frederick S. *Introduction to Stuart Drama*. Oxford, 1946.

Bowers, Fredson Thayer. *Elizabethan Revenge Tragedy: 1587–1642*. Princeton, 1940.

Boyer, Clarence V. *The Villain as Hero in Elizabethan Tragedy.* London, 1916.

Boyle, R. "Massinger," *Dictionary of National Biography,* XXXVII (London, 1896).

Bradbrook, Muriel C. *Themes and Conventions of Elizabethan Tragedy.* Cambridge, 1935.

Brooke, C. F. Tucker. "The Renaissance," in A. C. Baugh, ed., *A Literary History of England.* New York, 1948.

Bullen, A. H. "Cyril Tourneur," *Notes and Queries,* 5th Series, II (December 12, 1874), 465–66.

Byrne, M. St. C. "Bibliographical Clues in Collaborate Plays," *The Library,* IV Series, XIII (June, 1932), 21–48.

Campbell, Lily B. *Shakespeare's "Histories"; Mirrors of Elizabethan Policy.* San Marino, 1947.

Cervantes Saavedra, Miguel de. *Don Quixote.* Trans. Samuel Putnam. 2 vols. New York, 1949.

Chambers, Edmund K. *The Elizabethan Stage.* 4 vols. Oxford, 1923.

—— *William Shakespeare; a Study of Facts and Problems.* 2 vols. Oxford, 1930.

Charlemagne or the Distracted Emperor. Ed. J. H. Walter. Malone Society Reprints. Oxford, 1937.

Christ, Karl, *Quellenstudien zu den Dramen Thomas Middletons.* Leipzig, 1905.

Cole, George Watson. "Bibliographical Ghosts," *Papers of the Bibliographical Society of America,* XIII (1919), 98–112.

A Collection of Old English Plays. Ed. A. H. Bullen. 4 vols. London, 1882–85.

Courthope, W. J. *A History of English Poetry.* 6 vols. London, 1895–1926.

The Dance of Death. Introd. William M. Ivins, Jr. Washington, 1945.

Day, John. *The Ile of Gvls, 1606.* Introd. G. B. Harrison. London, 1936.

Dunkel, W. D. "The Authorship of *The Revenger's Tragedy,*" *PMLA,* XLVI (September, 1931), 781–85.

—— "Did Not Rowley Merely Revise Middleton?" *PMLA,* XLVIII (September, 1933), 800–805.

Eberle, G. J. "Dekker's Part in *The Familie of Love,*" in *Joseph*

Quincy Adams Memorial Studies. Ed. James G. McManaway, Giles E. Dawson, and Edwin E. Willoughby. Washington, 1948.

Eckert, Kurt. *Die dramatische Behandlung der Ermordung des Herzogs Alessandro de' Medici durch seinen Vetter Lorenzino in der englischen Literatur (Tourneur, Shirley, Sheil).* Königsberg, 1907.

Eliot, T. S. "Tourneur and 'The Revenger's Tragedy.'" *Times Literary Supplement,* XXX, 12 (January 1, 1931).

—— "Cyril Tourneur," in *Selected Essays 1917–1932.* New York, 1932.

—— "Thomas Middleton," in *Selected Essays 1917–1932.* New York, 1932.

Ellis-Fermor, Una M. "The Imagery of 'The Revenger's Tragedie' and 'The Atheist's Tragedie,'" *Modern Language Review,* XXX (July, 1935), 289–301.

—— *The Jacobean Drama.* 2nd ed.; London, 1947.

—— "*Timon of Athens;* an Unfinished Play," *Review of English Studies,* XVII (July, 1942), 270–83.

Empson, William. *Some Versions of Pastoral.* London, 1935.

Fabyan, Robert. *Fabyans cronycle newly prynted with the cronycle actes and dedes done in the tyme of the reyne of the moste excellente prynce kynge Henry the VII. father unto our moste drad souerayne lord kynge Henry the VIII. . . . Prentyd at London By wyllyam Rastell. 1533.*

Fleay, Frederick Gard. *A Biographical Chronicle of the English Drama, 1559–1642.* 2 vols. London, 1891.

Foakes, R. A. "On the Authorship of 'The Revenger's Tragedy,'" *The Modern Language Review,* XLVIII (April, 1953), 129–38.

Greene, Robert. *The Repentance of Robert Greene 1592.* Ed. G. B. Harrison. London, 1923.

Greg, W. W. *The Editorial Problem in Shakespeare.* Oxford, 1942.

—— *A List of English Plays Written before 1643 and Printed before 1700.* London, 1900.

Harbage, Alfred B. *Annals of English Drama.* Philadelphia, 1940.

—— *Shakespeare and the Rival Traditions.* New York, 1952.

Hazlitt, William. *Lectures on the Literature of the Age of Eliza-*

beth and Characters of Shakespeare's Plays. London, 1890.

Henslowe, Philip. *Henslowe's Diary.* Ed. W. W. Greg. 2 vols. London, 1904–8.

Herford, C. H. "Thomas Middleton." *Dictionary of National Biography*, XXXVII (London, 1896).

Heywood, Thomas. *An Apology for Actors, 1612.* New York, 1941.

Hillebrand, H. N. "Thomas Middleton's *The Viper's Brood*," *Modern Language Notes*, XLII (January, 1927), 35–38.

Holinshed, Raphael. *Historie of England. Holinshed's Chronicles of England, Scotland, and Ireland.* 6 vols. London, 1807–8.

Jenkins, Harold. "Cyril Tourneur," *Review of English Studies*, XVII (January, 1941), 21–36.

Jones, F. L. "Cyril Tourneur," *Times Literary Supplement*, XXX (June 18, 1931), 487.

—— "An Experiment with Massinger's Verse," *PMLA*, XLVII (September, 1932), 727–40.

The King's Office of the Revels, 1610–1622; Fragments of Documents in the Department of Manuscripts, British Museum. Transcribed by Frank Marcham. London, 1925.

Kurtz, Leonard P. *The Dance of Death and the Macabre Spirit in European Literature.* New York, 1939.

Lamb, Charles. *Specimens of English Dramatic Poets Who Lived about the Time of Shakespeare.* London, 1897.

Lawrence, W. J. "New Facts from Sir Henry Herbert's Office Book," *Times Literary Supplement*, XXII (November 29, 1923), 820.

Lee, Vernon (Violet Paget). "The Italy of the Elizabethan Dramatists," in *Euphorion.* London, 1899.

Lockert, Lacy. "The Greatest of Elizabethan Melodramas," in *Essays in Dramatic Literature, the Parrott Presentation Volume.* Ed. Hardin Craig. Princeton, 1935.

Malespini, Celio. *Dvcento Novelle Del Signor Celio Malespini, Nelle Qvali Si Raccontano diuersi Auuenimenti cosi lieti, come mesti & strauaganti. Con tanta copia di Sentenze graui, di Scherzi, e motti, Che non meno sono profitteuoli nella prattica del viuere humano, che molto grati, e piaceuoli advdire. Con Licenza de' Superiori, & Priuilegio. In Venetia, MDCIX. Al Segno dell' Italia.* 2 vols.

Marston, John. *The Plays of John Marston.* Ed. H. Harvey Wood. 3 vols. Edinburgh, 1934–39.

—— *The Works of John Marston.* Ed. A. H. Bullen. 3 vols. London, 1887.

Maxwell, Baldwin. "The Date of Middleton's *Women Beware Women,*" *Philological Quarterly,* XXII (October, 1943), 338–42.

Meslier. *Des amours tragiques, et estranges adventvres d'Hypolite & Isabelle Neapolitains. Par le sieur Meslier, Secretaire de feuë Madame la soeur du Roy. A Paris, Par Anthoine dv Brveil, au Palais en la gallerie des prissonniers. M.DC.X.*

Middleton, Thomas. *A Game at Chesse.* Ed. R. C. Bald. Cambridge, 1929.

—— *Hengist, King of Kent; or the Mayor of Queenborough.* Foreword Joseph Q. Adams. Ed. R. C. Bald. New York and London, 1938.

—— *Honourable Entertainments.* Ed. R. C. Bald. Malone Society Reprints. Oxford, 1953.

—— *Thomas Middleton.* Introd. Algernon Charles Swinburne. Ed. Havelock Ellis. Mermaid Series. 2 vols. London, 1887–90.

—— *The Works of Thomas Middleton.* Ed. Alexander Dyce. 5 vols. London, 1840.

—— *The Works of Thomas Middleton.* Ed. A. H. Bullen. 8 vols. London, 1885–86.

Middleton, Thomas, and William Rowley. *Middleton and Rowley's Spanish Gipsie and All's Lost by Lust.* Ed. E. C. Morris. Belles Lettres Series. Boston, 1908.

Mincoff, Marco K. "The Authorship of 'The Revenger's Tragedy,'" *Studia Historico-Philologica Serdicensia,* II (1939), 1–87.

Moryson, Fynes. *Shakespeare's Europe; Unpublished Chapters of Fynes Moryson's Itinerary.* London, 1903.

Napier, Henry Edward. *Florentine History, from the Earliest Authentic Records to the Accession of Ferdinand the Third, Grand Duke of Tuscany.* 6 vols. London, 1846–47.

Nashe, Thomas. *The Works of Thomas Nashe.* Ed. R. B. McKerrow. 5 vols. London 1904–10.

Old Plays; Being a Continuation of Dodsley's Collection, with Notes, Critical and Explanatory. Ed. C. W. Dilke. 6 vols. London, 1816.

Oliphant, E. H. C. " 'Anything for a Quiet Life,' " *Notes and Queries*, 12th Series, X (January 7, 1922), 11.

—— "The Authorship of 'The Revenger's Tragedy.' " *Studies in Philology*, XXIII (April, 1926), 157–68.

—— "A Dekker-Middleton Play, *The Bloodie Banquet*," *Times Literary Supplement*, XXIV (December 17, 1925), 882.

—— "Cyril Tourneur and T. S. Eliot," *Studies in Philology*, XXXII (October, 1935), 546–52.

—— *The Plays of Beaumont and Fletcher; an Attempt to Determine Their Respective Shares and the Shares of Others.* New Haven, 1927.

—— "Problems of Authorship in Elizabethan Dramatic Literature," *Modern Philology*, VIII (January, 1911), 411–59.

—— "Tourneur and 'The Revenger's Tragedy,' " *Times Literary Supplement*, XXIX (December 18, 1930), 1087.

—— "Tourneur and 'The Revenger's Tragedy,' " *Times Literary Supplement*, XXX (February 5, 1931), 99.

Owst, Gerald R. *Preaching in Medieval England.* Cambridge, 1926.

Parrott, Thomas Marc, and Robert Hamilton Ball. *A Short View of Elizabethan Drama.* New York, 1943.

Prior, Moody E. *The Language of Tragedy.* New York, 1947.

Reynolds, John. *The Trivmphs of Gods Revenege, against the crying, and execrable Sinne of Murther. . . . The First Booke. . . . London, Printed by Felix Kyngston, for William Lee, and are to be sold at his shop in Fleete-streete, at the signe of the golden Buck, neere Serieants Inne. 1621.*

Ristine, Frank Humphrey. *English Tragicomedy: Its Origin and History.* New York, 1910.

Robb, Dewar M. "The Canon of William Rowley's Plays," *Modern Language Review*, XLV (April, 1950), 129–41.

Roeder, Ralph. *The Man of the Renaissance.* New York, 1933.

Rosenbach, A. S. W. "The Curious-Impertinent in English Dramatic Literature before Shelton's Translation of Don Quixote," *Modern Language Notes*, XVII (June, 1902), 358–67.

Rowley, William. *William Rowley, His All's Lost by Lust, and A Shoemaker, a Gentleman.* Ed. C. W. Stork, Philadelphia, 1910.

Sargeaunt, M. Joan. *John Ford.* Oxford, 1935.

Schelling, Felix E. *Elizabethan Drama, 1558–1642.* 2 vols. Boston, 1908.

—— *The English Chronicle Play.* New York, 1902.

Schoenbaum, Samuel. " 'The Revenger's Tragedy': a Neglected Source," *Notes and Queries,* CXCV (August 5, 1950), 338.

—— " 'The Revenger's Tragedy' and Middleton's Moral Outlook," *Notes and Queries,* CXCVI (January 6, 1951), 8–10.

The Second Maiden's Tragedy. Ed. W. W. Greg. Malone Society Reprints. Oxford, 1909.

Segni, Bernardo. *Istorie Fiorentine dall' Anno MDXXVII al MDLV.* Ed. G. Gargani. Firenze, 1857.

Shakespeare and His Fellow Dramatists. Ed. E. H. C. Oliphant. 2 vols. New York, 1921.

Shakespeare, William. *The Complete Works of Shakespeare.* Ed. George Lyman Kittredge. Boston, 1936.

Spencer, Theodore. *Death and Elizabethan Tragedy.* Cambridge, 1936.

Stoll, Elmer Edgar. *John Webster.* Boston, 1905.

Swinburne, Algernon Charles. *The Complete Works of Algernon Charles Swinburne.* Ed. Sir Edmund Gosse and Thomas J. Wise. 20 vols. London, 1925–27.

Sykes, H. Dugdale. " 'Anything for a Quiet Life,' " *Notes and Queries,* 12th Series, X (January 21, 1922), 50.

—— "Cyril Tourneur: 'The Revenger's Tragedy': 'The Second Maiden's Tragedy,' " *Notes and Queries,* 12th Series, V (September, 1919), 225–29.

—— *Sidelights on Elizabethan Drama.* London, 1926.

Symonds, John Addington. *Renaissance in Italy.* 5 vols. in 7. New York, 1881–1908.

Symons, Arthur. "Middleton and Rowley," in *Cambridge History of English Literature,* VI (New York, 1910).

Thorndike, Ashley H. *The Influence of Beaumont and Fletcher on Shakspere.* Worcester, 1901.

—— *Tragedy.* Boston, 1905.

Tieck, Ludwig. *Shakspeare's Vorschule; herausgegeben, und mit Vorreden Begleitet.* 2 vols. in 1. Leipzig, 1823–29.

Tillyard, E. M. W. *Shakespeare's History Plays.* London, 1944.

Tourneur, Cyril. *The Plays and Poems of Cyril Tourneur.* Ed. J. Churton Collins. 2 vols. London, 1878.

Tourneur, Cyril. *The Works of Cyril Tourneur.* Ed. Allardyce Nicoll. London, 1929.

A Transcript of the Registers of the Company of Stationers of London; 1554–1640 A.D. Ed. Edward Arber. 5 vols. London, 1875–77.

A Transcript of the Registers of the Worshipful Company of Stationers; From 1640–1708 A.D. Ed. G. Briscoe Eyre. 3 vols. London, 1913–14.

Varchi, Benedetto. *Storia Fiorentina. Opere di Benedetto Varchi.* 2 vols. Trieste, 1858–59.

Vaughan, C. E. "Tourneur and Webster," in *Cambridge History of English Literature,* VI (New York, 1910).

Wagner, B. M. "Cyril Tourneur," *Times Literary Supplement,* XXX (April 23, 1931), 327.

Ward, A. W. *A History of English Dramatic Literature to the Death of Queen Anne.* 3 vols. London, 1899.

Webster, John. *The Complete Works of John Webster.* Ed. F. L. Lucas. 4 vols. London, 1927.

Webster, John, and Cyril Tourneur. *Webster and Tourneur.* Ed. John Addington Symonds. Mermaid Series. London, 1888.

Wells, Henry W. *Elizabethan and Jacobean Playwrights.* New York, 1939.

Wells, William. " 'Timon of Athens,' " *Notes and Queries,* 12th Series, VI (January–June, 1920), 266–69.

Wenzel, Paul. *Cyril Tourneurs Stellung in der Geschicte des englischen Dramas.* Breslau, 1918.

Wiggin, P. G. *An Inquiry into the Authorship of the Middleton-Rowley Plays.* Boston, 1897.

Wilson, F. P. *Elizabethan and Jacobean.* Oxford, 1945.

Young, G. F. *The Medici.* 2 vols. London, 1926.

Index